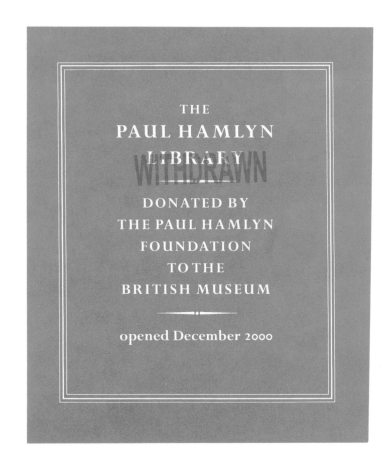

CHRISTIAN CELTS

Messages & Images

Charles Thomas

TEMPUS

For
FOUR LITTLE PEOPLE
(and any more to come)
who may one day read this book
and
ONE LARGER PERSON
who understood it from the beginning

First published 1998
Published by:
Tempus Publishing Limited
The Mill, Brimscombe Port
Stroud, Gloucestershire, GL5 2QG

© Antony Charles Thomas, 1998

The right of Antony Charles Thomas to be identified as the Author
of this work has been asserted by him in accordance with the
Copyrights, Designs and Patents Act 1988.

Typesetting and origination by Tempus Publishing Ltd.
Printed and bound in Great Britain.

British Library Cataloguing in Publication Data.
A catalogue record for this book is available from the British Library.

ISBN 07524 1411 9

Contents

List of Illustrations

The front cover shows a fragment of 350 Idnert

Preface

This book describes a particular accomplishment of Christian Celts who lived in Britain between the fourth and eleventh centuries AD. They were Celts in that their first language was Celtic — British, and later its daughter-tongues Cumbric, Welsh and Cornish — and Christian in that nearly all the people named here were baptised, raised, schooled and laid to rest as members of an orthodox British Christian church. Their accomplishment, long forgotten and unknown until its rediscovery in 1995, was the composition of certain Latin texts preserved because they were cut on stone. Most are memorials for the dead, though a few can be described as dedicatory and there is one Late Roman mosaic inscription to be considered. Many texts contain Celtic personal names alongside others (continuing-Roman) that were inherited from the Roman period.

These inscriptions make up about a tenth of the several hundred of post-Roman inscriptions on stone known from the west and north of Britain, southern Scotland, the Isle of Man, nearly all of Wales, and Cornwall and Devon with island outliers. What makes them special and distinctive is that their messages were thought out, structured and written for public display in *Biblical style*. That is the label for an elaborate composition style, as far as we are concerned in Latin (not Celtic), containing features known and used in the Roman world of letters before the fourth-century expansion and eventual triumph of Christianity. It can however fairly be called 'Biblical' because in Britain, and subsequently in Ireland when original Latin writings appeared, far and away the greatest example and stimulus came from the Vulgate, the Latin revision of the Bible by St Jerome and his circle. The Vulgate (*editio Vulgata*) was completed soon after AD 400 and parts at least seem to have reached Britain early in the fifth century.

Some features of Biblical style are recognisable as older Roman literary conventions. Some, certainly in post-Roman Britain and Ireland, reveal an intimate knowledge of the Bible because they depend on identifying minimal allusions, verbal and numerical. One component can be described as mathematical. This last feature the Romans took over, and preserved through education, from the works of the great Greek mathematicians. It concerns what we know as arithmetic and geometry. All these mathematical adjuncts of the style were introduced to bring patterns, proportions and a scheme of order to creations wrought from a stock of ordinary words and letters. Their incorporation had another side and purpose. In a way resembling cryptography, it made possible the inclusion of personal and Divine names, words, short phrases, Biblical allusions and even (rarely) absolute dates in Latin statements that, read at face-value, reveal nothing of these inner contents. Since there would have been no point in displaying messages so secret that nobody could read them the question is not how they are de-coded, but what percentage of readers is likely to have been able to do this.

We now have a much more remarkable discovery. Certain inscriptions (not all of those in Biblical style, but perhaps as many as half) have a further capacity to generate images; to suggest pictures, brought into focus and reality in the mind of the beholder (*mental images*). In some a picture may be suggested by the disposition of lines, lettering and simple ornamentation. In others a more detailed image is produced by arithmetical re-arrangement of a text indicated by a series of clues and pointers, and may be accompanied by an array of descriptive letters and words. Modern readers who are any good at crossword puzzles, anagrams, nonagrams, acrostics, codes of the *Boys Own Paper* kind and the extinct *John Bull* 'Bullets' will find themselves on familiar ground. They should know that the Romans were also fond of the whole spectrum of word- and letter-games. The historian Suetonius tells us that Julius Caesar, in private letters to Cicero and other friends, used a three-letter-shift code, in which A B C D became D E F G, etc., and Caesar would be written Fdhxdu; amusing, but not worthy to rank with anything like Samuel Pepys's private diary shorthand or the many nineteenth-century military alphabetical ciphers.

As far as is yet known, the rules of composition in Biblical style have not survived. It is not even certain that a rule-book existed. The methodology may have been taught, under the heading of *arithmetica*, as an aspect of general composition in Latin. Transmitted to generations of selected pupils in a system of schooling mainly directed by the Church, these rules and practices were largely (possibly not entirely) lost not long after the Norman conquest of Britain. They can be recovered. The process is slow and difficult, and the outcome certainly defective. Unless specifically mentioned in Greek and Latin, even the names of various tricks or devices are now unknown and new ones must be invented.

The present book is among other things a first attempt to write a guide or handbook to the inscriptional component of Insular (= British-plus-Irish) Latin Biblical style. Its larger purpose is to bring to a new readership not just the mechanisms, but the far more intriguing results, and (as I see them) some of the implications; and to give these in a narrative that is chronological and where possible geographical. If Wales dominates the story it is because that land was for centuries the major home of Britons who used a Celtic language alongside Latin and were, increasingly so from the fifth century, Christians. Were this book thrice its length I could have digressed into every conceivable detail of our Early Christian archaeology, art and imperfectly-documented history. Digressions are however few, and to illustrate points arising from what individual monuments may tell us. The notes on Further Reading (p. 203) will suggest recent and reliable publications to those interested in pursuing topics.

I wish that it had been possible to write on intellectual accomplishment during the same period in our sister-island Ireland. Though longer Latin Christian compositions in Biblical style were produced in Ireland (beginning with those of the fifth-century Briton, St Patrick the bishop) the developed *inscriptional* style was peculiar to Britain and, it begins to seem, in a less advanced manner to stone-cut Christian memorials after AD 400 in present-day Spain, Germany and probably France. This was because of a shared background of Latin and the Roman alphabet, the teaching of simple mathematics, the currency of long-established word- and letter-games, and above all the fixed *orthography*, spelling system, of Classical Latin and subsequently of the Vulgate. Though Ireland was in touch with Roman Britain and some knowledge of spoken and written Latin reached Ireland in the fourth century, full *romanitas* — the cultural and educational world of letters shared throughout the Western provinces of the Late Roman empire — did not. The oldest stone-cut inscriptions of the Irish show, in place of Roman letters, another script altogether (*ogam*: see Chap.5) invented to record proper names and a few repetitive words in the Primitive stage of the Irish language. It is now very likely that learned Irish scholars passed to their British colleagues in Wales and other areas, if so by the sixth century, writing with word separation and the page layout as we have it today (along with useful notions like the digraphs, two-letter sounds, written *ph, th, ch*), but these came from innovations in written Latin, not Irish. No British inscription written entirely in a Celtic language — and it is extremely unlikely that any *were* so written before about 700 — can be shown to have been composed in Biblical style. Because of the massive influence of the Vulgate and the legacy of Rome, that style was essentially Latin.

In no sense can I claim this book as complete or definitive; it pretends to be nothing better than an introduction. Given what the analyses of these Insular texts have revealed, it seems to me better to write it, and to expect the usual criticisms that the subject is too unfamiliar to be genuine or that the author has taken leave of his senses, than to connive in letting inscriptional Biblical style sink back into another eight or nine centuries of oblivion. Longer descriptive accounts of all the individual monuments have during the last two years been circulated to thirty or so colleagues, many kindly sending suggestions, corrections and fresh ideas. Some have understood and accepted these results; some have not. I have done my best to explain mathematical topics that I had first to learn, or re-learn, bearing in mind that almost all of them were once comprehended within everyday mental arithmetic. Translations of the Latin are given throughout, with some comments on Celtic names. It will be emphasised again, and can first be emphasised here and now, that this Insular Latin is invariably standard post-Classical and literary Latin, from men and women whose teachers had unbroken access to the best of models. What have been too often described in the past as barbarism, provincialisms, mistakes or ignorance and signs of a progressive breakdown in correct grammar and syntax are nothing of the sort. They are deliberate manipulations, designed to facilitate messages and images, by skilled users of a second language in which some writers may have been virtually bilingual. We have to picture a realm of endeavour in which composers of Biblical-style Latin, written with its own set of rules, could well have been composers of verse in their own Celtic vernacular ('neo-Brittonic', becoming Old Welsh); oral, and with an entirely different suite of rules. After several years spent in disentangling so many fascinating messages from what (to me) is a living past with real named people, my joint feeling is of admiration for such ingenuity and of gratitude for any opportunity to place these things in a printed record. I hope that at least some who read this book will, by the end, have come to share the feeling.

Acknowledgements

My greatest thanks are to David Howlett, pioneering discoverer and prolific exponent of Biblical-style composition in Insular Latin and other languages, for his help, encouragement, generous supply of ideas, improvements and corrections; and his unwavering belief in the reality of the inscriptional component. At a lecture recently it was remarked (not unkindly) that Howlett and Thomas had formed a two-man Mutual Credibility Society; if so, it is a band into which both would welcome any number of new members. Next, I am grateful to editors of three journals (James Kirk, Christine North and Donnchadh Ó Corráin) who have probably risked uninformed criticism by taking and publishing my papers on half-a-dozen of these inscriptions; and equally to many correspondents, friends and colleagues who having read circulated worknotes provided me with further encouragement and, more to the point, constructive criticism, elaborations and even likely new directions for research. Without committing any one of them to overt belief in all that I claim, I may mention Martin and Birthe (Kjølbye-) Biddle, Kemp Davidson, Nancy Edwards, Geraint Gruffydd, Mark Hassall, Peter Hill, Jeremy Knight, Dáibhí Ó Cróinín, Roger Tomlin and Michael Vickers, and single out especially Martin Henig and Kenneth Painter for particular inspiration and assistance. Third, in the last few years many of the ideas and illustrations given below were presented at university and society formal lectures or seminars — in Scotland, at Glasgow and Edinburgh (the 1997, first, John Jamieson Lecture); in Wales, at two University of Wales locations, Lampeter and Caerleon; in Cornwall, at Penzance, Porthpean and Devoran; and in supposedly non-Celtic England, at Yarlington and Oxford.

Drawings of inscriptions, when not by myself or Carl Thorpe, are from *CIIC* in which Macalister did almost all his own drawings, reproduced by courtesy of the Controller, Stationery Office, Dublin, and from *ECMW* in which staff members of the National Museum of Wales (so *ECMW*, p.1 n.1) were responsible, by courtesy of that Museum. In both cases, any modifications result from my inspection and numerous photographs. Acknowledgements appear in captions, but I must also thank Frances Mawer (*fig.13*), Kent Archaeological Society (*17, 19*), the shades of Sir John Tenniel (*48, 49*) and anyone else inadvertently omitted for permission to reproduce items; also Truro Old Cornwall Society, through Mrs Christine Parnell and Miss O'Flynn, for the use of their archive picture no.238 (here, *fig.80*). My special gratitude goes to Carl Thorpe, as draughtsman and fellow-explorer of the Cornish inscriptions, who spent so much time making new drawings from our photographs and checking them in the field. Lastly, if I may be permitted to write this as a contributor to a new series from a new publishing house, it is a particular pleasure to work again with a directing editor who (under another imprint) saw my *Christianity in Roman Britain to AD 500* (1981) and *Exploration of a Drowned Landscape* (1985) to successful conclusions; and who has been kind enough to take on board a rather different sort of book with enthusiasm and concern.

Abbreviations

CIIC	R.A.S. Macalister, *Corpus Inscriptionum Insularum Celticarum*, 2 vols. (Stationery Office, Dublin 1945, 1949)
ECMW	V.E. Nash-Williams, *The Early Christian Monuments of Wales* (Univ. of Wales Press, Cardiff 1950)
EWGT	P.C. Bartrum, *Early Welsh Genealogical Tracts* (Univ. of Wales Press, Cardiff 1966)
LHEB	Kenneth Jackson, *Language and History in Early Britain* (Edinburgh Univ. Press, Edinburgh 1953, and reprints)
RCAHMS	Royal Commission on Ancient and Historical Monuments of Scotland, Edinburgh, as publisher of *Inventory* volumes
RCAMW	Royal Commission on Ancient and Historical Monuments in Wales (earlier, RCAHM in Wales & Monmouthshire), Aberystwyth
RCHME	Royal Commission on the Historical Monuments of England, London (now Swindon)
RIB	*The Roman Inscriptions of Britain*; vol.i, *Inscriptions on Stone*, R.G. Collingwood & R.P. Wright (Clarendon Press, Oxford 1965), vol.ii (8 parts), *Instrumentum Domesticum*, various editors & contributors (Alan Sutton, 1990-95), plus 2 Index parts.
VSBG	A.W. Wade-Evans, *Vitae Sanctorum Britanniae et Genealogiae* (Univ. of Wales, Cardiff 1944)

The following are occasionally used:

NT	New Testament	pret.	preterite
OT	Old Testament	adj.	adjective
MW	Middle Welsh	nom.	nominative (case)
OW	Old Welsh	voc.	vocative
fem.	feminine	accus.	accusative
masc.	masculine	gen.	genitive
plur.	plural	dat.	dative
ind.	indicative (tense)	abl.	ablative

The symbol < means 'is derived from'
      > 'gives rise to'
      * is an inferred form, not attested in writing

Phonetic Equivalents

Where necessary, approximate sounds of words, syllables and vowels or consonants in contemporary speech are indicated thus /kat/, using a greatly simplified range of phonetic symbols, or equating them to modern English, as 'mile-goon'. A lengthened vowel is marked /uː/ 'oo', particular stress by a preceding tick /ˈkon/ and (Latin only) short vowels as ĕ ă. Our sounds of 'y' and 'w' (semi-consonants) are given as /y/,/w/ instead of the conventional /i̯/,/u̯/; ü/, as in German.

There are however certain vowels and consonants for which special symbols are inevitable. The obscure vowel, as e and o in 'the button', is always /ə/. Lenited m (see p. 69) is written either /ṽ/ or /μ/, and here I use the former; this sound, developed in neo-Brittonic, is quite important because its representation in the 20-letter ABC was variable. The sound as in Scottish 'loch' is /x/ and its harsher (voiced) version, which might be written 'gh', is /ʒ/. Our digraph *th* represents two sounds, as in *think* or *athwart* /θ/, and as in *bother* or *swathe*, written -*dd*- in Welsh and here /ð/. Again, the combination -*ng*- stands for separate things, but here /ŋ/ is as in *singer* or *banger*, and not as in *linger* or *anger*. Readers who consult some of the sources cited below will find in them more and different phonetic symbols, not always explained; they belong to a standard international system capable of notating all known languages (IPA, International Phonetic Alphabet) which is set out in all major textbooks on phonetics.

The rules governing length and quantity of syllables and vowels in Latin verse and prose (metrics, metrical scansion) are not really needed here; two marks denote 'long' and 'short' respectively, when these have to be shown, as in reciting Tūm-Tĭ-Tūm-Tĭ-Tūm (tum.ti.tum.ti.tum).

1 The Messages Within

Surprises at Much Binding

Join me in the following light-hearted episode. You are on holiday, your pastime is photographing old churches and, Hasselblad in hand, you are visiting Much Binding in the Marsh. Having parked, you walk along Church Street, noticing at No. 56 an old-fashioned shop announcing itself as W HANKS & SON ★ FAMILY BUTCHERS AND PURVEYORS ★ ESTAB 1894, and you enter the churchyard, heading for the south porch. A very recent grave (scatter of earth, faded wreaths, shiny granite headstone) attracts your attention and you pause to read it. It says

HERE LIES
WILLIAM HANKS
WHO DIED AGED 16 YEARS
AND 6 MONTHS
A GREATLY CHERISHED SON
(date)

Perhaps you ponder the wording and think, How sad to lose a son at this particular age, just setting out in the world; and then it occurs to you that this is a slightly unusual epitaph, and you are moved to count the words. Allowing the '16', and '6' and the (last line) article 'A' to be words on their own, you find that there are *sixteen* — same figure as the dead lad's years. Then you observe that a particular graph (any letter, number or symbol as a separate item), which has been cut identically as the 'I' in LIES or WILLIAM and the 'I' in the number 16, appears *six* times — same figure as the months shown below the sixteen years. This is so odd that you begin to add up the syllables, reckoning '16' as /six.teen/ (two syllables), and also 'YEARS' as two because we nearly all pronounce that word as a disyllable, /yee.erz/. By now you probably need your notebook and a biro, and you find:

here. lies	2
will.i.am hanks	4
who.died.aged.six.teen.ye.ars	7
and.six.months	3
a.great.ly. che.rished. son	6

When you tot up 2 + 4 + 7 + 3 + 6, they make twenty-two; and suddenly you see that this is *also* the sum of sixteen (years) and six (months).

Imagine next that, on holiday or at work, you are in love. If male, you are Neil and the girlfriend is called Joan; if female, the same names vice versa. Neil and Joan are rather serious; *Guardian* readers, and shared crossword-enthusiasts. In a saloon bar recently they played that game of adding up all the letters of their names (A is 1, B is 2, and so on up to Y, 25 and Z, 26), and were delighted to find that N E I L, 14.5.9.12, and J O A N, 10.15.1.14, both came to the same total; 40. Quite plainly, arithmetic smiled on their prospective union. So now, here in the churchyard, you as Neil or Joan happen to see that the *first* letter of William Hanks's memorial, H (=8) in HERE, and the very *last* letter, N (=14) in SON, happen to make 22; just like the syllables, the sum of 16 (years) and 6 (months). You continue, adding the first letters of all five lines; they are H W W A A, or 8.23.23.1.1, and they come to 56. Then you remember the street-number of the family butchers and, turning over the wreaths, sure enough you see one with 'In Loving Memory From All At No.56'.

Your reactions, at this stage, might include the following:

1. This is all a pure coincidence, though admittedly a most peculiar one.
2. You don't somehow feel able to go back and call at No. 56 Church Street to ask what is going on; but you do now peer around at any other recent headstones, to see if any contain similar letter- or number-games. None is worded in the same fashion, and no other inscription exhibits these inner totals.
3. You both have jobs that involve a lot of dealings with numbers, as teacher and accountant. However, something warns you not to mention any of this to colleagues, in case they think you are crazy.
4. You like thick books, listed under Fantasy, Science Fiction and New Age, in which some authors make fortunes from writing about lost secrets and vanished civilisations; books that involve numerologies, cryptic measuring (of Mayan temples or the Pyramids), codes known only to Freemasons and the Merovingian descendants of Jesus Christ and, if the writers are lucky enough, forewords supplied by Colin Wilson. But certain of your friends, intellectual friends, *real* scholars, keep warning you not to take any of this seriously; so you don't feel up to claiming that a secret numbers-cult of the dead is flourishing at Much Binding. More awkwardly still, you have a mad uncle who has proved, by numbers, that Bacon wrote Shakespeare, and you prefer to keep a low profile on these matters.

You and Neil, or you and Joan, check the Williams Hanks results and they won't go away. You now start adding up just about everything you see, car-numbers included, but with virtually no meaningful results; and you realise, eventually, that this game must have its own rules which you have yet to discover.

Thirteen years; In peace

Let us travel next to wildest Wales, back in time some 1500 years, to the rural churchyard of Llanerfyl; this is in (former) Montgomeryshire, and about thirty miles west from

Fig. 1 421 Rostece, mid-Wales, late 5th
or early 6th century (modified from
ECMW fig.190 by permission of
the National Museum of Wales).
Flaked-off letters are restored, dotted;
in line 4, small initial E, blacked, is
an undated addition.

Wroxeter. We find a battered stone pillar (*Fig. 1*), another sad little memorial, this time to a girl who died aged only 13, and whose proper Roman-style name might have been given as *Rustica*. Her epitaph is cut in capitals, very much as for William Hanks. Though one upper corner has been knocked off and there is damage from flaking, most of it can still be read and it appears to be in Latin. There are six-and-a-bit lines and some words are separated, not by modern spacing, but by dimples or dots like full-stops (points, *puncti*). The right way to transcribe an inscription is to put *square* brackets [ ] around missing or obliterated letters that can be supplied by analogy, or from common sense or near-certainty; *curved* brackets ( ) around missing letters that can similarly be supplied but, for any reason, were not cut; *dots* … where letters seem to be missing and it is uncertain what they were; and underlining of two (occasionally, three) letters that may be *ligatured*, which means cut or chiselled sharing a stroke. The layout is indicated by using a slash / to mark the divisions between lines; or else by copying the actual text. The transcription of 421 *Rostece* (which is how we shall refer to this particular stone, and similarly to any others mentioned)[1] therefore ought to go like this:

1   H I C [I N]
2   T V M̲ ̲[V̲]̲ L O I A
3   C I T . R [O] S T E
4   C E . F I L I A . P A
5   T E R N I N I .
6   A N I X I I I . I N
7   P A (ce)

If on a damaged modern tombstone we could read only IN LOV ... MEMORY OF, or IN LOVING M ... RY OF, we would unhesitatingly restore ING or EMO because the missing letters cannot be anything else. Above, in line one we can restore [I N] because HIC IN TUMULO IACIT 'Here in the tomb she/he lies' is a formula, like IN LOVING MEMORY. So too (lines six to seven) is IN PACE 'in peace', allowing (ce), CE, to be added. In line two both spacing and to some degree the shape of the flaking, which seems to have followed surface-breaking when cutting letters, allow MV as a two-letter ligature; in line three the missing letter was certainly an O, and in line six the ANI, for which the expected Latin would be ANNI 'years', appears to be deliberate. The message (the *text*) is: *Hic in / tumulo ia/cit Roste/ce/ filia Pa/ternini / ani XIII in / pace* 'Here in the tomb lies Rostece, the daughter of Paterninus. Years thirteen. In peace'.

Fig.1 gives what is called the *display* text; what any viewer, reader or visitor would see, fixed by being cut into a stone surface. Look closely at it; we may apply the William Hanks treatment. This poor child was thirteen, and that particular number will prove to be so central that we must designate it a *key number*. Latin 'I' or 'i', as well as marking a (long or short) vowel, and the semi-consonant or glide as a /y/ sound, was also a graph for a numeral; *unus* 'one'. Count the I's in *Fig.1*, remembering to include the flaked-off IN; h I c I n tumulo I ac I t rostece f I l I a patern I n I an I x III I n p a – and you will find they occur *thirteen* times. The letters C and M were also numerals, for *centum* 'hundred' and *mille* 'thousand'. Count (*Fig.1* only; what is visible) the M's and C's, and you will find C M C C, or M C C C, which stands for *thirteen* hundred. Then, remembering a new feature — that ligatured letters, like MV in the worked TV<u>MV</u>LO, must be reckoned as a *single* letter — count up all the letters preceding the age, XIII; they come to 39, *thirteen* times 3. Do not at this stage waste any professional mathematician's time by asking for calculations as to whether or not these results could have happened randomly or by chance, because there is more to come; and do not suppose that a computer programme (unless you want to write it yourself) would necessarily tell you any more than you can see quite easily in a text that was not created by any computer.

In the Much Binding stone for William Hanks, there would have been a distinction between the composer of his memorial (His father? The high priest of the indigenous number-cult?) who chose the exact words and decided exactly how they would be laid out; and the cutter, a commercial mason who carried out the composer's orders (the *model*), machine-cutting the text on imported Czechoslovakian grey granite at a pound a letter (this is the going rate in Cornwall, 1998). Projecting the relationship back into post-Roman times we would have *composers*, whose models (texts) were presumably worked out in written form on non-stone media; and *cutters*, available artisans who could ply the equivalent of mallets and chisels and whose sole job (on payment of a sheep, or whatever) was to reproduce, larger size and as a *display*, whatever model was provided. It is entirely possible (occasionally, more or less certainly so) that a composer might have scratched out, painted or charcoaled the desired letters. It is also possible that some cutters were illiterate. We cannot suppose, in the post-Roman world, perpetuation of the skilled Roman trade of the full-time *lapidarius* (on marble, *marmorarius*), the professional monumental-mason.

That 26-letter ABC, values of 1 to 26, used by Neil and Joan to intertwine their given names in arithmetical joy did not apply at the time of 421 *Rostece*. The relevant Latin, or

Roman, alphabet was a 20-letter one (this will be discussed again: p. 58), running

A	B	C	D	E	F	G	H	I	L
1	2	3	4	5	6	7	8	9	10

M	N	O	P	Q	R	S	T	U/V	X
11	12	13	14	15	16	17	18	19	20

and each letter had the value shown below; it takes very little time to commit this system to memory. Letter 19, conventionally written V in inscriptions (and in transcribing them), can be rendered as U,u when it serves as a vowel (as in our *push*, and *moon*) and V, v, when it is the semi-consonant or glide, which we can take as the sound of our /w/ for present purposes.

Now we can go on and set out 421 *Rostece* again, this time as the full, or original, or *model* text, with no abbreviations:

1   **H** I C I **N**

2   T V M V L O I A

3   C I T . R O S T E

4   C E . F I L I A . P A

5   T E R N I N I .

6   A N N I T R E D E C I M . I N

7   **P** A C **E**

Bearing in mind that anyone knowing Latin, in Wales and visiting this stone around 500 (its likely date), would have had no trouble in reproducing the above on a wax tablet or just by scratching it out knife-point on a bit of slate, we can apply the William Hanks approach for a second time. What does that reveal? The first and last letters overall are H E, 8.5 = *thirteen*. Within the first 20 letters the only two whose numbered positions correspond to their 'letters-as-numbers', or LaN, values (in: h i **C** i n t u m u **L** o i a c i t r o s t) are C and L, and C L, 3.10 =*thirteen*. The four words that describe Rostece are FILIA PATERNINI ANNI TREDECIM, and they have 26 letters; *thirteen* times 2. The four corner letters picked out above – top right, top left; bottom right, bottom left — are H N P E, 8.12.14.5, making 39 = *thirteen* times 3. The seven line initials are H T C C T A P, 8.18.3.3.18.1.14, making 65 = *thirteen* times 5.

Because it will be necessary and desirable to show most of the other inscriptions with a fuller analytical table, we can produce one for 421 *Rostece*; it breaks down, by lines, the totals of words (*W*), syllables (*S*) and two lots of letters, those in display (*LD*) and those in the postulated model (*LM*). Here it is:

		W	*S*	*LD*	*LM*
1	H I C I N	2	2	5	5
2	T V M V L O I A		4	7	8
3	C I T R O S T E		3	8	8
4	C E F I L I A P A	5	5	9	9
5	T E R N I N I		3	7	7
6	A N I (anni) X I I I (tredecim) I N	3	6	9	14
7	P A (pace)	1	2	2	4
		11	25	47	55

As if we had not already had enough of *thirteen* and its various multiples, yet another pops up; addition of totals *W*, 11: *S*, 25: and *LM*, 55 gives us 91, which is *thirteen* times 7. Though we can leave this for the moment, the whole arithmetical side of this short inscription — its *computus* — contains some other things. They may not be so immediately obvious but there is a use of *extreme ratio* (p. 75), reference to *square* numbers (25, 36 and 49) and, as the model letter total, 55 which is a *triangular* number (p. 76). All of them were intentionally built into the composition, just as were the many exhibitions of key number thirteen. In due course we shall see how.

At this point, forgetting Much Binding and William Hanks and these straightforward or first-order numerical indications, the author becomes temporarily, on paper, like a stage magician who in full view opens and closes an empty hand, and opens it again to reveal a large Union Jack or bowl with a swimming piranha fish. By logical steps, following ascertainable rules and clues, the unimpressive *Fig. 1* display becomes what can now be shown as *Fig.2*. It is a picture that has been waiting to happen; technically, a *mental image* in the shape of a *devised profile*, directly generated from the text through its computus. We see Rostece's burial 'in peace', below ground, her memorial stone at the left (her head) end. This is dominated by the Cross, from whose arm depend the letters making up her name. The image survives in modern hymnology; *Methodist Hymn Book* no.107, verse 3, 'I take, O Cross, thy shadow / For my abiding place'. When, in due course, one learns to accept the reality of this and of similar achievements in Insular Biblical-style creations, it is time to think very hard indeed about what we know, or don't know, or used to think we knew, in the areas of language and history and archaeology, and Latin and Christianity and education, proper to Britain in the post-Roman centuries.

Fig.2 *421 Rostece; generation of a mental image, a devised profile. Above, 49 letters omitting final IN PA (ce) as a square yield equal LaN totals for certain lines and columns, the '66' of line 2, col.4 marking the Cross. Below, how this might be developed. Col.1, 73, is the inscribed headstone and line 6, 73, the ground; the letters i n p a c e mark where her body lies and the letters of her name are pendent from the Cross standing above her grave.*

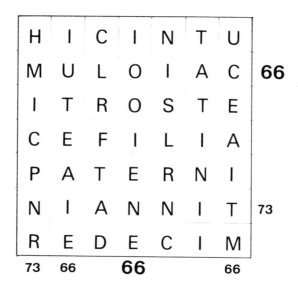

H	I	C	I	N	T	U	
M	U	L	O	I	A	C	**66**
I	T	R	O	S	T	E	
C	E	F	I	L	I	A	
P	A	T	E	R	N	I	
N	I	A	N	N	I	T	73
R	E	D	E	C	I	M	

73 66 **66** 66

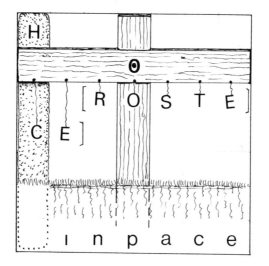

Could anything remotely suggestive of the *Fig. 2* image have been guessed simply by staring hard and long at the inscribed stone? Possibly; it may contain another kind of preliminary image. This is a Christian memorial and the set phrase HIC IN TUMULO IACIT is a Christian formula, one of two (the other being HIC IACIT, IACET, or IACENT (plural)) transmitted from Christian Gaul to western Britain late in the fifth century.[2] Rostece may well have died at the age of thirteen — given Roman marital customs, and those of early Wales later indicated by the Welsh law codes, it would not be unusual if she had died in childbirth. But *thirteen*, twelve plus one, is also a Biblically allusive figure, because it must represent Christ and his twelve Disciples or the first Apostles. It is of Christ crucified that the enlarged Cross (of the Crucifixion) stands as a

Fig. 3   *RIB 955; Carlisle, 4th-century tombstone of Flavius Antigonus Papias (drawn by R.G. Collingwood).*

primary symbol, even if not generally used in the West before the fifth century. The 421 *Rostece* inscription should not be dated far, if at all, beyond 500 for several reasons. Paterninus (extended from the commoner Paternus)[3] is a continuing-Roman name; so is Rustica, here spelled in a convention that is closer to the way it would have been spoken, / rozdeg / (the -T- and -C- in ROSTECE stand for /d/ /g/). The dots or *puncti* between certain words seem to have no computistic significance but are carried over from Romano-British inscriptional custom. What we cannot see is any trace of the ruled guidelines, either as light scribbling or (rarely) deeply-gouged lines, that appear (*Fig.3*) on some earlier inscriptions. Yet the *tops* of letters in line 3 have been aligned. If one draws a bar through them, and then another vertical bar with the I of IN, and the second I of FILIA, an outline cross emerges, its centre or junction as the circle of the O (flaked off) in ROSTECE (*Fig.4*). This must constitute a preliminary *display* profile image; *display*, because it is inherent in what we see, and not devised (i.e., generated by re-arrangement through some Biblical-style arithmetical device, as in *Fig.2*), and a *profile* because it is a side-on view, a picture in profile seen in the horizontal plane, of what is meant to represent a cross standing upright.

Contrary to a very different set of contemporary images, those generated through films that feature Indiana Jones and his all-purpose bullwhip, today's archaeologists (and historians and linguists) seldom if ever stumble across Lost Arks, Temples of Doom, and unrecorded civilisations seething away busily in photogenic jungles. Just occasionally, as

Fig.4   *421* Rostece; *another image,*
          a potential display profile *in*
          which letter-tops, line 3,
          make a horizontal, elements
          of letters a vertical, and the O
          of the name the intersection.

here, something unsuspected and unknown may turn up; when that happens it can demand a speedy account in print of all the known details, and (a harder need) the willing abandonment of notions that, however long cherished and defended, can be exposed as erroneous. The extent to which spoken and written Latin persisted after 400 or so in parts of Britain and Ireland is probably one such topic, calling out for massive re-definition. The nature of hundreds of stone-cut Latin memorial inscriptions, broadly related to 421 *Rostece* though by no means all exhibiting additional, internal, characteristics, is another. A whole parcel of popular views that might be identified through catchphrases like the Dark Ages, Celtic Christianity (Celtic 'spirituality'), and the Celtic Fringe and a supposed collapse of Roman-style civilisation is certainly a third potential casualty. For the time being we can concentrate on the inscriptions alone.

A data-base

Within those regions of Britain already specified (p. 7), there are about 300 inscriptions cut or pocked or chiselled on every variety of local rock (except for the south-west, where most are on granite). They have always been loosely dated between the fifth and eleventh centuries AD, the majority being of the *Rostece* type and pre-dating the eighth century. Most early stones are memorials by name to the individual dead. The wording, like the few instances of minimal accompanying art, tells us that these were Christians and the terms *inscriptiones Christianae* and Early Christian Monuments have long been applied to them, though we cannot exclude the likelihood of the odd non-Christian burial during the fifth century. As at least three extensive re-surveys of all these stones have begun or are now planned,[4] updating numbers and details with original and present locations — stones are, too frequently, moved around by well-meaning preservationists — there is no point in giving a reduced-scale map with hundreds of little dots. Instead, *Fig.5* serves to show the areas in question, each with approximate totals of all stones. Within them is one symbol only, marking inscriptions known (by the end of 1997) to have been composed in Biblical style.

The question that this map raises immediately is best shown by turning to another map, *Fig.13*, and comparing the two. Why do these concentrations of inscriptions relate neither to the spatial evidence for Christianity in fourth-century Britain, nor to the more Romanised (lowland, southern and eastern) part of Britannia, presumed home of spoken and written Latin and of the custom of erecting lettered tombstones in the Roman manner? We can address this problem in the next chapter.

Letter and languages

With rare exceptions the contents of the inscriptions, their *texts*, are in Latin. The personal names are either continuing-Roman ones, favoured survivals of the earlier Roman *cognomina* male and female; in a few instances, like *David*, they are Biblical and taken from the Vulgate or associated Christian writings; or they are Celtic. Most of the last sort come from British, but some are demonstrably Irish, outcome of minor settlements from Ireland starting in the late fourth century where Irish names were preferentially retained for some generations. There are also Celtic names common to British and Irish. Gender can usually, if not invariably, be determined by case-endings imitating the distinction in Latin; names in *-us,-i,-o* are probably masc(uline), those in *-a,-ae,-e* fem(inine).

Virtually all inscriptions, despite erosion through time, can still be read by experienced workers because the letters are either the familiar capitals, A to X, or known varieties of what will be called here *bookhand*, derivatives of Roman-period 'lower-case' or cursive scripts used for longer writings on other media. The two forms may appear as a mixture. A belief that monumental capitals (*capitalis*) were necessarily used earlier, and bookhands later, and therefore that the prevalence of one or other in a text offered a graduated timescale yielding approximate dates, would now be regarded as increasingly unsound. It fails to take into account an element of a composer's personal choice.

One worthwhile observation is that capitals in particular are frequently cut fairly large; certainly larger, and less closely set, than on most pre-400 Roman inscriptions. In Christian Gaul and probably generally in the other Western provinces memorial stones lay flat above, or besides, a burial, rather like many medieval slabs in floors of British churches. If ever set vertically, they were perhaps fixed into the walls of tomb-surrounds. Not only did the British have no access to flat smooth shaped slabs of marble and other fine limestones professionally quarried and marketed; the British (and Irish) obligatory preference for natural pillars, for large chunks of granite and other rocks, even earthfast

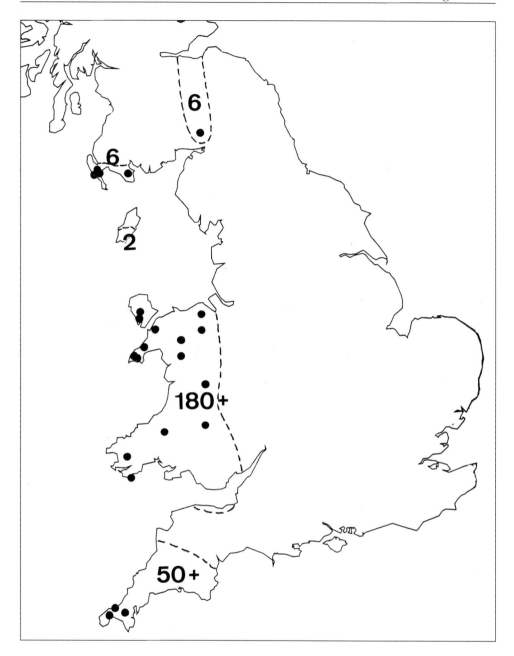

Fig. 5   Simplified distribution of post-Roman inscriptions in north and west Britain, with an
idea of totals; dots mark those (at end of 1997) known or suspected to be Biblical-style
compositions.

Fig. 6   487 Drustanus *(the 'Castle Dore Stone'), mid-Cornwall; large granite pillar, probably a prehistoric menhir re-used.*

boulders, owed something surely to far older pre-Christian customs, placing similar but of course *un*-inscribed stones at or near graves.

Verticality, if one can use that word, in British inscriptions carries further implications. One (see p. 123) is the influence exerted by the general model of the Irish ogam-inscribed stones. Another is that in western Britain the fifth-century innovation of the lettered text, intended as a public statement about a dead person of importance, was readily attracted to a vertical face. There are plenty of cases where a chosen pillar was pretty obviously a convenient menhir or standing-stone left over from deep prehistory. *Fig. 6* is an example from Cornwall, the Castle Dore 487 *Drustanus* stone, and its lettering was cut larger partly for visibility; the text (running vertically) is well above eye-level. Again, while inscriptions set flat are read from above, looking down on them as if upon a ground-plan, those set on upright surfaces (whether in horizontal lines like 421 *Rostece,* or reading up-and-down) are read in side-view; effectively, in profile. This must be linked to the Insular invention, apparently in the sixth century, of 'profile' mental images.

As for what the inscriptions say, while many of them contain no Latin beyond *hic iacit* 'here lies', or *filius/fili* 'son, of the son', individual texts help to expand the range considerably.[5] It has already been affirmed that the variety of Latin in use ranks with standard literary Latin elsewhere as the main vehicle of Christian ideas. What must also be said in no uncertain terms is that the Christian inscriptions of Britain have nothing to do with a supposed 'Celtic' Christianity, or the recently fashionable imprecisions now marketed as 'Celtic Spirituality' that nudge shoulders uneasily with New Age beliefs or, worse, what is being miscalled *shamanism*.[6] Thousands more of these inscribed memorials exist in Italy, Switzerland, the Rhine basin, many parts of France, and Spain and Portugal. They are in Latin and they also show a mixture of native and continuing-Roman (and Biblical) names. There is a basic unity, with regional and local characteristics. The common models are to be seen in earlier tombstones of pre- or non-Christian nature, and pre-400 stones in the Italian peninsula and several other Latin-using provinces. Those in Britain are, along with more extended texts surviving as manuscript copies, witness to an undivided Christian (not 'Celtic' Christian) faith. Throughout the West this was linked to, practised through, driven by, and at all periods bound up with, the Latin language.

For Insular protohistory the outstanding worth of these inscribed stones is that they make up the single largest body of evidence, not just for the post-400 spread of Latin Christianity, but for a concealed intellectual culture; inferentially, for a system of education; and obliquely, for the Early Christian archaeology of Britain, that overcrowded and eroded Atlantic isle. (The next most useful body of evidence is that of all the early place-names.) Where conventional archaeological discovery is concerned there is a new importance because, for economic reasons, factors that used to lead to so many new finds in the field are now present on a greatly-reduced scale. Yet, as later chapters show, it is apparent that 520 *Latinus* offers us potential new information on the long constructional sequence at Whithorn; 427 *Catuoconi* points to an unidentified funerary structure on Caldey; and 986 *Ioruert* allows a reconstruction of a lost, probably royal, double tomb. These and others are without exception to be taken as *archaeological* implications.

On that score the present book takes its place not among linguistic or epigraphic studies but on the shelf marked *Britain: Post-Roman Archaeology*. All stones are tangible monuments, many of them protected by antiquities legislation and quite a lot housed in national and local museums, labelled and spot-lit. All have been modified if not shaped by human-ordered activity, and most can be linked to commonplace archaeological sites. Together, studies of epigraphy — inscriptional form and contents — and of palaeography — development of the graphs or letters — make up the archaeology of one variety of writing. Study of the Celtic, British and Irish, name-forms and occasional words as evidence for contemporary speech or for sound-changes through time is simply an aspect of the archaeology of language (historical linguistics). As we shall find (*Fig.72*), even the mental images generated by some of these texts make sense, as a time-space phenomenon arising out of human achievement, only when presented in the guise of an ordinary archaeological typology. The added dimension of textual structuring in Biblical style, intrinsically a lot less complicated than many scientific techniques applied to archaeological material, calls for a fresh *intellectual* and partly intuitive archaeology (with its own tools and methods) to be joined to the other investigations.

This reads like a tall order. New ideas must expect to meet resistance from entrenched beliefs. It is no reader's fault that shortfalls in national education result in most of us knowing little or no Latin (let alone Greek), that few people have ever seen a reliable edition of the Vulgate, that mental arithmetic has become a lost art, and that a Celtic language once spoken all the way from Penzance to Edinburgh is now represented by road-signs on the motorway to Cardiff and Swansea or terrifying words like *llwynwst* and *rhwysgfawr*. There is a plus side. We deal with texts that are cut into stone; not wax, or beechwood slivers, or animal skins, or fragile papyrus. Unless brilliant undetectable forgers have been at work these texts are fixed; from the moment of model and display. In fact they are double-fixed, if in Biblical style. The system, on stone as with longer manuscripts (always prey to errors of copying and careless checking), possesses built-in safeguards to allow total recovery. If letters are missing now, frequently the arithmetic tells us which of possible alternatives must have been used because its numerical value is otherwise supplied. One gets the impression that some of these composers knew full well that, should the computus, inner content and any pictorial element of their texts be forgotten and lost, then sooner or later — as it has happened, a great deal later — some inquisitive reader would notice the first-order clues, work out the constructional rules and rescue the messages from oblivion.

A grieving father and a slaughtered son

Harking back to Indiana Jones and his Lost Ark, nothing has yet been said about how these inscriptional messages and images were recovered. A concise account may round off this first chapter. Biblical-style compositions in Insular Latin writings were first seen, explored, explained and fully demonstrated in a range of papers and books by Dr David Howlett. His work[7] arouses many reactions ranging from wilful disbelief (often, sadly, by avowed non-readers of it) to acceptance and participation, particularly by those who have applied the analyses and rules to unexamined material. In May 1995, studying certain longer Welsh inscriptional texts that I had used, but very much at face-value, in writing a historical account[8] it struck me that one in particular (350 *Idnert*, from Llanddewi-brefi in Ceredigion, Cardigan) showed two probable Biblical allusions; and that it seemed to possess some arithmetical structure. A subsequent realisation that quite by chance I had picked upon a late and just about the most elaborate and device-packed example of Biblical style in all Britain took a while to dawn, and its eventual publication required nearly fifty compressed pages.[9] What the discovery did provide, guided as it was by David Howlett's own descriptions, was a first outline of the rules — an outline to be modified, refined and expanded as more and more material emerged.

Today the Idnert stone is represented by two lettered fragments (*Fig.7*) built into an external corner of the restored parish church of St David at Llanddewi-brefi. Most fortunately the inscription was seen, and recorded when entire, in 1699 by Edward Lhuyd, a scholar on whose expert testimony we can usually place near-total reliance. This had been a tall slab or pillar, lettered vertically in three lines and a mixture of capitals and book-hand. It read as follows:

> HIC IACET IDNERT   FILIUS IACOBI
> QUI OCCISUS FUIT   PROPTER PREDAM
>   SANCTI DAVID

Fig. 7   *350* Idnert.
Surviving
fragments, the larger
40cm, (16in) long,
built during
Victorian
reconstruction into
the W face of the
external NW angle
of Llanddewi-brefi
parish church;
drawn in situ,
1995.

— and had long attracted a certain interest because it was thought that this may have been the earliest surviving reference to Wales's national saint. Without more debate the meaning is: 'Here lies Idnert, son of Iaco(bus), who has been slain on account of a depredation [*of the church, monastery, sacred site*] of saint David', a memorial for a man killed during some affray at a place that, on other evidence, had been of religious importance since around 600 and has a very long history of its own.

IDNERT is the Old Welsh name usually written *Iudnert, Iudnerth*. IACO, with a New Testament -BI (genitive), -BUS (nominative) added, represents a neo-Brittonic borrowing of the Vulgate *Iacob*, becoming Old Welsh *Iaco* /yago/; and DAVID /dawid/ is a similar borrowing. This text has 12 words, 25 syllables and 64 letters; no ligatures and abbreviations, and therefore display and model are the same. A deliberate division of the 12 words into 3 lines as 5.5.2 (or 5 and 7) arouses immediate interest when we see that the first *five* words contain letter I (=*unus*) *seven* times:

h **I** c **I** acet **I** dnert f **I** l **I** us **I** acob **I** = IIIIIII = 7

and conversely the last *seven* words have it *five* times:

qu **I** occ **I** sus fu **I** t propter predam sanct **I** dav **I** d = IIIII = 5

To spot Biblical allusions, which may come as only one or two words, does require a certain familiarity with the Authorised Version and the Latin Vulgate. I noticed two, both of which seemed to point to Jesus Christ. The prototype Jacob, *Iacob*, was the father of *twelve* sons, eponyms of the tribes of Israel. There are *twelve* words, and the genealogy of Christ set out in Matthew, chap.1, is taken back to the patriarch *Iacob* (v.2), incorporating King *David* on the way (vv.5,6). QUI OCCISUS, perhaps especially to lovers of Handel's *Messiah* using the libretto chosen by his friend Charles Jennens, is bound to recall 'Worthy the Lamb that *was slain*'. and thus Apocalypsis (the Vulgate name for Revelation), 5.12, *dignus est Agnus QUI OCCISUS est*. But 'the Lamb', we know, is Christ, from John, 1.36; *ecce Agnus Dei*, 'Behold, the Lamb of God!' cries the Baptist, as Jesus walks towards him.

By now it had crossed my mind, first that the composer of this memorial may well have been Iago, the dead man's father, and second that he may have been implying (extraordinarily so, to modern tastes) that his son's violent death should be placed alongside that of Christ on the Cross. Noting that both the name *Iesus* and, first in the text, the word *iacet* 'lies' begin with the letter *i* used to convey the /y/ sound, I wondered if any kind of acrostic-style spacing - using either 5 or 7 for the spaces — could produce this name. At a second attempt I found this:

hic / **I** acetidn **E** rtfiliu **S** iacobiq **U** ioccisu **S** / (28)

7   7   7   7

and then, counting letters, saw that the *span* from **I** to **S**, with its five letters IESUS and twenty-eight (4 by 7) intervals, came to 33 — which, by very early tradition, was Christ's earthly age when crucified; and that what followed the **S**, as 28 letters, was also a multiple of seven.

It would take up far too many pages, and would be unjustified because this has been already published elsewhere, to give the many other details, devices, clues, instructions and readings contained in this short but magisterial composition. Instead, I pick out one particular aspect; its pictorial component. Because there are 64 letters, and 64 is the square of 8, we are invited to set out the text as a letter-square; a common game from the Roman world, long antedating anything to do with Christianity. I had already worked out that this inscription was using a 20-letter A-to-X alphabet (not the longer alternative of 23 letters, with K,Y and Z) having LaN values of 1 to 20, because I knew that this is occasionally mentioned by early writers, and because we can see immediately these clues:

(a) First letter of text, H; last letter, D; H + D, or 8 + 4, making *twelve*, the same as the word total.

(b) First and last letters of the three lines are

H,	8		I,	9
Q,	15		M,	11
S,	<u>17</u>		D,	<u>4</u>
	40			24

together making *sixty-four*, same as the letter total, but doing so as 24:40, which represents — as David Howlett's work had shown me — the extreme ratio division (p. 75) of 64.

Fig. 8 is the next step. For this I added up all the values, first for the vertical columns and then for the horizontal lines, finding that cols.1 and 5 were equal with 71, and lines 7 and 8 too, with 67. When the square is drawn out, of course we see (col.4) IESUS again because we are back to (interval-7) plus (letter-1), but now additionally, col.3, the words

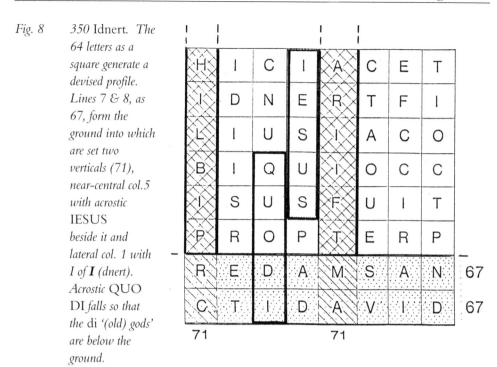

Fig. 8   *350* Idnert. *The 64 letters as a square generate a devised profile. Lines 7 & 8, as 67, form the ground into which are set two verticals (71), near-central col.5 with acrostic* IESUS *beside it and lateral col. 1 with* I *of* **I** *(dnert). Acrostic* QUO DI *falls so that the* di *'(old) gods' are below the ground.*

QUO DI — *quo di* ? 'where [are the old, pagan] gods ?'; answer, departed at the Triumph of the Cross. Indeed, if this shows what later I came to describe as a preliminary *devised profile* image, the abandoned deities are now below ground, allowing lines 7 and 8 to represent the earth. But, set into that ground, we see two matched uprights, cols.1 and 5. The second, near-central, has IESUS adjoining it; that on the left, the I of Idnert. And again we get the numeral allusion to the Crucified Christ because the four corner letters (H T C D, as 8.18.3.4) make *thirty-three*. Does this suggest, more pointedly, a depiction of Idnert 'crucified' alongside the True Cross?

The confident answer is: Yes, it does, and there is more to come. I pass over the catalogue of other details to be found — Iago (who may have been abbot of a monastery here, with his son Idnert, a priest, as his intended successor) did compose this, implies his age as 64 and Idnert's as 46 — the 18-years gap, at any rate, is believable — and also tells us the date: AD 806. There are internal rhymes (the text itself is metrical), any number of anagrams, two instructions to read the text backward giving both Idnert's name and the name of one of those, presumably, who slew him; at least five Fibonacci number-sets and the convention 5.7.12.19.31.50. (p. 75) used to mark extreme ratio; and a mass of numerical references. The main Biblical source was Matthew's Gospel, for some reason favoured in this and other Welsh inscriptions and to lovers of the Vulgate as a stylistic landmark arguably high among Jerome's finest work. After five months, on and off, studying the text and finding some new delight each time, I had discovered enough to formulate most of the rules governing this inscriptional style.

The text is in *three* lines; *three* proper names are mentioned; twelve words is *three* (times

Fig. 9   *350 Idnert. Because text has 12 words, there must be 11 intervals or blanks between them; 11 blanks plus 64 letters make 75, which can be set as a row of three squares of 25 (letters and blanks). In this further devised profile, basis for the depiction in Fig. 73, blacked-in blanks indicate a central Cross, and hint at two lower lateral ones; new horizontal readings appear (FUNCTI, IUS IIT).*

the four = gospels); Idnert is word no. *three*; the total of syllables, *twenty-five*, is the square of *five* which, with *seven*, is obviously a key number. Now any text of 64 letters, arranged as 12 words, must have eleven spaces between the words. Sixty-four (letters) plus eleven (blanks, non-letters) makes 75. We cannot 'square' 75, but taken as *three* times *twenty-five* it becomes patent that we *can* square 25, three times. *Fig. 9* is the result. Blacking-in at least the central blanks, the Cross appears in clearer profile. So, as horizontal acrostics, do new words. Lines 1 and 4, HIC . IACOBI, FUNCTI *hic, Iacobi functi* ('here (the work) of-Iago, who-has-made (it)', and line 5, IUS.IIT *ius i(v)it* 'Righteousness hath departed' (at Idnert's killing?).

This triple, fifteen by five, row of squares (oddly reminiscent of elongated and 'staggered' letter grids to give vertical acrostics, a feature that we meet in the next chapter: p. 50) is a threshold for a final depiction, *Fig. 73*. The unique aspect of this is that it never was a mental image, generated by the text. It existed already as a separate and genuine picture and, though lost for ever, we can infer that it was most probably a coloured (half-page?) miniature within a Gospel book, presumably the Matthew text; that it may well have been an eighth-century work, imported from Gaul; and that Iago began with this scene, Christ crucified on the hillock of *Golgotha, Calvaria* or Calvary between two thieves (Dismas, viewer's left; Gestas, viewer's right), Sun and Moon reddened by a dust-storm above the Cross, the Sponge-profferer on Christ's right and the Centurion with the lance, Longinus, on His left. A known earlier model for the scene survives in the Rabbula Gospels from Mesopotamia (of 586; since the fifteenth century, preserved in a library at Florence). What Iago did was to superimpose his son Idnert on the left cross, the one supposedly occupied by Dismas. At this final juncture we find a wealth of *labelling* (planned positioning of letters, or parts of words, so that they refer to components of a

Fig 10   *350* Idnert, *a selected detail from the final depiction (in Fig. 73); upper central part of square (b) in Fig. 9. The 'O' will become the nimbus around Christ's Head, the 'QUI' asks 'Who (is this)?' and the 'C' answers C(hristus).*

picture or image). This can be discussed later, but a small sample (*Fig. 10*) gives an idea. In the central square the upper three lines read: A C O B I / ★ Q U I ★ / O C C I S. For line 1, the 'C' goes up to form the crescent Moon, and the 'O' now forms the nimbus around Christ's head; line 2 asks Q U I? 'Who (is this)?', and (line 3) the central 'C' answers C(*hristus*).

By early 1996, applying the rules derived from analysing 350 *Idnert* to other inscriptions (at first, anything with more than 40 or so letters), I found that the earliest stone from Cornwall, 479 *Cunaide* — whose structure is very much like that of 421 *Rostece* — and also the earliest from south-west Scotland, 520 *Latinus*, were in full inscriptional Biblical style. The latter, suddenly and unexpectedly, revealed its own brilliantly-constructed mental image; a *display plan* fully labelled. When a first search through stones from Spain (Vives 505 *Anduires*) and the Rhineland (*Armentarius*; p. 96) showed related elements within these Continental memorials it became clearer that there must have been a common basis present before 400, probably throughout the West, and one that ought to be detectable at some point in Roman Britain. In due course, and thanks to the perspicacity and help of Dr Martin Henig, *RIB* 684 *Corellia Optata* and the Lullingstone mosaic text (both described in Chap.2) were tracked down to supply the evidence. The additional discoveries in their turn led to clarification and refinement of many of the rules governing, or seeming to govern, composition. At the same time the central role of intellectual life in Wales could be seen as the inventive force behind a secondary development of mental images as profiles, not just plans.

That is where we stand, and that (in outline) is what much of the book will try to describe and to illustrate. Certain further desirable lines of research suggest themselves. No proper search has yet been made among the hundreds, probably thousands, of post-Roman Gaulish memorials, a great many published long ago at levels of transcriptional accuracy that preclude confident analysis (for example, ligatures are often missed or misrepresented in print). It is now evident that, starting from the same literary basis somewhat earlier than 400 and then perhaps influenced in different ways by the growing circulation of the Vulgate text as a standard, Biblical style for longer Latin compositions went in one direction (described in David Howlett's successive books), and its inscriptional offshoot in another, making much greater use of the mathematical adjuncts.

Something about this can be repeated by way of conclusion; but we may now return to *Britannia*, pre-400 Roman Britain, and consider starting-points rather than ultimate developments.

Notes to Chapter 1

1. Inscribed stones are cited with the number (from Macalister, *CIIC*) and a relevant name; if from Wales, they may also carry a separate (Nash-Williams, *ECMW*) number; anything from Roman Britain carries its *RIB* number.

2. HIC IN TUMULO IACIT is less common than HIC IACIT; source and approximate dates are discussed by J.K. Knight, 'The Early Christian Latin inscriptions of Britain and Gaul; chronology and context', pp.45-50 in: N. Edwards & A. Lane, eds., *The Early Church in Wales and the West* (Oxford 1992).

3. 'Paternus' survived in Wales as (Saint) Padarn, of Llanbadarn, conceivably a figure of fifth-century SE Wales; Paterninus may have owed his name to a slightly earlier noted Christian.

4. The largest (general, including NW France) is the Celtic Inscribed Stones Project (CISP), a computerised data-base at University College London; for Wales, revision of ECMW has nearly finished; for Scotland, a separate exhaustive survey is now in a planning stage. For fieldworkers, shifting locations are probably the worst problem.

5. See my 'The Early Christian Inscriptions of Southern Scotland', *Glasgow Archaeol. Journal* 17 (1991-2), 1-10, which lists 40 words from Scottish stones and 52 from the thirty-odd inscriptions of N and NW Wales.

6. A shaman (from a Manchu or Tungus word) is or was a native Siberian magician priest involved with nervous ecstasy and trances; whatever vaguely comparable activities may or may not have characterised pre-Christian Ireland and Britain, it is a grotesque misapplication to talk of 'Celtic' shamans, and ludicrous to pose as a modern-day shaman.

7. D.R.Howlett's relevant books here are *The Book of Letters of Saint Patrick the Bishop* (1994), *The Celtic Latin Tradition of Biblical Style* (1995) and *British Books in Biblical Style* (1997), all: Four Courts Press, Dublin, and cited thereafter as 'Saint Patrick', 'Celtic Latin Tradition' and 'British Books'.

8. *And Shall These Mute Stones Speak ? Post Roman Inscriptions in Western Britain* (Cardiff 1994), cited as 'Mute Stones'.

9. 'The Llanddewi-brefi 'Idnert' Stone', *Peritia* (= *Journ. Medieval Academy of Ireland*) 10 (1996), 136-83, 5 illus.

10. See the article above for details; the Crucifixion-scene depictions have their own complicated history.

2 The Roman Background

The impact of Latin

Standing back somewhat and donning a historian's spectacles to view Roman Britain — far too large a field of study to discuss here beyond chosen aspects bearing upon this book's theme — one sees that the first four centuries AD were uniquely important in Britain's protohistory. Fully documented, we have the dated and certain (our first) introduction of a non-British language; and, by the close, the certain though less securely dated introduction of what was to become a national religion. In practice rather than theory, Latin is still with us (e.g., everyday botanical classification, the slightly mangled Latin of medical prescriptions). In theory, to judge from annual totals of baptisms, weddings and funerals alone, the religion is still national.

What Latin-speakers found from AD 43 was a Celtic vernacular not so radically different from Latin as to make it impossible for non-Britons to learn it, just as previously in Gaul (Gaulish and British, from what we know of both, were closely related). It can be doubted that there was much incentive to do so. There arose a familiar syndrome, the linguists' 'upper-lower' pairing,[1] in which almost all the advantages lay with Latin as the speech of the conquerors, their administration, armed forces and centralised trade. Latin was also the medium for the official Roman religion, and became a necessary item of baggage on any route to personal advancement. An advantage of British may have been its near-universality as a medium (the *Pretani* or Picts of the Scottish Highlands spoke an older sub-language but, from its remnants, one close to British). The distinction was that Latin arrived in a dual capacity. It was an Imperial speech current across much of Europe ranging from the mandarin to the vulgar, and also a written language with its evolved classical tradition, fixed spelling, several types of writing (from handsome capitals down to scrawled cursives) and for good measure a convenient, easy-to-learn, little scheme of numerical notation. The British language on the other hand had hardly ever been reduced to writing, except in late pre-Roman times as abbreviated names of native kings and their tribes on certain coins. From the first century AD, many more British nouns and adjectives *were* represented in writing because the Romans adopted them for place-names (mostly within a military network), but as the equivalent of the British in India choosing how to spell Darjeeling and Pondicherry.

Half a century back, students of both Roman and post-Roman Britain tended to accept uncritically one reading of conclusions advanced by linguists, Professor Kenneth Jackson foremost, to the effect that spoken British never *was* reduced to writing, and possibly that its sound-system was not fully portrayable in the Latin ABC. Today there would be rather less confidence in those views. It is conceivable that very occasionally people did write in British,[2] our problem being to distinguish words we do not necessarily know within *scriptio* (or *scriptura*) *continua*, strings of letters not showing any word-boundaries. The related Gaulish was frequently written, and not just as individual names, using several alphabets and favouring the Greek letters. A jolly inscription on a bottle[3] is quite legible as *ibetis uciu andecari biiete* and intelligible as 'Drink from this, you will be greatly lovable'. A Greek-lettered dedication on stone[4] is to MATREBO NAMAUSIKABO; *matrebo* is 'To the Mother-Goddesses', Latin *matribus*, the second word representing Namausos, Nemausos (city of Nîmes), adjective Namausik-os, -a, -on 'pertaining to Nîmes', dative plural feminine Namausik-abo (like the Latin ending -*abus*; *deabus*). One could reconstruct a British thought *carant sosan ceruesan* ('They love this beer!') and guess that the Roman alphabet renders it adequately. On Late Iron Age coins we can find purely British personal names, abbreviated, like a coin with two-line TASCI/RIGONI, read as the genitive of *Tasciovanos* who was *rigonos* 'Great-King, Divine-King'. Significant British and Gaulish Celtic names went on being written in the Latin ABC. Caesar's memoir *De Bello Gallico* is full of them, mostly those of native tribes, and elsewhere non-Roman names appear throughout Roman literature. These are particular cases. On the evidence of post-Roman stones, the first to exhibit actual short sentences in Old Welsh (*CIIC* 1033-4, Towyn, Merioneths.) and in Old Irish (*CIIC* 1, Inchagoill, co.Galway: p. 127) using exclusively a Latin bookhand are unlikely to be older than *c*.700. It may well have been the case for centuries that a perceived bond between the Latin language and Roman writing-systems was too strong to encourage serious attempts at writing British, but it would be unwise to see that as an immutable dogma.

A greater uncertainty today must concern the extent to which spoken and written Latin penetrated a population running into three or four millions, most of it rural and most of it an underclass. The older model would have it that Latin, the higher language of control and conformity, never went much beyond the sociological A-B categories; the wealthy who were agrarian landowners by descent or custom, those who could and did figure in the magistracy and the curial (local government) world, those who became enthusiastically Romanised and were schooled in Rome's culture. The analogy has been advanced of the Russian aristocracy who in their St Petersburg palaces and summer dachas affected conversational French, distancing themselves from the Slavic peasantry. Similarly, it has been suggested that Romano-British *ancillae*, *servi*, a large estate's house-servants and bonded farmhands, could pick up a certain amount of polite Latin from daily contact with their betters.[5]

No-one disputes that, on the evidence from place-names and from Old/Middle Welsh and Cornish alone, Latin words at several levels kept passing from (spoken) Latin into (spoken) British;[6] indeed, also into (spoken) Irish, a key topic in any consideration of Romano-British contact across the Irish Sea and the still opaque story of Irish Christian origins. Some words explicably were for purely Roman innovations (*fenestra* for any rectilinear masonry window-opening, not a feature of pre-Roman housebuilding). One extremely interesting case, a postulated colloquial-Latin *privat-us*, masc., *privat-a*, fem., perhaps the Late Roman legionaries' term for 'sweetheart, boyfriend/girlfriend, intended' (literally 'my bit-of-goods'), must lie behind later Welsh *priod* ('spouse, betrothed', etc).

Fig. 11   *The divisions (provinciae) of late 4th-century Britannia, the Roman civil diocese corresponding to modern England and Wales; the administrative centres are Ca(rlisle), Yo(rk), Lin(coln), Cir(encester), Lon(don). Smaller circles; centres of civitates. The dotted boundaries can only be schematic.*

Exceptionally there is a Welsh inscription of *c*.500 that contains this, obviously with some such meaning (p. 147).

What can fairly be pointed out is that the *archaeological* exhibition offered in the two thick volumes of *RIB*, thousands of illustrations of Latin writings long and short on every conceivable surface, as yet shows very little sign of a corresponding *historico-linguistic* impact. By that, I imply that *RIB*'s huge Britannic collection, updated annually in the journal *Britannia*'s supplement and now really necessitating a third volume for 1950 onward, forces a fresh model upon the thoughtful. It may not be the *highest* register of the use of Latin in Roman Britain that has changed — very probably 99 per cent of all fancier literature has perished — but the infinitely greater, popular or *lower* register. We now have a myriad tokens from a busy Britannia where employees, artisans, skilled and unskilled citizens in commerce, the rude soldiery, pupils and teachers and, for all we know, a sub-world of drunks, idlers, fun-lovers, dropouts and perennial scribblers on public conveniences habitually used Latin letters, the Roman numerals, names, words, abbreviations and technical terms in everyday life.

It is only to be expected that the material comes thickest from urban centres and military establishments, not just because these have been favoured archaeological targets but because one would tend to see countings and jottings more obviously associated with manufactories, offices, the taxation system and army stores, than with small farms. It is also true that this archaeological-scriptorial detritus fails to give us much by way of literary composition, but it may have been overlooked that a great many small objects classed as counters, tallies and tokens are probably aids to learning from primary education, and that frequent mis-spellings and clumsily-formed letters must be from the Man/Woman in the Romano-British Street; not from scholars and administrators.

RIB obliges us to re-think a much stronger probability; that right up to the end of Roman Britain both *spoken* Latin — as (British) Vulgar Latin, VL, with provincialisms and peculiarities of pronunciation — and *written* Latin, acquired through schools or self-taught slowly the hard way, were in no way marginal. Nor is there any compelling reason to see them disappearing overnight in 410 or 425 or any other arbitrary date for 'the end' of Roman Britain, or during the civil disturbances, coups, risings and riots that may have marked or marred parts of Britain during the fifth century. Rhetorical questions now pop up by the bucketful. *If* this was the linguistic scenario, did it apply beyond (or in the fringes of) the civil diocese proper of Britannia, shown with its eventual *provinciae* in the provisional map, *Fig. 11*? *If* we were transported to a latter-day villa estate, a 'gentleman's monastery' in south-east Wales of AD 475, could one enjoy a meaningful Latin chat with the person in charge? Would interesting and educated people who knew Latin, when encountered in fifth-century Cornwall or Caernarvon or Dumfries, all turn out to be refugees from the Lowland Zone buying their way into safety in the face of a dread Anglo-Saxon tide? Or would they be the stolidly indigenous gentry, Christians, quite well-read and still in the habit of sending out the odd letter, who knew both languages as a matter of course? Two final questions. Up to what time would any of these Latin-using post-Roman British have described themselves, when pressed, as both *Combrogi*, Britons, and *cives Romani*, Roman citizens like their forbears? And what, other than a Twilight-of-the-Raj nostalgia for past times under the House of Theodosius, could have been the bond, the motive, the social glue holding together an anachronistic attachment to *romanitas*?

These questions may be rhetorically-posed but they are central, unless we wish to conduct all future exploration of post-Roman times through lateral forays into core-periphery studies, the self-empowerment of elites, processual and post-processual interpretations of a poorly-represented material past, and other substitutes for an increasing dearth of hard and solid data. But what answers *can* be supplied? To point out that two British Latin authors, Patrick of Ireland in the fifth century and Gildas somewhere in Britain in the sixth, apparently regarded themselves as *cives Romani* is to cite what may be the only available authorities. Constant parading of fresh models must attend a not-so-constant supply of fresh evidence (among which, Biblical-style composition arrives as a high spot). Only two comments need be made now. One, to be resumed later (p. 70), is the suspicion that there *was* an intellectual-social compound; a deep-seated reaction to national events, combining a corporate sense of being British with a superior pride in memories of once having been genuinely Roman, and that this attitude hardened through time. The other is that *Latinitas*, some command of spoken and written Latin and a demonstrable retention of the older Classical literary culture, was in very large measure tied to Christianity. A parallel Celtic culture, far harder to delineate because it does not survive in writing (and is only now being properly discerned), remained independent of Christianity. Culturally, a poet could readily serve two masters. Latin, in its application from the fifth century onwards, may not have been exclusively Christian. We remember the likelihood of land-grants through written charters, first attempts at secular chronicles, probably a trickle of personal correspondence. That leaves untouched the fact that the Vulgate Bible, supported by a known repertoire of related (European) Christian writings, came to dominate Insular Latin composition. The unmistakable stylistic idiom of St Jerome and Rufinus the Syrian expanded the previous horizon; the Latin of Cicero, Ovid and Vergil. Throughout the West, untouched beyond centuries of barbarian turmoil and national scene-shifting, Christianity was first and foremost a faith whose induction, practice, sacraments and manuals were *only* in Latin.

Late and sub-Roman Christianity

An accurate, unassailable history of Christianity in Roman Britain has yet to be compiled. The task remains unattainable and the evidence continues to appear in discrete dribs and drabs; here a grave, there a diagnostic trinket. My earlier book,[7] a summary of what was known up to 1980, was written to counter a prevalent (European) view that arose, un-countered, in the post-War period. This was the impression that Christianity in Late Roman Britain was minimal, entirely urban, eccentric in certain respects, and insufficiently rooted to withstand the disruptions of the post-400 age. A British corollary, long-voiced, was that when physical manifestations of Christianity are produced for post-Roman western Britain, as probably too for Ireland, all this sprang from a more-or-less total reintroduction of the Faith by agencies that can be named for short as 'Gaulish missionaries'. There are those who appear to believe this still. British Christianity, expunged by a red tide of heathen Saxondom, bequeathed little or nothing to 'the Dark Ages', a long stretch in which Christianity was re-supplied from its unbroken existence on the nearby Continent. It is a venerable notion, offering a certain Anglocentric attraction because, allowing the Faith to have lingered on at best in a remote Celtic fringe, the decks were cleared to spotlight the AD 597 arrival of St Augustine.

The explanation involving Gaulish missionaries contains a strand of reality. Atlantic Gaul (the west and north-west of France) as the nearest seat of a continuing Church in direct maritime contact *was* a source, of literature, ideas, influential visitors and returning pilgrims. No-one would dismiss as marginal the arrival of Palladius and his team in Ireland in AD 431, a likely presence of un-named persons in south-east Wales slightly later and, on the evidence of inscribed stones, what one might well describe as mission-stations with Gaulish clerics in both north-west Wales and south-west Scotland, around 500 (p. 117). That cannot be the whole story. The obstacle to a clear recital of the mainland-British side of it persists, because we are forced to construct inferences, probabilities, that do not all possess graphic evidential support in the shape of time-space maps. If that reads as an excuse in advance for more speculation, turn to *Fig.12*, which shows the concentrations of Christian inscriptions from the fifth to tenth/eleventh centuries, and then here to *Fig.13*, which is supposed to reflect the establishment of Romano-British Christianity up to 400-odd. The two distributions barely touch. If these were maps of particular kinds of polished stone axes in the Neolithic they would be described as *mutually exclusive*.

In compiling *Christianity in Roman Britain*, I constructed various maps bringing together

Fig. 12   Location of
inscriptions, 5th
to 8th centuries;
concentrations
in Wales and
SW Britain
(broken lines),
outliers (dots) in
Scotland, Isle of
Man and
various islands.
In NW
England no
inscriptions are
known from the
150-mile
stretch, the Dee
at Chester to the
Solway at
Carlisle.

classes of Christian evidence, the firmest class (largest dots, most heavily-shaded squares) marking fixed evidence, sites like putative churches that do not move; and portable, easily-dropped items like finger-rings with Christian mottoes and symbols being shown as the smallest dots, having very little secure geographical connotation.[8] Another 'fixed' class is offered by certain place-names, which also do not move around. Those maps served their purpose (and are still worth consulting; relevant finds made since 1980 would add dots here and there, but would not change the emphases). There have been further essays in this direction. Conspicuously worthwhile as a contribution is Frances Mawer's (1995) *Evidence for Christianity in Roman Britain. The small-finds*.[9] It provides us with a rigid, minimalist catalogue of what *can* be accepted — beyond reasonable quibble — as the hard evidence, discarding some of the items I had earlier listed and adding some more.

It is therefore the Mawer map that is reproduced here (*Fig.13*), without embellishments, except the addition of dotted lines that enclose the main concentrations of post-Roman Christian inscriptions. These, omitting a very few outliers (four on the isle of Lundy; 498 *Brigomaglos*, Chesterholm) include the smallest, southern Scotland; the middle one, Cornwall and part of Devon; and the largest, most of Wales.

The stones, numerically about five or six times the total of the various Roman Britain

Fig.13   Placed alongside the occurrence of post-Roman inscriptions, Frances Mawer's 1995 map of (mainly 4th-century) Christian evidence from small finds, reproduced with her kind permission, shows a contrasting spatial emphasis and virtually no overlap except possibly in SE Wales.

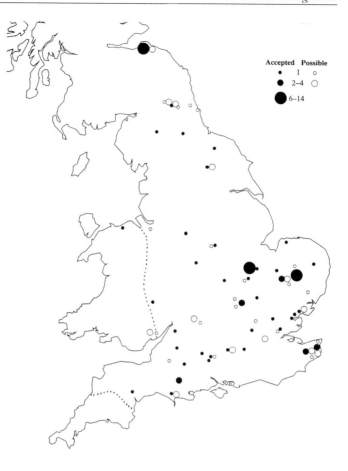

dots in *Fig.13*, form a different sort of evidence for Christian activity because the great majority can be associated with sites that have been church or cemetery locations for at least a millennium. The visible curvilinear bank-enclosure at Lewannick in east Cornwall (home to 466 *Ingenui*, 467 *Ulcagni*), still part of a parish churchyard, may in origin pre-date both Iona (563) and Augustine's Canterbury. Effectively *Fig.13* defines *one* state of knowledge — our picture, authentic as far as it can be, of the physical manifestations of *one* of the religions followed in Late Roman Britannia — and sets it alongside *another* state of knowledge, that of subsequent memorials on stone and nothing else. Like and like would be better matched, were it possible to compile a distribution of all post-400 small finds from southern Scotland, Wales and the south-west believed to have Christian associations (no-one has ever attempted so formidable a task).

In an attempt to circumvent the missing indications, *Fig.14* reproduces (modified) a 1981 map on which I brought together some of the evidence for fifth- and early sixth-century Christianity in Britain west and north of the blank area, marking the approximate extent by *circa* 550 of Anglo-Saxon advances and settlements. Cross-hatching refers to regions of (fourth-century) Britannia where any evidence of Christianity, from sites and small finds, was recorded — it should be slightly reduced in the light of Frances Mawer's

Fig. 14 From Christianity in Roman Britain to AD 500 (1981), *a map of sub-Roman Christianity beyond the English settlements (blank area), built up from non-archaeological evidence. 1, likely centres of pre-600 Christian activity; 2, survivals of Roman urban place-names; 3 & 4, types of place names with* ecles *'Christian community(?)'. Other details (five rulers named by Gildas, etc.) are less relevant than an indication that the post-400 Church in SW Scotland and N Wales ought in some measure to have survived from 4th-century Romano-British Christianity.*

work (as in *Fig.13*) — and the symbols are neither from archaeology, nor from inscribed stones. They refer to place-names; and place-names do not lie, nor confuse us. Important are the ten denoting urban centres where the Roman-period name was never wholly lost (like Luguvalium, *Carlisle*; Moridunum, *Carmarthen*; Corinium, *Cirencester*), and a class involving 'Eccles' on its own, or in compounds like Eccleston, Ecclefechan, because of the well-founded belief that this element survived through British into English (or English-Scots) from another extremely early loanword; the reflex of British VL *ecclesia*/egle:s(ya)/. It did not mean 'a church', unlike its much later manifestations as Welsh *eglwys*, Cornish *eglos*; in Late and sub-Roman times it is almost certain that it meant 'a Christian flock, community', very much its sense in the New Testament epistles,[10] and probably arose as a label given by neighbours, or isolated Christians, to anywhere distinguished by a Christian location and its adherents.

We have to say something about the most likely points of contact between the Church in pre-400 Britannia and the Church in the west and north, of sub-Roman (loosely, 400-500) and then post-Roman times. Given the distributions of inscribed memorials alone, three districts stand out. In the north-west, the oldest focus of Lowland Scottish Christianity (Whithorn and the Galloway coastal belt) must suggest continuity from Carlisle and the western hinterland of the Wall; this can be pursued in Chapter 5. In south-east Wales across the Severn — that is, in former Monmouth (now Gwent), most of Glamorgan, and some of Hereford — there are a good many grounds for thinking that much of the Roman way of life continued until after 500.[11] The English did not incorporate the Cotswolds into what was to be Wessex, and reach the Severn, until the recorded captures in 577 of Bath, Cirencester and Gloucester. For the north and north-west of Wales there is, comparatively, far less light. The evidence to be presented later points very firmly to more than one centre of intellectual and wholly Christian strength here (apart from a royal centre of the kingdom of Gwynedd, on the isle of Anglesey), but they remain to be identified; and there is far less evidence in this direction than for the south-east of Wales. As for the long south-west peninsula, Somerset, Devon and Cornwall beyond the Mendips — a post-Roman kingdom of *Dumnonia, Damnonia* — the maps tell the right story. In the Roman period the peninsula, outside and beyond *Isca (Dumnoniorum)*, Exeter, was barely Romanised (the main external interest was in its mineral resources of tin, and lead with silver). Overwhelmingly, the indications are that Christianity had virtually no impact here. The quite plentiful inscriptions with very few exceptions begin in the sixth century and they reflect a casual introduction of the Faith, along with casual settlement, from south and south-west Wales.[12]

As far as the evidence takes us, the Church in the pre-400 civil diocese of Britannia was organised in parallel with the Continent, after the 350s probably containing a double-figures list of bishops (*sacerdotes, episcopi*) whose seats were in towns and cities, whose congregations may never have been extensive and whose spiritual domains were organised geographically. It is only a guess that an episcopal network came loosely to correspond to the administrative-fiscal map of Britannia's (less than twenty?)[13] *civitates*, whose centres or 'cantonal capitals' functioned in a manner something like those of modern British first-tier authorities. It is much less of a guess that bishops, supported by attendant priests and deacons, held formal assemblies (synods) from time to time and that synodal meetings were possible, somewhere in Britain, considerably after 400. If one were forced to name Church centres from which any kind of authority percolated westwards into a Celtic, and partially Latin-using, world in the fifth century, they would have to be *Venta Silurum*, Caerwent, for south Wales;[14] *Luguvalium* (Carlisle) for south-west Scotland; perhaps also *Eburacum*, York, for a good two centuries of Celtic Christians in the Yorkshire and Derbyshire uplands, the least-explored of such regions; and for the northern half of Wales, the more strongly so as evidence for its fifth-century occupation grows, *Viroconium* (by Wroxeter). Remember that Llanerfyl, with 421 *Rostece* earlier, home of whatever *ecclesia* she and her father Paterninus graced, is only 32 miles from Viroconium. Features of her inscriptions do not have to be 'Gaulish' at all, in the light of what we shall soon find within Britannia.

There are other sides to the formidable problems of what, as *Kontinuität*, always sounds weightier in German; the British absence of so many things (bishop-lists, partial chronicles, quite reliable excavated evidence and the semblance of a historical record) that on the Continent bridge any (Christian) gap from the third and fourth centuries to the early medieval period. Some specific questions will be taken up in later chapters, notably what segments of society Christianity is likely to have covered, how the post-400 British Church may have been governed and to what extent the rich nomenclature from inscribed stones tells us anything beyond names and conventional sentiments. It can be the reverse of satisfying for any writer to have to admit that this account has gone about as far as it can, and to refer his readers to work already in print, but we are left mainly with *inferences*. The extent to which post-Roman Christianity among the Celtic British represented a direct legacy from the fourth century in Britannia rests as a matter of individual judgement and opinion.[16] Meanwhile we may turn to unfamiliar ground, and look at Latin compositions whose post-Roman counterparts do imply a kind of continuity, if very much at a rarified and intellectual level.

Corellia Optata's memorial

Romano-British inscriptions on stone as catalogued in *RIB*, vol.i, come in many categories. There are official Imperial and governmental entablatures; building-stones marking completion of temples and defensive works; a great many small sacrificial altars (*arae*); dedications to a straggle of deities, some native Celtic and some exotic; and personal tombstones. The last, broadly divisible into military and civilian, range in presentation from the competent and formal (often with a pictorial element) to the frankly crude and clumsy. No complete explanation has been provided why, in Britannia, the lettered-memorial tradition seems to have petered out during the fourth century, in contrast to neighbouring Europe. A handful of what are probably fourth-century stones can be suggested as Christian, on not very convincing grounds;[17] a puzzle is why there are so few of these.

If one started to look through the tombstones to find out if any exhibit traces of arithmetical content, acrostic readings or other elements diagnostic of post-400 Biblical style it would be sensible to concentrate on stones from urban centres most likely to have housed families benefiting from full Roman education in the liberal arts, people with literary tastes (and wealth), and that echelon of polite society in touch with a wider Roman world. London, Lincoln, York, Chester and Cirencester come to mind. In fact, the only instance so far detected comes from *Eburacum*, Roman York. It is the elaborate memorial to Corellia Optata, another girl aged 13, daughter of Quintus Corellius Fortis. Who he was we do not know but the family of Corellii can be traced in Italy and southern Gaul.[18] The top of this slab is missing. It must have shown a picture of the girl (her shins and feet remain), above a text which is fortunately complete and is headed by two roundels with D (*Dis* 'to the gods') and M(*Manibus* 'to the shades'). There is no reason to see it as Christian, and plenty of reasons to regard it as pagan; third century rather than fourth. It was found (in 1861) at The Mount cemetery, York,[19] and the accompanying burial is reported as a cremation, some of the ashes being in a glass flask.

RIB 684 *Corellia Optata* presents a text of eleven lines cut within a low-relief frame having corner-cusps and two side-cusps. It is in three parts; her name and age, five lines of (original) poetry in which her father mourns his loss, and the father's name and

Fig. 15   York: The Mount area, 1861, found with cremations and probably 3rd (or late 2nd) century. Incomplete partly-pictorial gritstone memorial (=RIB 684) for Corellia Optata aged 13; above recessed framed text, roundels with D (missing) and M, and from traces of shins/feet a frontal depiction of the dead girl. Photograph, RCHM England: Crown copyright reserved.

responsibility for the monument (*Fig.15*). There are 41 words. The display contains 199 letters. Expansion of ligatures, last-line abbreviations, XIII to *tredecim*, and a few *internalised* letters [20] would raise *LM*, the model's letter count, to 253.

Bearing in mind that rather later stone for another thirteen-year-old, 421 *Rostece* (p. 75), it might be spotted that (a) the *two* roundels with D and M, plus the *eleven* lines of text, happen to make *thirteen*; and (b) that line 6, which refers specifically to 'the semblance of the body', *simulacrum corporis*, is cut to read ET.SIMVLACRVM.CORPORIS.VM / (BRA, line 7) — that is, *four* words (as three-and-a-half) with *nine* syllables, also making *thirteen*. Then, allowing the obvious expansion of line 1, AN. to AN(NORVM) 'of years', it would be seen that the letter 'O' occurs exactly *thirteen* times. (The significance of that is that, in 20-letter LaN, *thirteen* is the value of O.) Because this resembles totalling of those letters that are also numerals (LNu), very careful inspection then reveals that between the two displayed names, hers as CORELLIA OPTATA and his as Q(uintus). CORE(llius).FORTIS, a visual-cum-mental expansion of ligatures and incorporations allows:

> x I I I secretI quI acherusIa dItIs IncolItIs lumIna
> vIte exIguIs cInIs sImulacrum corporIs InsontIs genItor
> InIqua mIserandus fInem

—which displays letter 'I' (here, as LNu *unus*), 26 or twice *thirteen* times.

Observations on this scale are good enough to reveal 13 as a key number prompted by her age; apparent use of (20-letter) LaN and of LNu; and too great a reference to *thirteen* to be dismissed as coincidental. We can give a full analysis, this time distinguishing the central line 6 as *B*, with *A* before and *C* after it.

A		W	S	LD	LM
1	CORELLIA. OPTATA.AN(norum).X I I I	4	12	20	29
2	SECRETI . MANES . QVI REGNA	4	11	18	20
3	ACHERVSIA . DITIS . INCOLI	3	10	20	20
4	TIS.QVOS . PARVA PETVNT POST	4	7	22	22
5	LVMINA . VITE . EXIGVIS . CINIS	4	11	19	22
	totals *A*	19	51	99	113
B					
6	ET . SIMVLACRVM . CORPORIS . VM				
	totals *B*	4	9	18	22
C					
7	BRA . INSONTIS GNATE . GENI	6	8	17	20
8	TOR . SPE . CAPTVS . INIQVA		7	18	18
9	SVPREMVM . HVNC . NATE	3	6	14	16
10	MISERANDVS . DEFLEO . FINEM	3	9	17	21
11	Q(uintus) .CORE(llius) .FORTIS.				
	PAT(er) .F(aciendum). C(uravit)	6	17	16	43
	totals *C*	18	47	82	118
	Overall totals:	**41**	**107**	**199**	**253**

The initials of the eleven lines, C S A T L /E/ B T S M Q, add to 117; that must mean something because it is *thirteen* by nine. The eleven last letters, as they stand, make only 102. But consider the final word, part of a stock-ending *faciendum curavit* ('took care of the making [of the stone]'). If the final letter were read, not as C(uravit) but as (curavi)*T*, the last-letter total would also become 13 by 9; 117. And we could revert to LNu, the numeral letters; central line 6 offers us, for higher values —

et si **M** u **L** a **C** ru **M C** orporis u**M** /

— which produces M L C M C M , or re-arranging them M M M C C L, or 3000 + 200 + 50 = 3250, *thirteen* times *twenty-five* times ten.

The opening means 'Corellia Optata; of years, thirteen' and the end, 'Q.Corellius Fortis, the father, took care of the making'. In between, the poem, a genuine and elegant expression of his grief, is:

> Secreti manes qui regna Acherusia Ditis
> Incolitis quos parva petunt post lumina vite
> Exiguis cinis et simulacrum corporis umbra
> Insontis gnate genitor spe captus iniqua
> Supremum hunc nate miserandus defleo finem

('O mysterious Shades, who inhabit the Acherusian realms of Dis' (*a name for Pluto*), 'whom the scant ashes and the shadow — vain semblance of the body — seek, after the little brightnesses of Life: I, the begetter of a blameless daughter, a pitiable captive of unjust Hope, weep over her final ending.')

There are patterns here, too. The line initials run S I E I S, a.b.c.b.a, and both S I and I S, as 17.9 and 9.17, make *thirteen* by two. In the third line, *et simulacrum corporis um* (= text, line 6) is preceded by *12* letters, followed by *3*. That is a 4-to-1 ratio, and counting words per line as we find line 2 has *seven*, the other four having *six* each; 6.6.6.6 and 7 is another '4 and 1' pattern.

We find, over and beyond key number *thirteen*, two elements. The first can be called the 'centrality' of *simulacrum corporis*, the reference to what remains of her body (cremated ashes) and what in Christianity would correspond to her soul. It falls in the central line. With 41 words, as 19.3.19, we have ET SIMULACRUM CORPORIS; with 107 syllables, as 53.1.53, et sim)**UL**(acrum; with 253 letters (model), as 126/1/126, simulacrum) **C** (orporis).

The second is a concept of a *square*. As in a good many later inscriptions, this is signalled in two ways; number *four*, a basic symbol for all and any squares, and *squared numbers*. The age, as X I I I, has *four* graphs and is the *fourth* word. The line initials and line last-letters, totalling 117 each, are like two equal sides of a square, the text itself being in a virtually square frame. In the display, line 6 (expanded), ET SIMVLACRVM CORPORIS VM, has as we noticed *four* words, and nine (= three *squared*) syllables, and its first and last letters E M, 5.11, make 16, the *square* of *four*.

Where does this lead? In what direction, to what outcome, are readers being gently pushed? Corellia Optata's grave was an accidental discovery, not a modern excavated site,

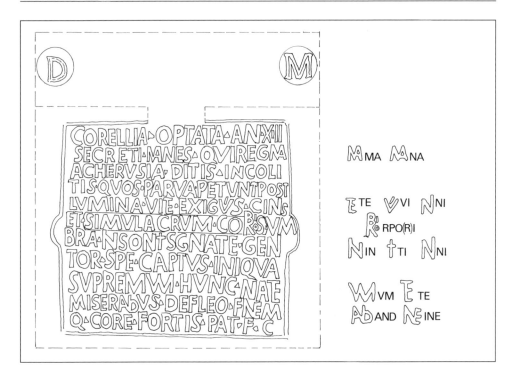

Fig. 16   RIB 684 Corellia Optata, York. Lower part of slab suggests an image, a small temple-mausoleum(?), in which line 6, SIMULACRUM CORPORIS, outlined, marks the transverse cremation-grave. The top is the front , where (Martin Henig's suggestion) the D(is) M(anibus) roundels are portico-columns; line 1, OPTA, below the picture of Corellia on the complete slab, marks the doorway (POrTA). Do corner-letters C I, I C (=12), C Q, Q C (=18) convey somebody's idea of likely dimensions in pedes? On the right, details of ligatures and internalised letters.

and we do not know in what physical setting it may have lain. But — examining a photograph of the stone (*Fig.15*) with its squared lettering-area and prominent recessed frame — is it meant to show a ground-plan? Is this not interpretable as a mental image (a *display plan*) of a small square construction, a little temple-like building above a rectangular cremation grave (vault, small mausoleum)? If so, that grave lies across the centre, as line 6, ET... and ...VM more or less by the two side-cusps. The roundels, D (defaced, top left) and M (top right), might represent two pillars supporting an external portico. The entrance or way-in (*porta*) should be in the middle of the top line; note **P O R T A**, and (corellia) **O P T A** (ta an xiii). *Fig.16* abstracts these details, and gives some idea of a plan that the composer may have had in mind.[21]

There is not much doubt, from mental images generated in post-400 Insular inscriptions, that the *plan* preceded anything shown in *profile*; and that drawn ground-plans must have been commonplace in the Roman world, from any sort of map down to a builder's first plan for a simple structure. *RIB 684 Corellia Optata* might be borne in mind as a first British record of image-generation. What its inscription contains is a key number (from age at death); LaN, to give short, long and multiple totals; LNu, for much the same; possible 4-to-1, or 1-to-4 (= quadruple) ratio, as one way of signalling 'a square'; and the idea of a square (plan?) from *four* and from squared numbers.

Lullingstone and Avitus

Our second example of original Latin verse, embedded in a public display that contains a great deal more than any casual glance could possibly suggest, comes from the heartland of Britannia; from what had become in the fourth century *Maxima Caesariensis*, the Home Counties and East Anglia with London and Colchester as the foci. The Roman villa at Lullingstone in the Darent valley of north-west Kent was thoroughly explored from 1949 to 1961.[22] We can picture it as a country estate with a succession of occupiers, the later owners being (in modern language) substantial gentleman-farmers whose mansion — the central villa-house — was altered or partly rebuilt several times.

Lullingstone has aroused much interest because, in what seems to have been its final phase, some upper rooms in the house were taken over, converted and richly decorated to become an internal church. Its Christian nature is shown by a remarkable suite of wall-paintings and it was used for a short while into the fifth century before the place was (accidentally?) burnt down. Late in the third century the occupiers enjoyed the use of the main house, outside which stood a kitchen-block, granary and gardens. Around 300, on a terrace behind and above the house, a square-plan pagan temple was added, covering a subterranean family mausoleum (burial vault). Impressive marble busts, probably portraying still-earlier owners, were brought into the house and displayed in a 'Deep Room' below the subsequent church; a basement area where, to judge from other fragmentary wall-paintings, a triad of local water-nymphs had been worshipped in a genteel setting.

Perhaps the most interesting development was a renovation that the excavator, the late Lt. Col. Meates, dated provisionally to *c*.330-60 (current views might place it a decade or so later). Across the central shorter axis of the house, a large rectangular reception room was created with, at its west end (the end nearer the terrace with the temple-mausoleum), a semi-circular apsidal extrusion as the normal provision for a dining area. Tasteful, impressive and we suppose costly mosaic floors were chosen and professionally laid. In the larger rectangle, the floor had a scene of Bellerophon between four roundel-portraits, representing the Four Seasons, surrounded by geometric designs. The much smaller apsidal mosaic had as usual a plain wide border on which couches for the hosts and guests would be placed. In that position, they would view the picture laid out before their gaze.

This, the 'Europa' panel, was recovered in near-complete state. It shows a conventional band of sea, above which is bounding a large horned bull, on his back a seated female partly unclothed and holding a veil above her. Two Cupid-style winged boys flank the bull (*Fig.17*). The chord of the apse is closed by a two-line mosaic inscription in letters big enough to be read with ease from around the border, and this (counterpart of an inscriptional *text* on stone) is legible still. In blue-on-white capitals and continuous

Fig. 17   Lullingstone Roman villa, Kent. The 'Europa' mosaic, showing 2-line text, pictorial element, and surround with 32 roundels. Reproduced by kind permission of Kent Archaeological Society.

writing, here for convenience divided into words, it reads

1   INVIDA SI TAVRI VIDISSET IVNO NATATVS   (= W,6: L,32)
2   IVSTIVS AEOLIAS ISSET ADVSQVE DOMOS   (= W,5: L,31)

If we shuffle the words of this neatly-constructed couplet into English and not Latin word-order, what it says is: *si invida Iuno vidisset natatus Tauri* 'If envious Juno had seen the swimming of the Bull', *iustius isset adusque Aeolias domos* 'the more justifiably would she have gone to the Aeolian halls (the halls of Aeolus)'. In Vergil's *Aeneid*, on which this is based, the goddess Juno visits the mountain halls of Aeolus king of the winds, demanding from him a storm to sink Aeneas and the Trojan fleet. Here the story-line has been changed a little,[23] and cultured guests at the villa would be expected to see and to applaud the subtleties. Zeus or Jupiter, Juno's consort, was charmed by the surpassing loveliness of a Phoenician princess Europa. Assuming the shape of a bull, the unfaithful deity approached Europa who, supposing the animal to be tame, obligingly climbed on its back; whereupon the Bull carried her over the sea to Crete and (as Zeus again) fathered Minos.

The entire mise-en-scène is sophisticated, completely Roman and pagan. We could just as well be in Italy or southern Gaul. What we do not know is how many of the postulated guests would see beyond the displayed words, the allusion to the *Aeneid* and the *Metamorphoses* of Ovid, and the competently-laid picture. For those who did, as we shall now, here are the first clues. Picture and text are united because the arc of red-and-white roundels has 32 roundels; same number as the letters in line 1. Lines 1 (32) and 2 (31) contain 63 letters; one short of 64, and the material for an eight-by-eight square. There are apparently two key numbers, *seven* and *five*. Each line has 14, twice *seven*, syllables; and line 2 has *five* words. More pointedly, though the mosaicists did not set out the letters evenly above each other, on paper (on a wax tablet, using a stylus) it is easy enough to jot down this revealing pattern:

$$\mathbf{I} \text{ nvida } \mathbf{S} \text{ itauriv } \mathbf{I} \text{ disse . tiunona . tatus} \qquad = \qquad 32$$

$$5 \qquad 7 \qquad 5 \qquad 7 \qquad 5$$

$$\mathbf{I} \text{ ustiu } \mathbf{S} \text{ aeolias } \mathbf{I} \text{ sseta . dusqued . omos}\star \qquad = \qquad 31\ (+\star)$$

With this very obvious 5.7.5.7.5 set, the paired letters — I, S, and I again — have values of 9.17.9, making 35, *five* times *seven*.

Next, those by now intrigued with the first revelations might think that the text holds more than its fair share of I's and S's. If we count, there are eight instances of initial I, last-letter S, so:

The text overall;	**I** nvida ... domo **S**
Line 1 overall;	**I** nvida ... natatu **S**
Line 1, last 7 syllables;	**I** sset ... natatu **S**
Line 2 overall;	**I** ustius ... domo **S**
Line 2, first 7 syllables;	**I** ustius ... Aeolia **S**
Line 2, last 7 syllables;	**I** sset ... domo **S**
First 7 words overall;	**I** nvida ... iustiu **S**
Last 7 words overall;	**I** uno ... domo **S**

Just about every combination of words starting with I and finishing with S is exploited here, in a framework dominated by *seven*. That might well arouse a suspicion that some further word in I … S, presumably of *five* letters, was being indicated. If any guest happened to be a Christian, one such word must have formed an obvious choice. The imbalance of certain letters is deliberate. We have I *eleven* times, S *eleven* times, and also U/V, *nine* times, and E *four* times. Add 11 + 11 + 9 + 4 to make 35 again. Our composer was playing with LNu as well as 20-letter LaN. That is obvious from line 1 alone; note the following —

$$\mathbf{I} \text{ n } \mathbf{VI} \text{ da s } \mathbf{I} \text{ ta } \mathbf{V} \text{ r } \mathbf{IVI} \text{ d } \mathbf{I} \text{ sset } \mathbf{IV} \text{ no nata } \mathbf{V} \text{ s}$$

— which he created to contain I, *unus*, 'one', *seven* times; and V, *quinque*, 'five', *five* times.

The Europa mosaic couplet is not a memorial. It is literary and sophisticated and its elucidation at a dinner-party might well have involved written demonstrations; boring the guests, as rigidly as contemporary guests who (dining among the chattering classes) are horrified to find that after-dinner paper-games are threatened. The messages here come in a literary shape; acrostics, and plenty of them. The key numbers *five* and *seven* are there to control the shapes of regular and staggered letter grids. Guided by the author (who is about to saunter forth) we now enter a Magic Garden of acrostical games, its many flowers kept in order by the two arithmetical elves Quinque and Septem. Here is both the composer and, as Martin Henig convincingly argues, the proprietor of the refurbished villa-house and selector of its new mosaic floors. The exhibition opens with a basic letter square, treating the text's 63 letters as if there were 64 of them by leaving a blank in the final space; observe how the first *five* columns are passed over before the reading.

```
(     5     )
i  n  v  i  d  A  s  i
t  a  u  r  i  V  i  d
i  s  s  e  t  I  u  n
o  n  a  t  a  T  u  s  8
i  u  s  t  i  U  s  a
e  o  l  i  a  S  i  s
s  e  t  a  d  u  s  q
u  e  d  o  m  o  s  ★
   •        8
```

Or to get the same as an initial acrostic we could cut out *seven* letters (first 5, last 2) and have a grid 8 across, 7 down:

```
invid)   A  s  i  t  a  u  r  i
         V  i  d  i  s  s  e  t
         I  u  n  o  n  a  t  a
         T  u  s  i  u  s  t  i  7
         U  s  a  e  o  l  i  a
         S  i  s  s  e  t  a  d
         u  s  q  u  e  d  o  m  (os
              • 8           2
```

We now have the name, *Avitus*.[24] Can you, reader, see another name, introduced by Avitus and marked above by underdotted columns? We can pick it up using the second line only of the mosaic text:

```
I  u  s  t  i  u  s  a
E  o  l  i  a  s  i  s
S  e  t  a  d  u  s  q  5
U  e  d  o  m  o  (s) ..
(S) .  .  .  .  .  .  .
           7
```

As might have been suspected by any Christian from *five* and I ... S, we find IESU or IESUS, Jesus. More interestingly, we get it again from a staggered grid, 12 across (= 5 + 7) and 7 down:

```
   .  .  .  .  i  n  V  i  d  a  s  I
t  A  u  r  i  v  I  d  i  s  s  E
t  I  u  n  o  n  A  t  a  t  u  S
(. . 5 . .) (. . 5 . .) i  U  7
s  T  i  u  s  a  e  o  l  i  a  S
i  s  s  e  t  a  d  u  s  q  u  e
d  o  m  o  s  (. . . 7 . . .)
```

Here, IESUS appears as the telestich but we also have (col.2) AIT, and (col.7) VIA. This is bound to recall John, 14,6, in the Vulgate; *dicit ei Iesus ego sum via et veritas et vita* 'Jesus saith unto him, I am the *Way*, and the Truth, and the Life...'. The text is earlier than the Vulgate; is it possible that an older version, a lost *vetus Latina* text (p. 87), actually had the alternative *★ait Iesus ...ego sum Via*?

The truth does indeed dawn. Avitus, if he wrote this, was either an established Christian or on the verge of becoming one, and his small literary masterpiece could be laid open to reveal as much. The rest of the display rather supports the notion of a recent convert , because Avitus now bids farewell to his previous religious adherence. It is done with considerable delicacy and taste; and at last we find out whose cult had formerly been upheld at the Lullingstone villa.

First we have to experiment with more grids, until we find one in modules of *five*, set out as 15 (*five* by 3) across, and *five* down:

```
(.  .  5  .  .) (.  .  5  .  .) (i  n  v  I  D
a   S  I  t  a  u  r  I  V  i  d  i  s  S  E
t   I  V  n  o  n  a  T  A  t  u  s  *  I  U  5
s   T  I  u  s  a  e  O  L  i  a  s  i  S  S
e   t  a  d  u  s  q  u  E  d  o  m  o  s  *

    2  3              8  9              14 15
```

What this was almost certainly planned to convey was (column-numbers italicised) *9* VALE, *14* ISIS, *15* DEUS; *Vale, Isis — DEUS* ('Farewell, Isis ; GOD!'). But what is also picked up, by chance and by the nature of Latin, is *2* SIT, *3* IVI, *8* ITO, lengthening the message; *Sit, ivi. Ito ! vale, Isis — DEUS* ('So be it, I have gone [from your worship]. Thou-shalt-go' (*ito* = so-called Second Imperative with future sense). 'Farewell' etc.). And as well as proclaiming his spiritual shift, Avitus names Isis a second time and again refers to Jesus in another staggered grid, *seven* plus one or *five* plus one across, *five* plus *five* down, in which we find:

```
          (.  .  .  7  .  .  .)  I
          .  .  n  v  i  d  a   S
5         .  .  i  t  a  u  r   I
          .  .  v  i  d  i  s   S
          .  .  e  t  i  u  n   o
                (     5     )
          (           7              )
          n  a  t  a  t  u  s   I
          u  s  t  i  u  s  a   E
5         o  l  i  a  s  i  s   S
          e  t  a  d  u  s  q   U
          .  .  e  d  o  m  o   S
                (     5     )
```

In view of the many other examples, we might guess that Avitus would have found this one, ringing the changes on 5 and 7, when searching for IESU(S) telestichs; would he also have noticed that the I of IESUS is letter no.33 in the whole sequence (p. 28)? The positioning of the two names carries the same implicit record of a spiritual transfer.

Fig. 18   R.G. Collingwood's drawing (1922) of faint graffito, LONDINI / AD FANVM
ISIDIS 'London, at the Temple of Isis', on a sherd from Southwark (Museum of
London); frequently reproduced, now RIB 2503.127.

We can go back to the couplet with its 5.7.5.7.5 structure, and look at it again:

I nvida **S** itauriv **I** dissetiunonatatu **S**   = I S I S
            5   7   16

I ustiu **S** aeolias **I** ssetadusquedomo★ **S**   = I S I S

This time it is less a signboard for *five* and *seven* than a reminder of Isis, linked to *sixteen*
(square of a square, four). The small Lullingstone temple on the terrace, a shrine that
Colonel Meates considered was already falling into disrepair when these mosaics were
laid, had the usual square plan; from the publication, 12.2m (or about 40ft), probably laid
out as 40 *pedes* (of 11.6in). It appears that in its last phase this temple was dedicated to Isis,
goddess of both motherhood and produce, encountered in Egypt by the Romans and
brought north and west mainly by the army (an unlocated Temple of Isis stood in London,
from a graffito on the well-known Tooley Street potsherd, *Fig.18*).[25]

Lastly as the guests — perhaps Christians among them — joined Avitus in reclining
around the pictorial apse, looking at the design and the intriguing couplet and probably
admiring the delicacy of this syncretistic squire's dismissal of the gentle Goddess, it is
certain that sharp eyes detected a second meaning in the picture. Ostensibly, the amorous
Zeus-Bull gallops off with lovely Europa, one cherub urging him on, the other pretending
to grab the tail. Yet what it *also* shows is Isis. She is seated upon her consort, the god Osiris
in his manifestation as Serapis, another Bull; and Serapis rides off with her, right out of
the scene, out of the little sphere of Avitus's worshipping, out of his life. Was there, in this
neo-Christian's mind, a tiny bit of remorse? We may think so. Look at the second line,
immediately over the picture (*Fig.19*), and see how we can drop selected letters:

    i u s t i u s a e o l i a s i s s e t a d u s q u e d o m o s
    I S I S   O I S I S   V E

'Isis, o Isis…' is the farewell cry. If we extend or produce the triangle of the right cherub's
chubby left hand, it meets the letters V E (of adusqVE), because now they stand for
V(AL)E 'Farewell!'

The foregoing interpretation cuts right across many pages of discussion devoted to the

Fig.19   Lullingstone, the pictorial element and lower line only of the apsidal mosaic. In this presentation the lady on the Bull may be Isis upon Serapis, moving away right; behind her 'ISIS O ISIS' can be brought down from the text, while in front of her the cherub's hand could point to letters V E, VALE 'Farewell'.

mosaics of Late Roman Britain, and to one particular theme; whether or not these and similar Vergilian or other literary depictions [26] can be construed in a Christian sense. For instance is Bellerophon on Pegasus, as here, really the Christian God as master of the annual cycle (the Seasons)? What we have at Lullingstone in a pre-Vulgate, late fourth-century Biblical-style verse text with its key numbers, LaN, LNu and multiple acrostics is explicit witness to one family's abandonment of a pagan cult and a transfer of allegiance to DEUS, manifest as IESU(S), worshipped in the subsequent domestic church. One could venture to propose that the evidence, for *Avitus*, *Isis*, and the Christian phraseology, all given through a coherent system controlled by 5-7 countings and so many acrostics, is not only cumulatively too strong to be set aside; it conforms to one view of Late Roman villa-owing society as having been very much part of a polished literary culture, combining Christianity with full retention of Classical learning and predilections.

Anything more about Lullingstone would divert us from the main theme. The villa-house with its telltale mosaics seems to have been abandoned as a dwelling before about 400. The converted church continued in use for a while until the final fire, and in another place it could be proposed that the site functioned as the centre of some private monastery. Our concern is with the combined witness of *RIB 684 Corellia Optata* and *RIB 2448.6*, the Lullingstone couplet; the former, pagan, (late?) third-century, the latter crypto-Christian and late fourth-century, and both textually antecedent to the range of post-Roman Insular memorials. Both are completely Classical with admirable metrical compositions of originality and taste. They display arithmetical adjuncts of Biblical style. We have seen a prominent signalling of key numbers; 20-letter LaN, with internal totals and the adding of initials and final letters; LNu, in part to reinforce key numbers; in the second, wide use of acrostics and telestichs, with squares and both regular and irregular grids. Corellia's memorial generates an image, a ground-plan. Avitus's shorter verse does not but it is hard to see what purpose would be served, given its nature.

These are compositional devices that we shall encounter again and again in the further half of mainland Britain, along with others whose mathematical bases might have been known from *arithmetica* taught in Britannia's private schools (triangulars, certainly so), but which are not as such apparent in the two specimens analysed here. The significance of these findings is that it links the Latin tradition of (Christianised) Britannia, mainly in the east and south of the country, to the not dissimilar Latin tradition of subsequent Christian Celts in the west and north. It may not yet be possible to reflect any such link, or transfer, through the usual channel of archaeological distribution-maps. Nevertheless it renders it unsound to suppose that we have to look solely to re-introductions from Christian Latin learning in Gaul and elsewhere, to explain phenomena from fifth- and sixth-century Wales. Westward diffusion took place, and it is incumbent upon us to explore that claim. By far the most likely conduit would have been a surviving system of formal education, tied to an active Church rather than to secular aristocracy.

Notes to Chapter 2

1. For this, see standard discussions like Leonard Bloomfield's, *Language* (1935 and many reprints), chap.26.
2. R.S.O. Tomlin, 'Was ancient British Celtic ever a written language? Two texts from Roman Bath', *Bull. Board of Celtic Studies*, 34 (1987), 18-25.
3. Examples are from Wolfgang Meid, *Gaulish Inscriptions* (Archaeolingua, series minor 1, Budapest 1992); here, p.51.
4. Meid, *ibid.*, p.25 and Fig.19, showing large and confident Greek capital letters.
5. This greatly compresses the relevant passages in *LHEB* (chap.III).
6. A long selection was listed by Henry Lewis, *Yr Elfen Ladin yn yr Iaith Gymraeg* (= 'The Latin Element in the Welsh Language') (Cardiff 1943); more words and names might be added.
7. *Christianity in Roman Britain to AD 500* (1981; 2nd impr. with new foreword, 1985).
8. See above, *Fig.16*, and explanation at p.137.
9. F. Mawer's book is *BAR*, British Series 243 (Tempvs Reparatvm, Oxford 1995).
10. And to Saint Patrick in the fifth century; Patrick enlarges it to mean 'the Church universal (or in Britain)', *ecclesia plorat et plangit* 'the Church cries and bewails', *Deum et ecclesiam ipsius* 'God and His Church'. A group of fixed nouns meaning 'a church as a building' is uncertain before the sixth century, and there was considerable regional variation in preferences.
11. This has been pursued, mostly in secular terms and in a good many publications, by Professor Wendy Davies; summarised in her *Wales in the Early Middle Ages* (Leicester 1982).

12. My *Mute Stones* (1994) sets out a range of evidence for this; an exception is 479 *Cunaide*, Hayle, for which here see p. 149.

13. The most up-to-date map, a brave venture, is *Map.5:11* in Barri Jones & David Mattingly, *An Atlas of Roman Britain* (Blackwell Reference, Oxford 1990).

14. Admirably summarised in consecutive papers, *The Early Church in Gwent*; George C. Boon's 'I: The Romano-British Church', *Monmouths. Antiquary*, 8 (1992), 11-24, and Jeremy K. Knight's 'II: The Early Medieval Church', *ibid.*, 9 (1993), 1-17.

15. Cf. R. Geraint Gruffydd's O'Donnell Lecture 'In Search of Elmet', *Studia Celtica*, 28 (1994), 63-80, an essential introduction.

16. It is only proper to warn readers that such continuity is much more readily credited by Celticists and students of post-Roman matters than by those whose principal interests are within the Roman period.

17. *Christianity in Roman Britain*, 127-8; *RIB* 690 *Simplicia* (also from York, probably fourth-century) is the least unlikely.

18. See *RIB*, under the entry (unhappily we can forget the novelist Marie Corelli, whose real name was Mary Mackway!).

19. RCHME *York Inventory*, vol.I, *Ebvracvm*, Roman York (1962), under Index; Plate 50 (73), a fine photograph, is reproduced here and the glass flask (H.G.53) is shown in Plate 66.

20. See *Glossary* at end; internalised letters (Roman, but none in post-Roman, Britain) are tiny ones placed within normal-sized ones, as an alternative to ligaturing.

21. The suggestion that a mental image of a ground-plan lurks here was Martin Henig's and I am most grateful to him for this lead; some idea of an actual rectangular vault from The Mount, York, is given in RCHME *Ebvracvm* (no.19 above), 95, Fig.72.

22. See under *Further Reading*, selected from a considerable body of Lullingstone publications.

23. Implying general familiarity with Ovid, *Metamorphoses*, bk.ii, where the princess 'dared to climb upon the Bull, little aware on whose back she was now reclining' and later 'her fluttering garments floated in the wind' (exactly as the mosaic shows).

24. This, too, was first detected by Martin Henig (by starting at (invid)*A* and counting intervals of 7; I would however now prefer to explain all the readings as essentially by acrostic method).

25. Note that there was a Serapaeum, a temple of Serapis-Osiris, in York, set up by a named *legatus legionis* (equivalent to an army colonel; had he served in Egypt ever?). See below, *Fig.36*.

26. For Lullingstone particularly, see A.A. Barrett, 'Knowledge of the Literary Classics in Roman Britain', *Britannia*, 9 (1978), 307-13. He shows that the inscription 'written to accompany the mosaic', itself 'designed specifically for the setting', may be primarily Ovidian and indicates 'a close familiarity with the poems of Ovid'.

3 Education and Commemoration

Within limits, this chapter has a nuts-and-bolts character, because an explanation of many inscriptions that possess cryptic messages and pictorial potentials ought to be preceded by an understanding of what these monuments are; why they continued to be written in Latin; whom they commemorated and (looking outwards from Roman Britain) if comparable memorials can be detected anywhere else.

Keeping the lamps of Latin alight

Moving directly into the sixth and later centuries, a picture of one obvious way of perpetuating a knowledge of correct Latin in Celtic Britain — through organised education — can certainly be sketched, but not from direct evidence. No Insular inscription mentions a learned teacher (*doctor*) or famous master of a school (*magister*). No strictly educational site has ever been excavated.[1] Rather oddly, however, we may have an uneven sample of educational aids. Latest in time might be the Kilmalkedar, Co.Kerry 'alphabet' stone, *CIIC* 913 (*Fig.20*), a pillar decorated with incised ornate crosses and the abbreviation DNI, *Domini* (for '[cross, sign ?] of-The-Lord'), all this being perhaps *circa* 700; and subsequently enriched down one edge with bookhand letters, abcdefghiklmn / opqrstuxz et (the '*et*' ligatured, and the layout resembling those Victorian dames' school slates that ended with '&', *and*-per-se-*and* = 'ampersand'). Strongly suggestive of rustic open-air teaching, a particular interest of this addition is that it shows the 23, not 20, letter alphabet with K, Y and Z. It may be later than 800.[2] Then, if we go back to Roman times, there are some fragments of possible display-alphabets (with capitals)[3] but, more to the point, from a number of places we have a considerable quantity of small counters or discs made from stone, pottery and (predominantly) bone, among them many marked with a single letter or numeral.[4] Undoubtedly many must be construed as gaming-pieces for board games or varieties of gambling, and perhaps some as shop and warehouse tallies. An alternative suggestion that they include counters to help small children learn the Latin ABC and the numerals, *and* possibly the convention of LaN values for the twenty letters, should not be overlooked. *Fig.21* shows just a selection. It is unnecessary to point out that, while contemporary Early Learning shops sell for infant use sets of letters stamped out in bright plastic (and letter-*shaped*), these have replaced an immemorial aid, the full range of letters, numbers and even some punctuation-marks printed or painted on little squares of wood. They are eminently worth considering (*Fig.22* shows some that are known to date

Fig. 20   *913 Kilmalkedar, Co.Kerry; the 'Alphabet Stone', drawing by Macalister. Tall double-
face cross slab, late 7th ? 8th century ? with* d n i *(=DOMINI) on one edge, to
which the 23-letter ABC, with final ET ligatured, was added in ? 9th century.*

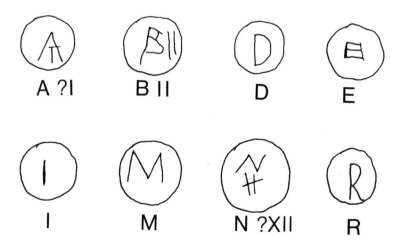

Fig.21   *Selection of small bone and stone discs or counters from Roman Britain, urban sites, redrawn from a number of sources; are any of these educational aids rather than gaming
pieces or commercial tallies?*

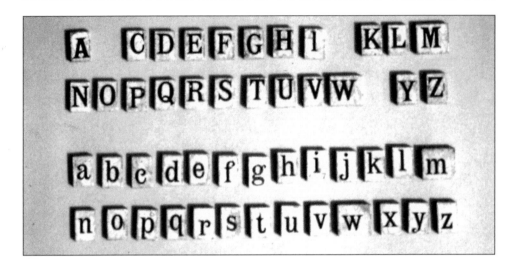

Fig. 22   Painted/printed wooden counters for teaching small children their letters capitals and lower case; survivors of a large set known to date from the 1890s (photo: author).

from the 1890s) because we must ask: Have these, or their like, ever *not* been around since Roman times?

One indication is contained in the Latin life, the *Vita Prima*, of the bishop and saint Samson of Dol born into a well-to-do family in Demetia, south-west Wales, in the late fifth century. Surviving versions of this Life contain an historic core that was composed in Brittany in the early seventh century.[5] When he was a small child, perhaps only five, Samson's parents Amon and Anna decided to send him to school. The boy was taken to *scolam egregi magistri Britannorum Eltuti nomine* 'the school of a famous *magister* of the Britons, by name Eltutus' (= Iltut, Illtyd). This lay right across south Wales, at Llanilltud Fawr or Llantwit Major in the coastal plain of Glamorgan. Little Samson, we read, took to learning instantly. In one day he mastered (chap.10) *vicenas aleas thessarasque* and within a week was able to string letters into words. The Latin means 'the dice' (with numbers; *alea*, a die, gaming-counter) 'and the little square pieces' (with letters? *tessera* was also a mosaic square or checker) 'twenty-of-each'. The allusion must be to a primary acquaintance with the 20-letter ABC, but can it further imply that numerals I-II-III up to XX were learnt in parallel to inculcate LaN values?

Other Latin Lives of saints, particularly some from Wales that, if they do happen to contain far earlier memories and traditions, were not composed until the eleventh century, make similar reference to aristocratic, royal and future-saintly infants being handed over to Christian *magistri* for prolonged training. Samson's Life, as an earlier record, is valuable because of what is obliquely said. Illtud was a *presbyter*, priest, skilled in the Old and New Testament, all manner of philosophy, *metrica* (theory of Classical verse composition), *rhetorica*, *grammatica*, *arithmetica* and, in short, all the branches of accomplished learning. Schooling, dictated by an angel's promise to Anna that Samson would become *sanctus et sacerdos summus* 'holy and a highest priest', was exclusively Christian. The child longed to attend *Christi scolam* 'a school of Christ' in order to attain priesthood. The adolescent Samson (chap.11) came to explore the inner and deeper meanings (*altioribus intellegentiis*) of the Scriptures and, meeting problems, he and his master Illtud explored *cunctos tractatus*, implying at least a library with a range of Biblical commentaries.

This is a post-Roman Christian biography in an altered recension, not factual history. The Breton author certainly imposed his own embroideries, but one is inclined to accept the *nature* of the school, the statement of Illtud's own attainments (out of the usual order, they represent the seven liberal arts of antiquity) and the record of the 20-letter alphabet with or with LaN values. For our purposes there may be rather more here.

The school, chosen by a family who were important people at the Demetian royal court and regarded themselves as superior to the clergy (chap.6), was part of Illtud's *magnificum monasterium*. The monastery was real; it apparently existed in the later fifth century (Samson's lifespan was from 480 x 490 to some time after 561/2, and the *Vita prima* author repeated a belief that Illtud was a disciple of St Germanus who died in 448); and, as an establishment, it is mentioned in later sources.[6] A link, at any rate in Wales, between monastic sites and traditional Christian schooling — as if this were the optimum educational option for Christians, conducted in the language of the Bible — figures in other Lives of later date. *Catmail* or *Cadocus* ('Cadog'), grandson of a king, child of a prince and princess, was entrusted when aged seven to an Irish *doctor* Meuthius for instruction in the liberal arts and Godly doctrines. The *doctor*, who had a great many pupils (*plurimi discipuli*), seems to be an eleventh-century duplication of an Irish *Tatheus*. In the latter's (separate) Life[7] the expected monastic establishment and school (together called *civitas*) is at Caerwent, the former *civitas* centre. *Vita Tathei* has Cadog being taught at this school and, on leaving it, to have excelled beyond all its pupils, *omnes discipuli*. Quite separately in the late eleventh-century Life of St Cadog, and using one of a number of named-place anecdotes of some antiquity that Lifris, the Llancarfan (Glamorgan) author, apparently found at Brecon, we encounter Cadog as a young man. He visits *Brecheniauc*, Brycheiniog, the upper Usk valley and kingdom of his grandfather Brachan. Cadog has been in Ireland where for three years he mastered the Seven Liberal Arts at the monastery of Lismore. A *famosus rethoricus nuper de Italia*, a renowned rhetorician lately from 'Italy' (for which read probably 'the Continent'), has come to Brycheiniog. Cadog is eager to be instructed in *Romano more Latinitate*, a mastery of Latin in the Classical manner. The *doctor* or *scolasticus*, whose name was Bachan or Pachan,[8] agreed to receive Cadog as a pupil. The point of the tale happened to be authentification of a grant (by king Brachan to his grandson Cadog, and thence by eventual descent to Llancarfan in pre-Norman times) of a *monasterium* at *Lannspitit*, Llanspyddid. A more likely reading is that, whether or not Cadog (later sixth century) comes into this, it preserves a memory of a small monastic school headed by 'Pachan' and famed for its Latinity, at a site that may have begun in Roman times as a civilian cemetery near Y Gaer, the old Roman fort by Brecon; and by 500-odd was a *lann*, Christian location.[9]

Can we really know what was taught in these places? Patrick's *Confessio* depicts a Briton, from a Christian and curial family; if his 'late' dates are preferred, born around 415 (dying in ?493), if a 'northern' geography is preferred, coming from a country *villula* somewhere east of Carlisle.[10] When, aged about 15, he was captured from his home by Irish raiders he must have left school. He tells us little of his education. We suppose his first (home) language was British. In later life he must have learnt conversational Primitive Irish, and Latin could have been acquired at school and around the home. What we *do* now know, from David Howlett's analysis of the writings, is that Patrick's schooling in Latin composition and a version (mostly older than the Vulgate, p. 87) of the Latin Bible produced a writer whose standing has been misunderstood for centuries. Far from being *rusticissimus*, 'an inarticulate artless man of simple piety burdened by a sense of his educational and intellectual inferiority',[11] Patrick the Briton was an Insular Christian Latin author, a master of Biblical-style composition whose surviving work is of great complexity and immense power. If he is a sole witness to his own end-of-Roman-times schooling, it was a system able to teach and to nurture an author of astonishing competence.

The drift of all these remarks must be clear. By and large, chance references and fortuitous individual survivals may have to serve, and we simply do not know up until *when*, and if so *where*, specimens of the older *scola grammatici* (a grammarian's private academy, with fees) may have been maintained. Of course individual tuition, especially when inspired by anyone's reading of God's will, continued; Patrick himself mentions (*Epistola*, 3) a presbyter whom he had personally taught *ex infantia*, from the age of 7, presumably in Latin. What we shall find in the brief texts cut on stone are signs of an elaborate Latin schooling that does not have to be regarded as any sort of post-400 Continental reintroduction; and centuries later than 400 we encounter Celts sufficiently confident to bend the strict rules, to manipulate their second language (of the Church, *and* the surviving Classics), in a manner unthinkable without an unbroken educational basis.

Reference to monasteries is important, as long as we are clear that 'monastery' means several things. Monasticism describes a very large and colourful sector of the Christian life ranging from the pure Soldier of God, the hermit in his cave close to his Maker, to (in Ireland) what were really specialised towns with agricultural and industrial activity, both lay and clerical inhabitants, subordinate territory and on occasions a propensity to nothing less than offensive or defensive warfare. The ascetic monasticism that developed during the third and fourth centuries in Egypt and the Levant, a world of Greek- and Coptic-speakers conveyed to the West by the medium of Latin-translation descriptions and manuals, first reached Ireland (in this inspirational literature shape) in 431 and, probably southern, Wales rather later; in both cases, *via* Gaul. This brand of the monastic life, whether eremitic (hermits) or coenobitic (as strict communities modelled on those of pioneers in Egypt), cannot have bridged a gap between the culture of Late Roman Britannia and the Christian Latin learning of the post-Roman west and north. What we may well now bear in mind is a separate, but not particularly long-lived, movement to which (without any disparagement) the label 'gentleman's monasteries' can be given.

Professor John Percival draws attention to twenty-two places through France,[12] many of them subsequently medieval monasteries or *abbayes*, where there is evidence that as Christian establishments they date from the later fourth, or fifth, century and in any way overlie Gallo-Roman villas. The classic instance is Ligugé[13] where, following St Martin of Tours' visit in 360-1, a church (rectangle with apse) was built *within* a basement granary wing of a very substantial villa-house. Some of Percival's sites ought to represent a specific wave of (Gaulish) monastic enthusiasm, partly inspired by the fame of Martin and his pioneer monasteries. The notion of the well-to-do Christian turning his or her home into a private monastery (not necessarily run entirely on ascetic lines) is found beyond Gaul; St Jerome's friend Marcella, a pious and rich Roman matron inspired by reading of the Desert Fathers, set up just such a private monastery in her mansion on the Aventine in the 370s. Aristocratic Gaulish letters into the fifth century show us plenty of *prominenti* supporting private chapels on their estates.[14] There is a, generally Roman, character to this movement that tends to set it apart from the more Orientally-inspired monasticism we find by the sixth century in Celtic lands and, because of the different and more intensive Romanisation of so much of Gaul, it was accompanied by an ongoing educational system[15] — in Latin: the Gaulish language, unlike British, had by 400 shrunk to obscure rural pockets and was no longer a real vernacular.

We cannot yet tell if before 400 there was a British counterpart to this; but Lullingstone might be seen as an instance, rather than an (improbable?) insertion of quite a sumptuous church by Avitus and family for general use by estate-workers and neighbours. (The wall-painted row of *orantes*, surely portraits of identifiable persons richly clad, suggests more than one explanation.) What must also come to mind, though further into the fifth century, is the status of more than one site in south-east Wales. If we allow *Eltutus*, Illtud, to have lived between about 430 and 510 there is a strong probability that his magnificent monastery and school, at heart a private establishment, was based upon the large Roman villa at Llantwit Major. There remain uncertainties as to firm dates for a late fourth-century abandonment of the villa-house, to which (as at Lullingstone) a mosaic floor was added around 350.[16] A second possibility would be the villa at Llandough (= *lann* + *Docco*) because (on recent excavational evidence) this was accompanied, certainly in the early sixth century, by a very extensive Christian cemetery, just across a small coombe and around the parish church.[17] (Caerwent and the sixth-century monastery of Tatheus is much less likely to offer an instance of such a sequence.) Llantwit stands as the best candidate for a 'gentleman's monastery' and a likely setting for a retained tradition of formal pre-400 schooling. It might be noted that two supposed offshoots — the smaller house under abbot Piro on Caldey (from Llantwit, so the Life of Samson) and the first-known Cornish monastery near St Kew on the north coast (from Llandough? this was still *Landochou* in the tenth century) — do not, either of them, suggest extreme asceticism.[18]

The subsequent inscriptions: who was commemorated?

Estimates of the all-Britain population by AD 400 range from about two million to an archaeologically-favoured four million. In what is now Wales with its present population of almost three million, in AD 400 the figure may not have been much above a hundred thousand, the same as the (1086) Domesday estimate. Precise totals do not matter. Assuming both high infant-mortality and generally a low life-expectancy, between AD 450 and 750 Wales will have seen about a million and a half deaths. Many (not all) were marked by graves and burials. Increasingly through time these would have been Christian burials; the later we go, the more readily identifiable. Over that same period we know of about 150 inscribed memorial stones, or one per ten thousand dead.

Obviously the stock of surviving stones is far smaller than the total of all erected. We cannot know by what factor; but even an excessive assumption of 15,000 stones would still be only one per hundred potential graves. What might favour the idea that in those three centuries there never were more than 500-1000 stones is that during the last fifty years Wales, like most of the country, has seen more change and erosion in the countryside (and to the urban scene and entire housing-stock) than in the previous millennium. Yet in both Wales and the deep south-west, Cornwall and Devon, the rate of discovery of new inscribed stones has remained steady at just about one per decade.[19] In no sense have they ever been archaeologically common, and concerted searches have failed to yield the hoped-for results.

If we accept that provision of a memorial-stone inscribed in Latin was always rather a rare privilege we might ask: Who was given them? Was a king a hundred times more likely than a cowherd to be commemorated? Were they only for the upper reaches, an aristocratic minority; or only for Christians, also a minority but one that was disproportionately represented by the ruling castes? The former idea can be, and occasionally has been, argued from the nature of the (British) names. Today it has been too long for most of us to remember what the originals of names like Rex and Basil meant in Latin and Greek. The British (male) names represented are stiff with elements meaning king, prince, lord, notable, fame, valour, greatness, battle, strength, and hound/wolf as a symbol of aggressive masculinity. Could these ever have been favoured names for peasants?

Concentrating on Wales as the largest sample-area we find that a minority of the displayed names may be called Roman or, better, *continuing*-Roman; in the sense that nearly all are known from Britannia and other provinces. As cut, spellings are on the whole correct; fixed, because perceived as unalterable items in written Latin – 393 *Carausius*, 389 *Eterni* (gen.), 360 *Paulinus*, 373 *Severi* (gen.). The same goes for names of Biblical origin. 350 *Idnert* supplies IACOBI (gen.; the New Testament *Iacobus*) and DAVID. A few names were added from patristic or monastic writings. 403 (corrected in *ECMW* 268) MACARI, 470 MACARI in Cornwall and a new (1997) two-line memorial from west Cornwall, 1212 MACAR. (*Fig.23*) are genitives of *Macarius*, Greek *Makarios*, an interesting feature.[20] Minor deflections follow known provincial variations; an O-for-U substitution, for example 389 *Iovenali* (for *Iuvenali*, 'Juvenal') and 421 *Rostece* (properly, *Rustica*; short *e* - short *i* is a common shift). As long as relatively decent capital letters were used, there is not much to choose between the display of an ordinary Roman male name in a Roman context, and its sixth- or seventh-century reproduction. A very different state of affairs greets us when we turn to that majority of Celtic personal names, male and female, that had to be spelled and cut in the Latin 20-letter ABC (see next section).

The mundane facts, urged on us by close observation, are that society in post-Roman western Britain was by modern liberal standards unreformed. All men counted for more than most women, there was an intricate stratification allied to birth, family and wealth, the Church exercised considerable influence and the unfree at the bottom counted for nothing. A suspicion exists that if we had a thousand inscriptions to read the social mix would be much as it now seems. Broadly speaking, those memorials we possess may have been confined to rulers, aristocratic landowners, members (occasionally female,

Fig. 23   Three 6th-century instances of MACARI, *genitive of the name Macarius borrowed from Greek (Makarios). Top, 403, Glamorgan (but from ECMW; MACARI and TINI (adj.?) are separate). Mid, 470 N Cornwall, MACARI, correcting Macalister's drawing in situ. Below, a new (1997) 2-line memorial, provisional no. 1212, W Cornwall;* MACARI?.../CARASIMILIVS, *with many inverted and and reversed letters.*

occasionally young, like *Rostece*) of their families, and a Christian clergy associated with, and drawn from, these higher levels. It is possible to pick out the names of six kings (who varied in importance), shown in *Fig.24*. Giving their names in later forms, they are (1) *Clotri*, a native kinglet in part of Pembroke, fifth century; (2) *Triphun*, an Irish-descended king in north Pembroke, late fifth century; (3) *Guotepir*, an Irish-descended king of *Demetia*, Dyfed, mid-sixth century; (4) *Riuallon*, king of Brycheiniog, mid-seventh century; (5) *Cadfan*, king of Gwynedd (north-west Wales), reburied in the later seventh century; and (6) *Catgocaun*, king of Dyfed, early eighth century. Only (5) has the word *rex* 'king'; (1) and (4) contain an element *ri-* (<*rigi-*), meaning 'king' in British (oblique stem); and (6) is a dedication-stone, not a memorial. We round off the royalty with a Scottish memorial, 515 (the Yarrow Stone, Selkirk), to (7), *Nudus* and *Dumnogenus*, two sons of Liberalis, who are called INSIGNISIMI PRINCIPES 'the most distinguished princes'.[21]

Four of the stones selected also have crosses of various kinds, an unusual addition (*Fig.24*, bottom). Nos. (3) and (7) as texts contained the word MEMORIA, perhaps implying a larger than usual grave, a grave-plot with above-ground features. More to the point and closer to the subject of this book, four of them — (3) (4) (5) (6) — are compositions in Biblical style. Two of them certainly, (4) and (5), with (3) as a possibility

Fig. 24 *'Top People' commemorated? selection of kingly names, Cornwall to Scotland, drawn from Various photographs and other sources. 1, 435* Clutorigi; *2,* bone mimori *(of a son of-) 476* Tribuni; *3,* memoria *(of-) 358* Voteporigis; *4, 986* Ruallaun; *5, 970* Catamanus rex; *6, (...for the soul from) 427* Catuoconi; *7,* memoria *(of two famous princes), 515, The Yarrow Stone. Below, crosses accompanying names, as numbered, mid-6th to early 8th centuries. (2, Cornwall; 7,Scotland; the rest, Wales.)*

here, have texts that generate mental images. Stone (1), which reads (435) CLVTORIGI / FILI PAVLINI / MARINI LATIO ('Clutorigi; of the son of Paulinus Marinus, from Latium (?)'), is neutral in this respect but the other six are demonstrably Christian from their wording (some, also from contexts).

Epigraphically, socially, by internal structure, and also spiritually, these are from the top of society. Their appearances, applying criteria of what aristocratic Roman tombstones looked like, are of much less moment than their content and application. We can make a tentative proposal about audience-identification, for the viewership and sufficiently-informed readership these displays presuppose. It may not be possible to quantify it, but it must have corresponded to this commemorated segment of society.

Spelling conventions and 'Inscriptional Old Celtic'

Throughout the last two millennia certain forenames have appeared unchanged in writings on all and any media; familiar Classical names (Alexander, Julius, Lavinia, Viola) and the popular choices from the Latin Vulgate. Transmission has been essentially written, and for at least half the period the written vehicle was Latin. In contrast to these nominal fossils, we have two large language-families (Celtic and Germanic) where many names originated in, and for a long period were transmitted through, *speech*. Whether 20 or 23 letters were to be used, elements of choice and preference, uncertainty and variations, were inevitable.

There is one peculiar feature of the way in which Celtic names are spelled and cut on Insular inscriptions that is well-known, but hardly ever explained. If we pick out three, on sixth-century stones from Wales, Cornwall and Scotland (327 DVNOCATI, 468 CVNOVALI, and 515 DVMNOGENI), we could wonder why their clear portrayal with four syllables each does not in fact represent accurately the way these names were pronounced when the men died. For the first, spoken as /düngad/, or / dünəgad/, why was it not shown as DINCAT, an acceptable neo-Brittonic representation of the spoken version, instead of the artificial DVNOCATI ? Or — somewhat later, about 725-750 perhaps — we can notice 427 CATUOCONI (see further, p. 169). Analysis reveals that for both mathematical and metrical ends this is supposed to be five syllables, and presumably read out as /cad.oo.wo.gon.i/, being (long-long) (long-short-short). In that sense it harks back to its British components, *cat*- 'battle', plus -*u*-, compositional vowel, plus an adjective we can write as *wo-con(os)*; meaning uncertain. But at the time it was a spoken trisyllable, and is still with us as (Welsh) Cadwgan, (English) Cadogan; three syllables only, not five.

Before seeking an explanation we can take a look at two other substantial catalogues of post-Roman memorials and related short texts, in which non-Latin names are embedded in Latin and also use 20 letters. The first is from the diocese of *Hispania*, Spain and Portugal. Earlier names are mostly Roman and Biblical, with some Latinisations of others, presumably proto-Basque and Iberian. In the sixth and seventh centuries much of Spain came under the rule of Germanic-speaking (Christian) Visigoths, a wave of conquerors including Suevi, Vandals and Alans who entered Spain after 410.[22] We can set out a table of names (inscriptions on stone, a few coins). Column (*a*) is for name-forms of kings, queens and notables commonly used in historical writings; (*b*), as they appeared in contemporary Latin sources, with suffixed -*us*, -*i* (males) or -*a* (females); and (*c*), the same or similar names from inscriptions, numbered after Vives [23] and with dates.

(a)	(b)		(c)
Chindasuinth (642-53)	*Chindasuinthus rex*	366	[CHI]NDASVINTVS (642) Chindasvintus (*coin*)
Ermenigild	*Ermenigildus*	364	ERMINIGILDI REGIS (573) Ermenigildi (*coin*)
Gundemar	*Gundemarus rex*		Gundemarus (*coin*) Condemarus ri. (*coin*)
Leovigild	*Leuuigildus rex*	364	LIVVIGILDVS REX Leouigildus (*coin*)
Reccared (586-601)	*Reccaredus rex*	302	RECCAREDI REGIS (587)
Reccesuinth (649-72)	*Reccesuindus rex*	259 174	RECCISVINTI (650) RECCISVINTHVS,deacon (643)
Sisebut (d.621)	*Sisebutus*	263	SISEBVTI REGIS (614)

Now what this table shows is that, allowing for a near-universal later Latin short-vowels *e-i* alternation and D,T,TH as ways of putting -*th*- as in English 'other', the *written* inscriptional and historical forms pretty well agree; and enough is known of early Germanic to say that, here, writing mirrors contemporary *speech*. We can go on to look at a second gathering, from Christian Latin tombstones, late fourth to eighth centuries, in the Middle Rhineland. Ordinary Roman names (Agrippina, Crispinus, Florentius, Victor, etc.) are joined by Germanic ones, mostly Frankish. The people are commoners, not kings, and do not figure in historical records. We can match name-elements instead of names, using (*a*) two Latin sources, Gregory of Tours' *History of the Franks* (completed, 594) and the *Fourth Book of the Chronicle of Fredegar* (seventh century), against (*b*), inscriptions, numbered from Walburg Boppert's book.[24] (*Fig.25* shows a representative sample.)

(a)		(b)
Fifth-sixth century		
Ingitrudis	145	INGILDO
Siggo	164	SIGGO
Sixth-seventh century		
Audofleda, Audovera	21	AUDOLENDIS
Bertegundis	26	BERTISINDIS
Chrodechildis, Chariberthus	130	CHRODEBERTUS
Leudemund	56	LEUTEGUND
Bertetrudis	68	MUNETRUDIS
Grimoaldus, Sigoaldo	26	RANDOALD
Seventh century		
Badegisilus	24	BADEGISELUS
Childebertus, Belechildis	108	BERTICHILDIS
Pitto	72	PANTO
Radegundis	78	RADELINDIS

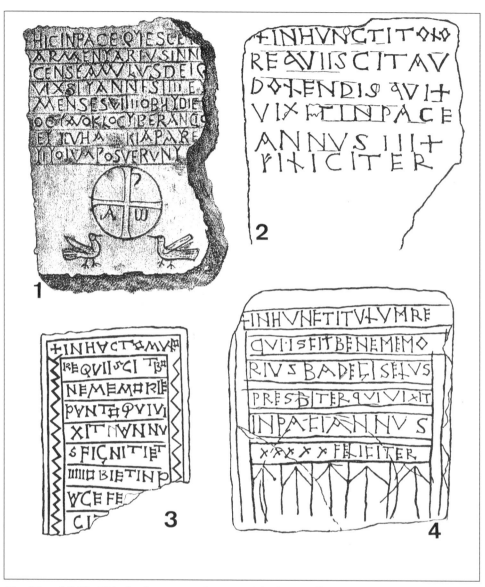

Fig. 25   Middle Rhineland; representative memorials, from Walburg Boppert's corpus as numbered. 1, 125 Armentarius, early 6th, Boppard. 2, 21 Audolendis, later 6th, Mainz. 3, 72 Panto, 7th century, Mainz. 4, 24 Badegiselus (presbiter), c. 700, Mainz. (Nos.1 and 3, and marginally no.2, contain Biblical-style computus.)

This looks, and is, very much as for Spain. Again, inscriptional forms are reasonable and direct approximations of contemporary speech. Frankish was a kind of linguistic great-great-uncle to German and English and the elements' meanings are known; many occur now in (unfashionable) proper names.[25]

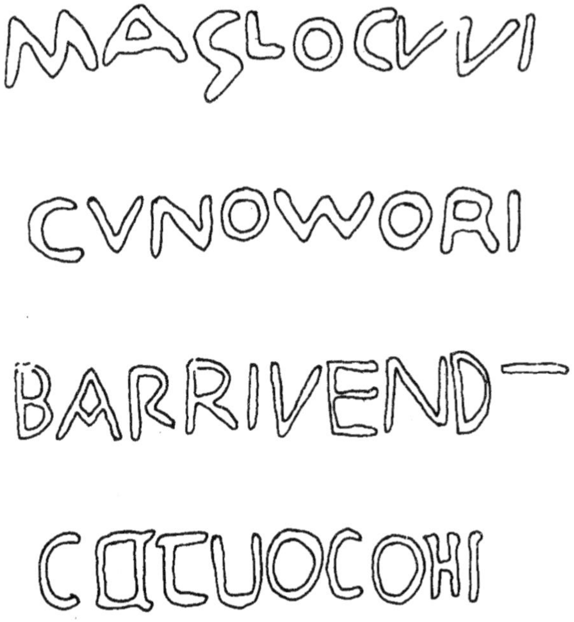

Fig. 26   *Sample of male British names, all in 'epitaphic-I', exhibiting Inscriptional Old Celtic spellings. 446, MAGLOCVNI (VN-ligature botched) early or mid-6th; 487, CVNOMORI (with inverted M as –W-), mid-late 6th; 368, BARRIVENDI (final –I horizontal), 6th century; 427, CATUOCONI, early 8th century. (487, Cornwall; the rest, Wales.)*

MAGLOCVVI

CVNOWORI

BARRIVEND-

CATUOCONI

These lists are both from regions of Rome in the West; from widespread Christian Latin matrices in which other-language names are successfully spelled out in a Latin medium. Is there any reason why, if we selected ten complete male and female Celtic names in the 20-letter ABC from Christian Latin *British* memorials, they should not all likewise approximate their spoken versions? And if not, why not? What special considerations might have intervened?

There is no question, as was shown earlier, that the Latin alphabet *could* be used to record both British and Gaulish. We know this from the place-names of Roman Britain.[26] Many, for military establishments, simply took over what we suppose to have been local names. LITANOMAGUS (Scotland) is British *litan-os,-a, -on* 'wide, broad' and *magos* 'plain'; CAMBOGLANNA (Castlesteads) is *camb-o(s)* 'curved, bending' and *glanno-* 'river-bank'. A very close parallel is the brief economic 'conquest' of the Malaysian tin-bearing gravels from about 1900. Place-names for brand-new mining settlements were made up from Malay, a relatively straightforward Indo-Pacific language; Ayer Hitam (water' + 'black') Sungei Besi ('river' + 'iron'). We could guess that a few Roman purveyors and officials who needed to penetrate native life knew some British, on the scale that various Cornish mining engineers found it useful to learn Malay.

One would thus expect that some of the names in *Fig.26* were being spoken, at the dates indicated in the captions, more or less as they were spelled; rather as if they were syllables in Latin. There were minor differences. Letters C and T occurring medially (inside words, between vowels) were pronounced G and D, as they had been in the spoken Latin of Late

Roman Britain. But medial M (for the British) had become a sound we do not use, *lenited m*, written /ṽ/, a very nasalised /v/, something like /m/ and /v/ spoken together. That means (*Fig.26* again) MAGLOCVNI ought to stand for /mag-lo-goo-nee/ and CVNOMORI for /coo-no-ṽor-ee/; four syllables each, just like (on 421 *Rostece*) PATERNINI, /pad-er-nee-nee/.

But all the indications from linguistic research are that, by the year 550 (which will serve for these two examples), they were not as above. In British speech they would have been far closer to sounds we can indicate approximately by 'mile-goon' and /cun-ṽor, con-ṽor/. The *Fig.26* spellings give a good idea of something that affected many, but not all, British names rendered inscriptionally; deliberate archaism. They are not (as in Spain) what we could call 'Reccesuinth' spellings. A better label is 'Inscriptional Old Celtic' (IOC).[27] It was a learned, artificial and obsolete style of spelling but, at the same time, it was intentional. For quite a lot of those inscriptions in Biblical style, the arithmetical side (the computus) will only work because IOC spellings have been used.

Modern times offer no complete parallel. A man wanting a fancy tablet for his parents Albert and Audrey might settle for mock-Latin *Albertus* and *Audreia* (as many have done for *Henricus* and *Georgius*). The true equivalent to IOC would be to etymologise them and go right back to the oldest-known elements; for Albert, the Frankish *Adalberht* or Bede's (Kentish) *Aedilberct(us), Æthelberht*; for his mother, *Æthelthryth* or the later *Etheldreda*. In case of difficulty the man would have to find a linguist, an onomasticist, a professional scholar. Are we to infer that in post-400 Britain, up to the eighth century, there were scholars who *still* understood name-elements and compositional forms of ancestral British, a language not spoken in its fully-inflected guise since the Roman period?[28] Why do we not detect this antiquarianism within Continental inscriptions? What was the *point* of IOC?

There *are* possible answers, and the one put forward shortly seems to me to gain support because it goes beyond language alone. But at once we find ourselves tangled up in certain unresolved debates. The best illustration comes from the writings of the British cleric Gildas, and his tract *De Excidio Britonum* of about 540.[29] Gildas attacks the records and behaviour of five named British kings, all then alive. Two have continuing-Roman names (*Constantinus, Aurelius Caninus*). Two more, addressed in the vocative (ending -*e*, not nominative -*us*), have British names; *Maglocune, Cuneglase*. Gildas knew what the second meant (*cun* — 'hound, wolf, fierce beast' + *glass-os* (older *glast-os*) 'grey, tawny', also, confusingly, 'blue, blue-green') because he gives its *Romana lingua* translation, *lanio fulve* ('tawny mangler, butcher'). Name-records are disappointingly rare from post-400 Britain. Patrick leaves us only Roman names (*Calpornius, Patricius, Potitus*). Gildas has this very rare record of IOC forms — *Maglocuni*, 446 MAGLOCVNI; *Cuneglase*, elements seen inverted in (from Ireland) 159 *GLASICONAS* in ogam, 'Grey-Wolf', genitive (the words were common to Irish and British).

We could believe, with Professor Kenneth Jackson,[30] that Gildas 'was *not* using an archaic form, but was spelling *as well as he could* the name which was in his time something like *Maʒlogun(əΣ)*'. Italics are mine; the symbol /ʒ/ is a kind of 'gh' sound, and the /Σ/ is our 'sh'. That would mean that *Maglocune*, written in manuscript, and probably MAGLOCVNI on stone 446, are really 'Reccesuinth' names; writers spelling them out in 20-letter style more or less as anyone would have spoken them. Or we could believe, as

Sir John Morris-Jones did in 1918 [31] and as probably most students do now, that in 540 this king of Gwynedd's British name was spoken more as /maʒlgun/, or with diphthong as /mailgun/ ('mile-goon') — and that under other circumstances Gildas and any of his learned friends would have put it down in neo-Brittonic style as: m a i l c u n. Similarly, for *Cuneglase*, which is IOC, we could have had: c o n g l a s (or else c i n g l a s — the first vowel is not so important as the fact that four syllables are reduced to two). But this is what we *do* have from written Old Welsh; *Conglas*, probably eighth-century, from *Land* [32] and *Cinglas, Cenlas* (the faint -*g*- lost) from two early genealogies.[33] Again, there was a British adjective that could also be a name, *maglac-os* ('princely'). Gildas would presumably have addressed any bearer of it as *Maglace*. On the opposite view, by 540 it would have been spoken /mailog/, 'my-log', and written: m a i l o c. An émigré Briton, or possibly British-descended Breton, of this name became a bishop in north-west Spain; at a church council at Braga in 572 he signed as, or had his name recorded as, *Mailoc*.[34]

Our first explanation must assume that in post-Roman Celtic Britain, certainly in Wales, there was a class of people fully conversant with Latin, but also with the ancestral and Roman-period stage of their everyday language (in Gildas's day, not properly still British but developed into Neo-Brittonic, or (Archaic) Old Welsh). If these folk, in their Christian schooling, properly learnt the structure of Latin, a fully inflected language, so that the word *laudabamus* was correctly analysed as *lau.da.ba.mus* and not *laud.a.bam.us* (wrong), then analogically a few scholars still knew the structure of British as a comparable, once-inflected, language; certainly enough to dictate the shape of important names in IOC. In other words, was Gildas ever taught that Conglas (in speech) went back to (nominative) *cu.ne.gla.sos*, with (Latin-type) vocative *cu.ne.gla.se*?

To credit any perpetuation in the odd monastic school of these rarified interests is no harder than to credit many of the Biblical-style compositional heights discussed later; or the growing hints that some of our composers knew some Greek and were even aware of Hebrew.[35] Nothing of this so far tells us *why*, and to that we turn.

Adversus gentiles?

This writer sees the curious Insular use of IOC for names on inscriptions — a very interesting, though actually marginal, feature — as one manifestation of a much more far-reaching movement. It could be described as the gradual construction of an *intellectual bastion*, initially centred in Wales, and it was *adversus gentiles*; against the heathens. These were external foes, their greatest threat lying eastward; the inexpungible pagans, the Anglo-Saxon invaders and conquerors and the Early English settlements. Not until well into the seventh century, when enough of the English kingdoms had been converted, could the defences be lowered. Inside 'Fortress Britain', what was so strongly emphasised was anything held to characterise Britishness. This extraordinary attachment symbolised by IOC — of a power inherent in the language of ancestors who faced, and might be regarded as having absorbed, Rome? — has no parallel elsewhere in the Late Roman Empire, and is only loosely matched in contemporary Ireland (p. 129). The British ruling classes were Christian, and linked by orthodoxy and culture to a Christian world beyond the barbarians. Their forebears had been Roman citizens entirely versed in the principal language of the Empire, with its vast literary culture. There was every incentive, as latter-day *cives*, to perpetuate language and culture through correct schooling. At a rarified summit, composition in Biblical style was not only maintained but enriched by specifically Insular developments. In part because of maritime contacts (we have just enough archaeological evidence to suppose these were never broken) there was both an Irish adoption (p. 125) and a British re-adoption of the inscribed memorial, as an appropriate token to the notable Christian dead. Even the stone memorials became defensive statements because they were blackboards on which to chalk up Christianity, Latinity, IOC, and intellectual superiority in the shape of messages and images.

The description, or definition, is summary. It is not expected that every reader will want to believe it as I state it. What must be added, however, is that almost nothing of this 'intellectual bastion' could be found through the exercise of conventional archaeology, or by continuing to study these (and other) elements in isolation — continuing to look at inscribed stones as specimens of epigraphy, very occasional art, and limited evidence for literacy. The accompanying historical record remains a grossly defective source. For any search, we are obliged to fashion what amounts to an *intellectual* archaeology. This book presumes to put itself forward as a preliminary manual.

Notes to chapter 3

1. Unless in County Down, by H.C. Lawlor; *The Monastery of Saint Mochaoi of Nendrum* (Belfast 1925), where one rectangular room (no.22) was quite plausibly identified as a school.

2. On inscriptions, the shift lay between 350 *Idnert*, AD 806, 20 letters; and 1051 Penzance Cross, AD 1007, 23 letters. Other considerations (OW orthography, for one) suggest *c*.850-950, but the 23-letter basis had been used in MSS (by Bede, certainly).

3. A tiny piece (personal?) with ABCD..., Traprain Law, *RIB* 2131; larger block, Chesters, *RIB* 1492, interestingly showing D E F G H I K. (The Latin Bible used K,Y and Z.)

4. *RIB* II, fascicule 3, contains the bulk of these small objects.

5. Full discussion, with reference not repeated here, in my *Mute Stones*, chap.14; I am among those convinced that the essence of *Vita Prima Samsonis* dates from the earlier seventh century.

6. A series of ninth- to eleventh-century sculptured cross-shafts, etc., some lettered, from here is described in *ECMW*, nos.220-226.

7. *Vita Cadoci, Vita Tathei*; texts and translations in A.W. Wade-Evans, *VSBG*.

8. Bachan in the *Vita* proper, chap.11; Pachan in an associated charter (chap.58); I believe this to represent 'Pachom(ius)', after the name of a founding-father of Egyptian monasticism.

9. Llanspyddid churchyard has a seventh-century cross-slab reputedly marking the grave of Anlach (Cadog's great-grandfather, died *circa* 500!). More the point, trial

excavations recently found a quantity of Roman pottery in the southern bank (with ditch, and two inner graves) of what may represent the first enclosure - *Archaeology in Wales*, 35, for 1995 (1996), pp.50, 60.

10 I support this in *Christianity in Roman Britain*, chaps.13 & 14, but others prefer 'early' dates of *c*.385 to 461 and not everyone credits the northern location (as against, say, the Severn). The reference here is to the texts in Howlett, *Saint Patrick*.

11. Howlett, *op.cit.* 119 – citing this view to demolish it.

12. In 'Villas and Monasteries in Late Roman Gaul', *J. Ecclesiastical History*, 48 (1997), 1-21 (without map).

13. Above, no.10 on list; *Christianity in Roman Britain*, 106-7, with Fig.22, plan made *in situ*, 1979.

14 Good survey in Nora D. Chadwick's *Poetry and Letters in Early Christian Gaul* (Bowes & Bowes, London 1955).

15. The standard account is T.J. Haarhoff, *Schools of Gaul. A study of pagan and Christian education in the last century of the Western Empire* (Witwatersrand Univ. Press, Johannesburg 1958).

16. For these Glamorgan sites see, *Glamorgan County History II* (=*Early Glamorgan, Prehistory and Early History*), ed. H.N. Savory (Cardiff 1984), with detailed references.

17 The post-Roman part of Llandough awaits publication; see note in *Archaeology of Wales*, 34 (1994), 66-8 with plan.

18 Landochou: *Mute Stones*, 229. John Morris, *The Age of Arthur* (1973), 356 ff., anticipated me in pointing to the evidence for a phase of 'gentleman's monasteries'.

19 Wales: since *ECMW* appeared (1950), four have been published. The south-west: since *CIIC* (1945, 1949, but really completed by 1939), eleven have been found, four of which were already known (but not to Macalister). The post-*CIIC* Cornwall and Devon stones are provisionally numbered from 1200 upwards in my *Mute Stones* (1994), 330 ff.

20 All probably inspired by incoming Desert Fathers literature (to south Wales, later fifth century); Macarius, disciple of St Antony, was a famous hermit.

21. Macalister's *CIIC* reading must be replaced by C.A.R. Radford's in *RCAMS Selkirkshire Inventory* (Edinburgh 1957), 110-3.

22. Convenient guides to this are E.A. Thompson, *The Goths in Spain* (Oxford 1969), and Edward James, ed., *Visigothic Spain, New Approaches* (Oxford 1980).

23. Spanish inscriptions are cited by number and italicised name, as with *CIIC*, from D. José Vives, *Inscripciones cristianas de las España romana y visigoda* (Barcelona 1942, revised edn, 1969).

24. Rhineland inscriptions by (page) number and italicised name from W. Boppert, *Die frühchristlichen inschriften des Mittelrheingebietes* (Von Zabern, Mainz 1971).

25. 'Bertha' (French *Berthe*) is directly from a pet-form of *berht*-'bright' (as 26 *Berti*sindis); 'Gertrude' contains *trudi*-'strength' (as 68 Mune*trudis*).

26. A.L.F. Rivet & Colin C. Smith, *The Place-Names of Roman Britain* (1979).

27. This expands the 'Old Celtic', proposed in a similar sense for Roman-period British and Irish, by John T. Koch in his 'The Conversion and the Transition from Primitive to Old Irish, *c*.367-c.637', *Emania*, 13 (1995), 39-50.

28. Koch (*above*) assumes in Ireland 'a far more conservative and less localised learned language, which stood closer…to…Old Celtic than to Old Irish…This educated language was mastered by only a relatively small minority…' I am proposing a similar scenario, reading *British* for Irish.
29. Conveniently, Michael Winterbottom, *Gildas. The Ruin of Britain and other works* (Phillimore, Chichester 1978); analysis of the king's names, Kenneth Jackson, '*Varia*: II. Gildas and the Names of the British Princes', *Cambridge Medieval Celtic Studies*, 3 (1982), 30-40.
30. *LHEB*, 189-90, with wider discussion.
31. In his long study 'Taliesin', *Y Cymmrodor*, 28 (1918).
32. *Land* here and throughout = *Liber Landavensis*, the Book of Llandaff (for all names, see Wendy Davies, *The Llandaff Charters*; NLW, Aberystwyth 1979).
33. Bartrum, *EWGT*, at 10 (Harleian 3859, no.3) and at 48 (Jesus College 20, no.39).
34. *LHEB*, 464; there may even be a seventh-century Welsh record, as *m a i l a c /mailog/ in the place-name *Landeuailac*, now Llandyfaelog-fach (*Mute Stones*, 139 ff.).
35. For the lattter, rather surprising, conclusion see D.R. Howlett, 'Israelite learning in Insular Latin', *Peritia*, 11 (1997), 117-52.

Interlude:
The Mathematical Side of
Inscriptional Texts

This is a pause between narrative chapters. We need to acquaint ourselves with the *arithmetical adjuncts*[1] of Biblical style, as they appear in inscriptions; here, described individually as *devices*.

Proportional composition

A sentence plucked from today's paper, 'Promising Start For Cultural Crusaders', lacks a verb and means very little, but above all has no *structure*; no pattern. A language-teacher says to a student, 'This is all wrong. Welsh has a nasal mutation. Don't you know it yet?' — and gets the reply (which we can mark as having two parts) 'I *don't* know (=a). No-one's taught it to me (=b).' Overlook the apostrophes and approach this as a piece of writing. Part (*a*) has 3 words, 3 syllables, 9 letters. Part (*b*) has 6 words, 6 syllables and 18 letters; and is therefore twice as long as (*a*) in all respects. The proportion, the *ratio* of (*a*) to (*b*), is 1 to 2, or (inverted) 2 to 1 — called 'duple ratio'. If we look back at 421 *Rostece*, which has *eleven* words, there might be an (*a*) and (*b*) on these lines; (*a*) is about the girl and her father, HIC IN TUMULO IACIT ROSTECE FILIA PATERNINI, and (*b*) about her age and repose in peace, in the model form ANNI TREDECIM IN PACE. With words only, (*a*) has 7, (*b*) has 4, total 11. A ratio of 7 to 4 (7:4), or the reverse, 4:7, is not the same as 2:1 or 1:2; in fact, it looks quite uneven. But suppose we have a number-set, like this: 1.3.4.7.11.18.29.47.76.123... (on as far as you like) in which, after the '1' and '3', each is the sum of the two preceding (4=1 + 3, 7 = 3 + 4); this is a pattern, and it would cover (Rostece) (*a*), 7 (words), and (*b*), 4 (words), making 11 in all. It is a pattern that can be written as 4:7 → 11. It is also an instance of *extreme ratio*.

A pious spinster living with two companions regularly attends Matins at the parish church, but she cannot stand the Vicar. One Sunday evening she writes to her aunt. Here are two sentences from her letter. Again we can divide them as (*a*) and (*b*):

(*a*)   This very morning, we attended Divine Service.   (38 letters)
(*b*)   Had the Vicar not played his guitar, Our Lord's
        presence would have been felt.   (62 letters)

That makes one hundred letters. The division can be written down as 38:62 → 100 (and we shall see what that means shortly). The *words* are once more (*a*) 7, (*b*) 14, 1:2, duple ratio. The *syllables* come out as 13 to 19, which is not a recognised ratio. However, preserving the totals of words and letters as they are, one could adjust the text to convey the same meaning, but now reading:

(*a*)   This very *morn*, *three* attended Divine Service.
(*b*)   Had the Vicar not *abused* his guitar, Our Lord's
           presence would have been felt.

Now the syllables are (*a*) 12, and (*b*) 18; 12 to 18, or 2 to 3, or a familiar ratio 1:1½(called 'sesquialter ratio'). The whole passage has a coherent structure. Words, syllables and letters, *W, S, L*, exhibit (as between (*a*) and (*b*)) acceptable proportions.

To compose in this way, to adjust one's thoughts and words in any fixed-spelling written language, Latin in particular (including all the inscriptions considered here), is to impose order where there might be randomness, muddle, chaos; to write in accordance with *Number*, which stands outside feeble humanity and is of God, a part of Divine Creation; and to show in one's handiwork a fitting attempt to copy God's precepts. With a little practice it can be done at speed and many writers in antiquity seem to have done it automatically. At the simplest a text can fall into equal halves; division by symmetry or *mean ratio* (written 1:1). Common ratios, 1:2, 1:3, 1:4, have their own names (duple, triple, quadruple).

Quite different, indeed possessing its own philosophy, is another that has many names — *extreme ratio* (ER), as shown just now, also the Golden Mean, Golden Section, *sectio divina*, Divine (or ideal) proportions.[2] Its full guise is 1 : 1.6180339 (continued as a non-recurring decimal). As 1.618 (for short), this is a constant known as *phi* (ϕ); among its properties, *one* divided by ϕ, and ϕ minus one, both equal 0.618. A geometric theorem that had been worked out by the Greeks, and would have been taught by the Romans, gives the value of ϕ from proportional drawings that yield an equation of $= \frac{1}{2}(1 + \sqrt{5})$; or half of $(1 + 2.236)$; or half of 3.236 $(= 1.618)$. Spatially, imagine a rectangle whose shorter side is 100 units, and longer side 161.80339 (say, 162) units (*Fig.27*). This shape, known to architects and some artists, has been regarded as having the ideal, the most harmonious (the most God-inspired) of, proportions.

It is more or less certain that in Roman times, and for these later inscriptions, the normal way to find extreme ratio was from memorised sequences or sets of Fibonacci numbers.[3] In these, as we saw, each from the third onward is the sum of the two preceding, and those two numbers are in extreme ratio within their sum. The first set runs 1.2.3.5.8.13.21.34.55.89.144... If you calculate 55/144, and 89/144, they come to 0.3819444 $(= 0.382)$ and 0.618055 $(= 0.618)$. In practice only the first five or so sets were used (1.3.4.7.11.18..., 1.4.5.9.14.23..., 1.5.6.11.17.28..., 1.6.7.13.20.33...) and the higher the numbers the closer they fall to correct ratio. We shall meet the use of two other sets (non-Fibonacci conventions) which for some reason were popular. The commoner is 5.7.12.19.31.50..., and there is also 4.9.13.22.35.57.92... (in the eighth century, both were found necessary for the computus of 427 *Catuoconi*, p. 169.) Doubling the numbers in the first convention gives 10.14.24.38.62.100 (and naturally 0.382 and 0.618 of a hundred are

Fig.27 *Extreme ratio or the Golden Mean in a very simple graphic guise. In the upper, aesthetically-pleasing rectangle, sides m, M are in ER as 1:1.618…, drawn here at 50 and 81mm. Progressive division of rectangles, clockwise, into squares and remaining rectangles, gives squares whose sides (smallest upward) are now 5, 7, 12, 19, 31 and 50 mm — an extreme-ratio sequence. Visually, 5 + 7 = 12, 7 + 12 = 19, etc. A curve (incremental spiral) drawn through the centres of squares is found in Nature, as is the series 1.2.3.5.8.13.21.34.… (e.g., on pineapples, fircones; see D'Arcy Wentworth Thompson,* Growth and Form *[2nd edn. only; Cambridge 1942]).*

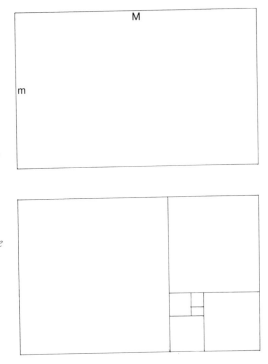

38 and 62); this is what we had in the Vicar-hating spinster's note, as its letter count.

We can see at least four reasons for composing a text to show extreme ratio at one, two or all three levels, *W, S* and *L*. The first is to advertise a composer's competence and is a statement that a composition is in Biblical style; the second, perhaps more important, is to exhibit conformity with a Divine model (seen extensively in the Vulgate). Third, the break-point, the *extreme section* (ES), is used to emphasise a name; mostly of the deceased, sometimes of the composer. 479 *Cunaide* has 13 words (p.150), divided 5 and 8, from 1.2.3.5.8.13.21… and goes *Hic pace nuper requievit* **CUNAIDE** / *hic in…*; and as 4:7 → 11, 421 *Rostece* would read — *Hic in tumulo iacit* / **ROSTECE** *filia Paternini…* In 350 *Idnert*, twelve words as 5:7 → 12 (that convention), ES of both syllables and letters come at the same point (*hic iacet Idnert filius Iac* **O**) / *bi qui…*) to indicate the author and to give his correct name *Iaco*, not *Iacobus*. Fourth, we have to identify the conventions or Fibonacci sets used (and there can be more than one in a text) because the terms give the intervals in precession-and-interval readings (see shortly).

Triangular numbers

A *triangular* (number) from N, any whole number, is the sum of all numbers from 1 to N inclusive; $1 + 2 + 3 + 4 + 5 + 6 = 21$, and 21 is 'the triangular from 10', written Δ10. Probably discovered by Pythagoras among the various *figured* numbers that could be worked out with pebbles and counters, equations to find them are: $\Delta N = \frac{1}{2} N (N + 1)$ —

thus Δ6 is 3, times 7 (21); or $\frac{1}{2}$N-squared $+\frac{1}{2}$N — thus Δ12 is 72, plus 6 (78). We can be sure that in the Roman *arithmetica-geometrica* curriculum the first twenty triangulars at least were learnt by heart. These are

(1)	(1)	8	36	15	120
2	3	9	45	16	136
3	6	10	55	17	153
4	10	11	66	18	171
5	15	12	78	19	190
6	21	13	91	20	210
7	28	14	105		

Playing around with pebbles also demonstrates that any *square* number will be the sum of two triangulars, as the diagram shows:

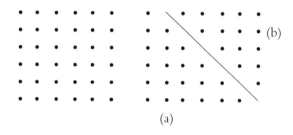

(a)

with the equation $N^2 = \Delta N + \Delta(N-1)$. The square of 6 is turned into a pattern, of a triangle from 6 and another from 5. On the right, straightening them into equilaterals, (a) is called a *pyramid*, and (b) an *inverted* (triangle).

The purpose of arranging a text so that its letter total is triangular (like CHRISTMAS IS COMING SOON; 21 letters, or Δ6) is to lead to *triangularisation*; writing it out thus —

```
            C                        C   H   R   I   S   T
          H   R                      M   A   S   I   S
        I   S   T                      C   O   M   I
      M   A   S   I                    N   G   S
    S   C   O   M   I                    O   O
(a)  N   G   S   O   O   N      (b)        N
```

—and then treating these as what amounts to *numerical* acrostics. We can add the LaN values on the two diagonal sides, the level base or top, and also the three *apicals* (angle letters). In Biblical style computus (*computus* is a useful term for the entire mathematical aspect of a composition) these give, not new words, but new *totals*; primarily, symbolic or allusive numbers.[4] When a text is analysed, presence of a triangular (generally, a total of letters) can be taken as an implied instruction: Triangularise this.

Square and perfect numbers

Square numbers may have both a practical and a symbolic role. A square letter total suggest, at once, that a text is to be re-cast; 64 letters are to be written out as 8 by 8. In this case, the intended products are likely to be *verbal*; words and names that we do not read in the display. They are read downwards as part or whole columns; *acrostics* for the first (left-side) and internal columns[5], and correctly *telestichs* for the last (right-side) column. (The Lullingstone mosaic offered fine examples.) There may also be minor numerical messages, from adding LaN of all four corners. Allied to these square dispositions are *grids* (also seen at Lullingstone), *regular* if simple rectangles from even-numbered totals, *staggered* if they contain blanks (whose totals ought to be related to key numbers).

A *perfect* number, a figured discovery we seem to owe to Euclid, is equal to the sum of all its factors including 1. The first is 6 ($1 + 2 + 3 = 6$), the second is 28 ($1 + 2 + 4 + 7 + 14 = 28$), the next two are 496 and 8128 (known to Nicomachus in the first century AD but hardly relevant to these inscriptions), the seventh appears in the fifteenth century ($33,550,336 = 2^{12}(2^{13}-1)$) and curiosity has led recently to a perfect, the 33rd, with 517,430 digits(!). Some special emphasis is apparent in inscriptional computus on 28, which is also $\Delta 7$, and on 36, which is very special; the *square* of 6 (which is both perfect *and* triangular) and *triangular* from 8 (which is the cube of 2).

Anagrams

We come to devices that are both numerical and verbal. The anagram is always with us. Who has not sat in a train and watched a fellow-citizen with a newspaper struggling to rescue BEN ELTON from NOBLE TEN? Inscriptions may hide ordinary anagrams; in 970 *Catamanus*, OPINATISIMUS is to be shuffled into OPTIMUS ASINI (p. 167). A particular development within Insular style was the emergence of anagrammatic *rursus*, *retrorsum*, both meaning 'backward', as a signpost to inverted readings.[6] But these, and sometimes other words, are found as *split* anagrams; as tricky as clues in the old *Observer* crosswords. Here is an ordinary anagram in an unstructured sentence, itself a clue:

He was a large composer (large = L A R G E = **E L G A R**).

And here, within a longer sentence using extreme ratio and several patterns, is a split anagram:

O, he was a great and real composer then, I am sure

It has *twelve* words (and involves the convention *5.7.12.19.31...*). The anagram (Elgar again) is contained thus: letter totals shown.

O, he was a / **GREA** t and rea **L** / composer then, I am sure
$\qquad$ 7 $\qquad\qquad$ 12 $\qquad\qquad\qquad$ 19

The 12 letters from G to L are the *span*. Within them, 5 letters are used, GREAL, and 7 are not (5:7 → 12). Letters-before, plus the span, total 19 (as 7:12 → 19); the span, plus letters-after, give 12:19 → 31. Both the composition of the span, and its exact positioning, follow the designated extreme-ratio structure. They are *validated*. When they are (and only when), we accept them as intended. Here is a ninth-century example from 350 *Idnert*, a 12-word text (as 5:7 → 12) dominated by 5 and 7 as key numbers. We are given *rursus*:

hic iacet Idne / **R** t fili **US** Iacobi q.ui occis **US** fuit p **R** / opter
12   5   7   7   5   5

The letters R.US.US.R (= RURSUS) are arranged a.b.b.a., and so are intervals of 5.7.7.5; the span is 5 times six letters; before it are 5-plus-7 letters, after it 5, and the remainder of the text has seventeen, 5-plus-7-plus-5, letters. It is wholly validated.

Precession-and-interval

This names a device required to give a reading, in the right order, of letters making a name or word (if a name, generally the author's) that occur in a longer letter-sequence, but separated by planned intervals. We can find 'Mary', within 'Fro**m** a lot of **a**ccounts, gin's a **r**ollicking sort of liquor for **y**ou'; where the precession-and-interval scheme of 3 . **M**. 6 **A**. 12. **R**. 24. **Y** (2) simply shows intervals being successively multiplied by the (2) (from **Y** *ou*) at the end. When the device was first identified (1995), I assumed that it was widespread from the fourth to eleventh centuries. However, when intervals are regular or equal throughout, it is safer to see them as really indicating acrostics. The reading of the name AVITUS (p. 50) could be seen as (5) **A**. 7. **V**. 7. **I**. 7. **T**. 7. **U**. 7. **S** (for the same IESUS in 350 *Idnert*, p. and *Fig.8*); but both are no more than regular-intervals rewriting of what are primarily acrostics.

True precession-and-interval ranks as a cryptogram, probably invented in Wales some time after 600; it is applied to backwards (inverted, reversed) arrangements of a text, a disposition that is suggested by split anagrams of *rursus* and *retrorsum*. The intervals are usually unequal, and taken from an extreme-ratio sequence (a Fibonacci set; or either of the conventions 5.7.12.19, 4.9.13.22) offered by the textual computus. This may itself involve a choice. 350 *Idnert* makes use of four Fibonacci sets, as well as 5.7.12.19. The final choice — and like the whole de-coding process it requires a good deal of trial and error before the right answer is given — is the *application* of the intervals-sequence. Taking 1.2.3.5.8.13.21 as an illustration, we could select the seven letters having those numbered positions in the reversed text (*indicated* letters). Or we could indicate the first letter and then skip over the intervals, reading **X** . 1 . **X** . 2 . **X** . 3 . **X** . 5 . **X** . 8 and so on; and a variant would be to *open* with an interval (1 . **X** . 2 . **X** . 3 . **X**). Nor is this all. The full reading, indicated letters and unequal intervals, might constitute a span, with a number of left-over letters following the last indicated; and that total itself ought to be related to the interval-sequence, or a key number or ratio.

Precession-and-interval has now been detected in six, possibly seven, texts, four of which (all from Wales) also have 'reversal' anagrams. As these are demonstrated in later chapters a single instance will be enough now; it is from 350 *Idnert* again, using the part that contained a *rursus* split-anagram (p.). Since the span contained *qui occisus fuit* 'who was slain' (i.e., Idnert) it seem likely that any concealed name will have been that of one of his killers. We reverse the twenty-five (key number 5 squared) letters in

(hic iacet Idnert fi) / lius Iacobi qui occisus fuit p / (ropter)

25

to give: p t i u f s u s i c c o i u q i b o c a i s u i l

and then, using the first Fibonacci set of 1.2.3.5.8.(13.21.34.55…),

read: **P** t **I** u f **S** u s i **C** c o i u q **I** b o c a i s u i **L**

1   2   3   5   8

It gives PISCIL (this would have been spoken /pisgil/), conceivably an Old Welsh personal name ultimately derived from Roman *Pisciculus*. The whole span is 25; letters *after* final L (those *before* it in the unreversed text) total 16, and 16:25 → 41 is a correct extreme ratio by calculation — 41 x .382 = 15.7 (16); 41 x 0.618 = 25.3 (25). (This is introduced by a 'demonstration' reading, with split anagram of *retrorsum*, within the last 5 words; precession-and-interval applied to these, reversed, using the same intervals produces IDNERT.)

These constitute the principal devices identified in the texts. There are a few others, less complicated, that can be pointed out in appropriate places. The writer's sympathies are wholeheartedly with readers whose reactions include 'I was never any good at maths', 'I don't trust any of this Bible Code stuff' and 'You can prove anything with numbers, especially in a dead language'. An inescapable problem, a massive (and, to many students, tragic) Black Hole in our knowledge of Roman times and early Latin learning, is that we do not have the exercise books, the chalked-up blackboards, the primers and manuals and wall charts; the sort of details from which visitors from the future, exploring a modern comprehensive school preserved in aspic, would be able to reconstruct most of a curriculum and its content. The Roman versions have not survived, or not nearly enough of them. From Classical mathematicians we know some of the words for some of these adjuncts; a 'perfect' number (*teleios*), Theon of Smyrna's clear statement of his discovery of $N^2 = \Delta N + \Delta(N - 1)$, *heteromekes* ('oblong') as one basis for the grid, *trigonous arithmous* for 'triangular numbers'. Most Latin equivalents can be found; the extra vocabulary to describe their textual application is lost. A reaction that would *not* be justified is any over-hasty dismissal of everything involving numbers and patterns in Insular inscriptions that this book tries to describe, to explain and perforce to name, just because it is unfamiliar, unexpected, needs some understanding, and is at odds with popular depictions of Dark Age Celtic Britain. One might point to a growing body of evidence that closely-related proportional composition systems were used in art (constructing 'carpet-pages' in greater manuscripts) and in architecture (ground-planning major buildings), as they still were in the Middle Ages. Inscriptional style was a particular and specialised development of Insular Latin composition, as the latter has been so richly explored by David Howlett. Though it has escaped the notice of most Biblical scholars, some of this *arithmetica* is common in the Vulgate (p. 89).

Above all, behind it all, this was a Christian world and the conviction that God is

Number, and Number is of God, who inspired it. The astronomer Carl Sagan's novel *Contact* (1985) is not, first or foremost, about earthlings travelling to Vega down a worm-hole in their space-machine built from coded instructions. Sagan's grander theme is the contingency that if the constant *pi*, 3.14159... (non-recurring), could be calculated to trillions of figures, we might — years ahead — encounter a configuration; his own idea was that it would be expressed as a perfect circle ('the artist's signature'). Classical mathematicians and the composers of Insular inscriptions did not use base-11 arithmetic nor contemplate the possibility of resolving constants through years of computer-time, but (like Carl Sagan) we can borrow a thought from Nicomachus of Gerasa, whose own *Arithmetica* dates to about AD 100. It constitutes a view that we can be quite certain was held by many Christian Celtic authors in the centuries that followed:

'The universe seems ... to have been determined and ordered in accordance with *Number*, by the forethought and the mind of the Creator of all things; for the pattern was fixed, like a preliminary sketch, by the domination of *Number* pre-existent in the mind of the world-creating God.'

Notes to The Interlude

1. This, David Howlett's definition, distinguishes them clearly from the wholly literary figures like chiasmus, parallelisms and any metrical characteristics.

2. Specialist works are: H.E. Huntley, *The Divine Proportion. A Study in Mathematical Beauty* (New York 1970), and R. Hertz-Fischler, *A Mathematical History of Division in Extreme and Mean Ratio* (Waterloo, Ontario 1987).

3. Generally so-named (by the mathematician Edouard Lucas) for Leonardo ('Fi'Bonacci') of Pisa, a medieval sage who recovered the first set. The geometrical properties of the Fibonacci series are as interesting as their arithmetical ones.

4. As will be clear later, triangularisation was disproportionately often used (because it is a way to signal numbers over 100) in arriving at symbolic 144 (= the Heavenly City), or at 153.

5. I use 'acrostic' for medial as well as initial readings; but again, strictly, a medial reading is called a *mesostich* (a word absent from the *OED*).

6. There are other words with the same meaning (*retrorsus, retrovorsum, retroversus,* (post-Classical) *retrocessim*) but these are the only two found in the Insular split anagrams.

4 The Priesthood and the Word

It does not follow that, because introduction and circulation of the newly-translated Latin Bible, the Vulgate, in fifth-century Britain was a prime stimulus to compose texts in what *we* call 'Biblical style', all compositions long and short were the work of priests. Some certainly were, like the *Catuoconi* statement, p. 174. Others probably were, but we also have 493 *Carausius*, an impressive creation, with a female and therefore lay author(ess). On the other hand a system of education perpetuating the knowledge and use of Latin, together with the ways in which it could be used, seems to have become largely a monastic preserve and in any series of public statements — which is what the inscriptions are — so closely tied to religious teaching and beliefs, one would expect the custodians of that religion to have played a full part.

The Priesthood

Knowledge of the Church hierarchy and its orders in post-Roman Britain is built up from isolated references. Unlike the Continent, we have no bishop-lists going back to 400 or earlier and, from Roman Britain, merely the odd mention of clerics attending meetings elsewhere.[1] For the fifth to eighth centuries there is an unresolved (or, perhaps, debatable) question associated with the growth of monasteries of several kinds, leading to diversified patterns of Christian sites in much of Britain as well as in Ireland. Did there arise *two* systems, potentially in conflict? One, as argued for fourth-century Britannia, would have seen bishops at the head of geographical dioceses, ruling over priests and deacons and lesser orders of clergy attached to churches; this is the norm for other parts of the Late Roman world, a sort of early counterpart of the way that the Church of England is historically organised. The other pattern, by 600 or so, would have been of monastic establishments ruled by abbots and *praepositi* (priors) who, though priests, were not necessarily also bishops; and whose geographical rule or sphere-of-influence (*paruchia*), in no way tied to any map of the former Roman civil administration, was necessarily linked to a later network of very loosely-defined native kingdoms. Informed ideas[2] tend to see this duality as perhaps exaggerated. With the virtual disappearance of the Roman towns by 500, if not earlier, an older concept of town-based bishops might give way to a belief that most British bishops in the sixth-seventh centuries — their episcopal standing essential to many Christian sacraments — were attached to courts and royal households rather than to fixed locations possessing major churches.[3] Since there remains considerable ignorance as to the real total of British kingdoms, both the larger and longer-lasting ones and any spread of sub-kingdoms within them,[4] it is perfectly possible that in (say) AD 700 the Christian Celtic episcopate was well into double figures.

Bede tells us[5] that around 600 Augustine of Canterbury held a conference, a *colloquium* conducted naturally in Latin, somewhere in the West Midlands or the Cotswold area, to which *episcopi sive doctores*, bishops and learned men/teachers, were invited 'from the adjoining province of the Britons'; i.e. Wales. In their party, or as a rapid follow-up, were seven such bishops and many very learned men (*doctissimi*). Some had come reputedly from a large and famous monastery that Bede knew as *Bancornaburg*; Bangor-on-Dee or Bangor Is-coed, in Flintshire, the very north of Wales. This actually tells us no more about the organisational background of the British church — were these *episcopi* from courts, fixed territorial dioceses, or monasteries, and in what proportions? — than do the complaints of Gildas about the clergy a century and a half earlier.[6] Gildas's strictures concerned individual conduct rather than organisational shortcomings (if there were any). He wrote of *sacerdotes*, *pastores*, *sacerdotium* (= the priesthood generally), and the separate orders of bishopric, *episcopatus*, and priesthood, *presbyterium*. What he does imply in another passage of *DEB*[7] is that in the early sixth century there had been Britons who, unable to attain ordination as priests or consecration as bishops at home, had 'first sent urgent messages ahead'; and then, 'sailing across seas and traversing wide lands', had managed improperly to acquire these offices abroad. This, the ecclesiastic sin known as simony, from the suggestion that the offices were more or less bought, presumably occurred in Gaul (or northern Spain or even parts of what is now Italy).

If Gildas dwells on the downside of his Scenes From Clerical Life, there is a pleasanter implication. He complains of such men, stiff with purchased pride, returning home; 'their gait, which had been erect before, erecter still'. Where transgressors could apparently with little difficulty engage in transmarine trips so could worthier men. The seventh-century *Vita Prima* of Samson (p. 58) has an episode[8] when the young Samson is at the island monastery of Caldey, off the Pembroke coast (p. 169); we are early in the sixth century, and within Gildas's lifetime elsewhere. Samson meets there a small party of *peritissimi Scotti de Roma venientes* 'very skilled and expert Irish, coming from Rome', no doubt on their way to Ireland, perhaps going overland and then in a boat from Cardigan Bay. Conversing with them Samson finds them to be genuine *phylosophi* 'learned scholars'. Whether or not *Roma* here means 'Rome' or 'the orbit of the Church of Rome in the Western provinces' is immaterial. These learned voyagers can stand equally well for others — the inscriptional heroes, the incoming phylosophi — whom we shall meet in these pages with 391 *Senacus*, and then 516 *Viventius* (p. 120).

But how many inscribed memorials do really commemorate priests? It is too simple to rely on an older assumption, that any stone with a male name on its own, and no filiation-statement ('the son of X'), should denote a cleric because the text would reflect a Biblical injunction, especially binding upon the priesthood. This occurs in Matthew, 23.9: the command to 'call no *man* 'your father' upon the Earth, for *One* is your Father, which is in Heaven'. Sometimes, but not often, a context suggests a priest. *Fig.28* is a granite block, pillow-like to sit on a grave, from St Kew in north-east Cornwall. The name IVSTI, *Iusti*

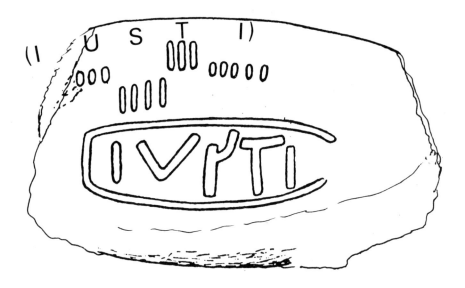

Fig.28   Heavy granite block, 74cm, from St Kew, Cornwall; gravestone for Iustus *(a member of the monastery at Landocco?). In the frame,* IVSTI *'of-Iustus'; ogam characters (I missing),* U S T I *(R.A.S. Macalister's drawing, CIIC 484).*

'of-Iustus', appears in the cartouche and is repeated in ogam as *IUSTI*, a common Roman name and frequent among Christians.[9] It would be difficult *not* to connect this with the local monastery of Landocco (as we may call it), according to the Life of Samson existing there by about 500. This would be for a grave of one of the brethren and, if the monastery was an offshoot of a larger and earlier establishment in Wales, we would expect persons of mixed Welsh and Irish descent (hence the ogam). The same goes for 466 *Ingenui* from Lewannick, near Launceston in east Cornwall (*Fig.29*), also dating to not much after 500. It marks the *memoria* 'memorial, monument, ?grave-plot' of Ingenuus, a Roman name. With the ogam *IGENAWI MEMOR*, we are given a very fair rendering of the name spoken aloud, because INGENUI and *IGENAWI* both represent phonetic /iŋenawi/; the word *MEMOR* / meṽor ?/ being what we would expect Latin *memoria* to become, when borrowed into spoken Primitive Irish. The parish churchyard at Lewannick still contains the prominent circular embanked cemetery of the sixth century, and this stone to Ingenuus ought to have marked the burial of its founding priest.[10]

For the written sources, Patrick in the later fifth century stated that his grandfather had been *presbyter*, a priest, and his father *diaconus*, a deacon. He mentions other un-named *diaconi, presbyteri*. Priests in general are *clerici*. Patrick calls himself *episcopus* 'a bishop', using this word rightly because his standing and labours were akin to those of any Late Roman bishop, *civis Romanus* (Roman citizen), led by God to oversee a vast diocese — he had in this case been appointed to all Ireland (*Hiberione constitutus*).[11] *Fig.30* brings together wordings that mention clerical grades. To avoid sheets of discussion (but see later, p. 115), *sacerdos* is taken to mean 'consecrated as a bishop, but not necessarily acting as a diocesan or

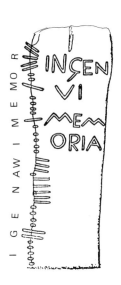

Fig.29 466 Ingenui, *Lewannick, east Cornwall; pillar of reddish granite. Much of the ogam, visible in 1892 to A.G. Langdon but by the 1920s 'in very bad condition' when Macalister drew this, is now barely detectable.*

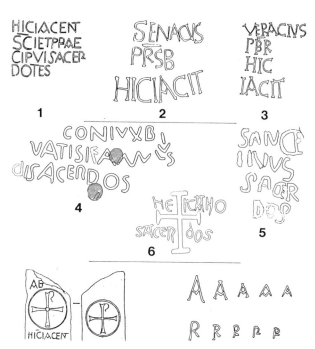

Fig. 30 Memorials to clergy. 1, 516 Viventius et Mavorius, sacerdotes *2 and 3, 391* Senacus *and 392* Veracius, *both* presbiter. *Probably later (6th century) are 4, detail from 325* Audiva, *wife of* Bivatisus, *the sacerdos, and 5, 384* Sanctinus, *also* sacerdos. *No.6, Peebles, late 7th or early 8th, is to* Neitano sacerdos *(not in CIIC). Below, some letter forms, 'angle-bar A' and 'sideways R' from nos.1 to 3; of the six shown here, nos.1 to 4 are variously composed in Biblical style. (Drawn from different sources; any from ECMW are by permission of the National Museum of Wales.)*

territorial bishop'; *presbiter* (Latin: one form of Greek *presbyter*) 'a priest', the grade below bishop and above that of deacon.

We cannot distinguish those at the top of *Fig.30*, all dating to around 500, no.1 from Scotland, nos. 2 and 3 from Wales, from the three below (4 to 6) which are later, describable as firmly *native*, and epigraphically separate from the first three. Of Sanctinus (5) we know nothing. The British-named Neitan (6) was perhaps a bishop around 700 in the Tweed basin of southern Scotland. Bivatisus (4) whose wife (*coniux*) is commemorated here could have been an early sixth-century court bishop of Anglesey to the rulers of Gwynedd, a kingdom of north-west Wales once ruled by Gildas's *Maglocune* (p. 69).

The special interest of nos.1, 2 and 3 is that a very strong case can be make for seeing these men — the *sacerdotes* Viventius and Mavorius at Kirkmadrine, south-west Scotland, the *presbiteri* Senacus and Veracius at Capel Anelog, Aberdaron, north-west Wales — as incomers from Gaul; their monuments executed by companions, *fratres*, in two isolated little groups of immigrant clergy that in modern language had set up mission-stations. These texts contain HIC IACENT (IACIT) 'here lie, lies', one of two standard Christian formulae, the other being HIC IN TVMVLO IACIT that we met earlier with 421 *Rostece* (p. 15), which became very common in later fifth-century Gaul and seem to have been copied thence in parts of south Wales, later still in south-west Britain.[12] Epigraphically nos.1 and 3 exhibit certain letter-forms, fashions rather than substitutes, that also became common in Gaul and the Rhineland before 500.[13] They are shown at the bottom; angle-bar A, and sideways-R. The practice of showing on stone as well as in manuscripts any abbreviations (either contractions or suspensions) by *overlining*, putting short bars above the affected words, survived widely after the Roman period on the Continent but was almost unknown in post-Roman Insular memorials.[14] Its presence on nos.1 to 3 again points to external models; the next instance in point of time is on the Welsh 986 *Ioruert Ruallaunque* stone (p. 156), at least two centuries on. On no.1 in *Fig.30* the motif of the encircled chi-rho with open or hooked (not closed-loop) rho (the P element) is unquestionably Gaulish.[15]

It is therefore of extreme relevance that two of these possible 'mission-station' memorials (Nos.1 and 2) are not only exercises in Biblical style of a high order — they have elements in common, but differently handled to give specific information — but no.2, 391 *Senacus*, to be examined next, generates a mental image in the same vein as did Corellia Optata's stone earlier. As we go on, attention can be directed to these linked questions; of any later fifth-century Gaulish input, whether due to genuine immigrants or to the better of Gildas's returning clerics accused of self-advancement, and also of course of any evidence for similar traits in contemporary inscriptions *outside* Britain. Immediately however, because one strand in this supposed external contribution was a strong recourse to Biblical allusions, it is as well to clarify what (in post-400 Western Britain) is meant by 'the Bible'.

The Vulgate

The languages of the Bible were Hebrew for the Old Testament, and at first principally Greek, the predominant Christian language in the eastern half of the Empire, for the New.

Spreading the Word across the West necessitated Latin versions. These existed by the fourth century as a series of translations, collectively known as the Old Latin or *vetus Latina* Bible. We can certainly allow one in pre-400 Britannia and parts of this were certainly read and quoted until at least the sixth century; they must have been from whatever Biblical writings happened to be available at remoter or poorer places. In 520 *Latinus* (Chap.5) the opening *Tè Dominum laudamus* 'Thee, Lord, we praise' is not apparently from the Vulgate, and may be either from a liturgical prayer or a lost passage of a *vetus Latina* book.

The turning-point, emergence of what would stand as the cornerstone of Western letters for centuries, was the preparation from new translations and revisions of earlier ones of a standard Bible in Latin, the *editio Vulgata* or Vulgate produced between 382 and the early 400s. It was the work of St Jerome (*c*.347-419) and his associates; a systematic preparation of the whole of the existing Old and New Testaments. Jerome himself knew Greek and learnt enough Hebrew to monitor the Latinisation of the Old Testament. He did not translate everything himself and one of his known assistants, Rufinus the Syrian, can be credited with some of the books and with general editing; authorship is not always certain for parts of the Vulgate but Rufinus's work followed the standard of Jerome's. To the latter, born in Dalmatia as Eusebius Hieronymus, European culture has been, and remains, indebted twice over since the fifth century. Along with many other writings Jerome transmitted to the Latin-speaking world the riches of Greek and Hebrew literature, and he is rightly represented as the Prince of Translators. Second, Jerome possessed and communicated by his work a literary culture and a magisterial Latin style that differed from, and came to overshadow, that of most other Early Christian Fathers.

We lack hard information about this, but there seems to be no reason why the four Gospels, the Psalms, many of the Pauline Epistles and at least the first five (or eight) Old Testament books in the Vulgate form could not have reached the Church in Britain as early as 420-30. This would have been as books of the Vulgate brought in from Gaul or further afield, then copied locally for internal circulation; from church to church, later from monastic centre or school to individuals. There is much in the context of inscriptions to suggest that, by 500 or so, this superior Latin scripture was widely available and preferentially consulted.

When the claim is made that both the literary and arithmetical sides of Biblical style can be found in short texts on stone was well as in longer compositions, it should be understood that the model provided by the Vulgate reinforced and extended features of Insular Latin that must already have been familiar from Classical literature. Here we can notice a few such features, starting with the non-mathematical ones, to show how early they appear on stones. Repetition or parallelism comprises a limited statement immediately followed by a second of comparable length and pattern that repeats the sense in other words (paraphrases it).[16] Isaiah, 1.10, reads

> (a)   *Audite verbum Domini, principes Sodomorum*
> (b)   *Percipite auribus legem Dei nostri, populus Gomorrae*
> or: 'Hear the word of the Lord, you rulers of Sodom:
>   Give ear to the teaching of our God, you people of Gomorrah'

Effectively (b) is the counterpart of (a), differently expressed. In the fifth-century inscription 479 *Cunaide* (p.) the first nine words are

> (a) Hic pace nuper requievit
>   CUNAIDE
> (b) Hic in tumulo iacit

'Here in peace lately went to rest / Cunaide / Here in the tomb she lies'. Each half is *four* words, starting HIC and ending -IT, and (b) is simply a paraphrase of (a).

Chiasmus is a statement followed by its re-statement in reverse or inverted order. Here is a doggerel example of it:

a	I rushed
b	to the market
c	to buy me
d	some bread.
d'	A loaf
c'	for to purchase,
b'	shopwards
a'	I sped.

The matched elements, the *chiastic terms*, can conveniently be denoted by a,b,c,; c',b',a', etc. Chiasmus is extremely common in the Vulgate, usually in long passages. Elements of short and simple chiasmus do occur in inscriptional texts. For instance, 970 *Catamanus* (seventh century; p. 163) has

a	Catamanus *rex*	'king'
b	*sapientisimus*	superlative
b'	*opinatisimus*	superlative
a'	omnium *regum*	'of kings'

But there is a different kind that we can call *inscriptional chiasmus*; where terms are matched by related meaning, contrasts (e.g., general-specific), as parts of speech, and by inversion of shared letters. Examples are given in other chapters. We can go back again to 421 *Rostece*, eleven words, and set it out chiastically with explanations.

a	Hic in tumulo	space *general* (hic), then *specific* (in tumulo); letters **I C I N**
b	iacit Rostece	word (verb) qualifies name; letters **I A I T E**
b'	filia Paternini	word (noun) relates to name; letters **I I A T E**
a'	anni tredecim in pace	time *specific* (XIII), then *general* (in pace); letters **N I C I**

This kind of interlocked and multiple reversal, which overcomes the obstacle that a short text cannot possess sufficient appropriate words for a full verbal chiasmus, is not uncommon among Insular inscriptions. The earliest examples seem to be 421 *Rostece* and the similarly-organised 479 *Cunaide* from Cornwall (p. 151), both later fifth century. As purely stylistic (non-arithmetical) constructs they are quite subtle. The model of the Vulgate apart, it suggests that chiasmus continued to be taught as a desirable component of all Latin composition along with parallelism (with which it can be elaborately combined, as it constantly was by Jerome).

Beyond and beside the commonplace literary ornaments like chiasmus and repetition which were integral to any Latin writing that aspired to elegance, style, and imitation of the approved models of Roman literature, we can detect a low-level combination of recourse to 20-letter LaN, the adding of initial and last letters and the arranging of desired totals of words, syllables and letters, throughout the Vulgate. Mostly it appears to have been done for the sake of doing it and we can suppose that Jerome, Rufinus the Syrian and others chose and disposed their words to produce these little arithmetical patterns almost automatically. With Latin (far more readily than with English) this is a practice not especially difficult to master. At various points in the book I include examples — like Jerome, with John, 21 (p. 190) — that involve subtlety of a high order and were provided to underline or emphasise some particular recorded event. For the general run of the Vulgate, *arithmetica* is often found when the Bible mentions anything concerning numbers and dimensions.

Let us observe Jerome at work; Exodus, 26.2, with instructions for making the curtains (*cortinae*) for the Tabernacle. The sentence reads *longitudino cortinae unius habebit viginti octo cubitos* 'the length of one curtain shall be 28 cubits'. We could guess that, far back, Hebrew sages settled on this arbitrary '28' knowing perhaps some or all of its properties (a perfect number; the triangular from *seven*; sum of *seven*, plus the triangular from six; *seven* times four, etc.). What do we find in Jerome's Latin? There are *seven* words and 49 (*seven* squared) letters; as a letter square the corners are L U C S, 10.19.3.17, or *49* again. Every *seventh* letter (U R N E I O S) gives 91, *seven* times 13; word no.7 (*cubitos*) has *seven* letters, and CUBITOS adds to another square (81).

Two more simple instances can be drawn from Matthew's Gospel, in Jerome's impressive Latin. The first is the catalogue of names of the twelve disciples specific to this Gospel, in Chap.10, verses 2-4 (I do not give this, or the next, in full but readers can look them up in any reliable Vulgate edition). Preferring for the second name of the last disciple 'Iscariotes', against Scariotes, the list from *primus Simon qui dicitur Petrus* to *qui et tradidit eum* has 36, 3 x *12*, words and 84, 7 x *12*, syllables. The Twelve are marked by God's *three*-fold nature and the *seven* (days) of God's Creation. In Matthew, 18, 12-13 we have the compact parable of the Lost Sheep Found; the man who had 100, the one stray sheep being when rescued a cause for greater joy than with the 99 sheep that never strayed. From *quid vobis videtur* to *quae non erraverunt* 'which did not stray' is 46 words, and by LaN the first and last letters are Q T, 15.18 = 33. The metaphor is of Jesus (as 33) rescuing Man (as 46, from the Greek LaN for AΔAM). The passage contains exactly *ninety-nine* syllables, for the sheep that did not err. The stated numbers are picked out by extreme ratio. With 38:61 → 99, the section falls at…nonne relinquet *nonaginta novem* / in montibus 'doth he not leave the 99 on the hill?' In the first 28 syllables, from the ratio 15:23 → 38, the section is at…si fuerit alicui *centum* / oves 'if someone should have 100 sheep'. Three and seven may come into this again because allowing the reading *super ea* (against *eam*) from the best source, codex A (the Amiatinus), the two verses contain 231 letters — that is, *three* times *seven*, times eleven. Here we find counting of totals of W, S, and L, 20-letter LaN, and extreme ratio (for the Sheep, from the set *1.7.8.15.23.38.61.99…*).

Understandably perhaps, Biblical scholarship ignores this component (mechanical rather than theological) of the Vulgate. Recalling how Sir Isaac Newton, last and greatest of the Late Antique wizards, was entrapped for decades in the *arithmetica* of the Book of

Ezekiel, it could be thought: This way, madness beckons. But all we have here is an embellishment to Latin composition, using totals of units and totals of letter values, to stress figures that occur in the supposed Word of God (Who is also Number), or to incorporate certain numbers that in the Word, notably in Gospel teachings and parables, are openly linked to aspects of Christian life and death. The point is not whether *we* can find this — any reader is invited to trawl through the Vulgate and spot dozens of similar instances — but that this particular arithmetical adjunct, which must have predated Jerome, was most certainly perceived, studied and imitated by the composers of Insular inscriptions. (It was, also, by Gildas; see p. 201) Here is one more illustration centred on the number 21 which, as *three* by *seven*, worships God as *Three* Persons in One and, in the beginning, the Ordainer of the *Seven* days of Creation. Whether by Rufinus, or inserted slightly later, Apocalypsis, 1.8, reads like this — it has both a parallelism (I, II) and an internal *triple* parallelism (i, ii):

I	Ego	sum
	i	Alpha
	ii	et Omega
	i'	principium
	ii'	et finis
II	dicit Dominus Deus	
I'	Qui est	
	i'	et qui erat
	ii'	et qui venturus est
II'	Omnipotens	

('I am Alpha and Omega, Very-Beginning and Very-End, saith the Lord God: Who is, and Who was, and Who shall be, the All-Powerful.') That is its stylistic or figural pattern. For the arithmetic, there are *twenty-one* words; and both Dominus, and Deus (the central eleventh word), have D S, 4.17 = *21*. Whoever arranged the Latin version knew Greek. Words nos.7 and 14 are both *et*; E T E T, or 5.18.5.18, make 46, the Greek LaN total for God's first created Man, Adam (AΔA M, 1.4.1.40 = 46). The Greek version also has *21* words, with Theos (= Deus) as central; overall, the initial is E (*Ego*) and the last letter is R (Pantokrato*r*), and in Greek LaN, E R, 5.100 = 105, or five times *twenty-one*.[18]

I have to assure readers once more that there is absolutely nothing esoteric, cryptic, mystical, still less lunatic, about this. It shows an instant appreciation of ordinary letters, and conventional (LaN) values, and an ingrained practice of very rapidly adding units of a written text; and, because it was common to select and add initials and last letters, a further instant recognition of word-boundaries even in continuous writing. We do not ourselves do this. We do not *need* to do it, and any driving force of God as Number has been replaced by one of Mechanical Intelligence as God. To understand the work and accomplishment of these, our devout and learned fellow-humans of a past culture upon which our own is so largely built, is to regress along most unfamiliar paths; but the journey is neither impossible nor, after the start, particularly difficult.

391 Senacus, 392 Veracius, at Cefnamwlch, Aberdaron, photograph by Jean Williamson.

391 Senacus (from ECMW, by permission of the National Museum of Wales). In line 2, abbreviation of PReSBiter by both contraction and suspension is marked by a small overlining bar. Details of the double and triple ligatures are shown, right.

A man's life in seven words

One of the most impressive of the early insular memorials shows admirably how a structure continuing from Roman times was enriched by the Vulgate model. This is 391 *Senacus (Fig.31)*. It may date from around 500 and it comes (with the much shorter 392 *Veracius*) from an unexcavated site, Capel Anelog, near Aberdaron in the Llyn Peninsula, the 'pig's ear' of north-west Wales.[19] For the moment we can envisage a small community (*fratres*) of churchmen, either Gauls or Britons returning from residence in Gaul; and that Senacus and Veracius, both priests, were buried and commemorated by their fellows in geographical but not cultural isolation.

The memorial reads: SENACVS /PR[e]SB[iter] /HIC IACIT / CVM MVLTITV / DINEM / FRATRVM, six lines with rather unusual ligatures, overlining in the second word and use of angle-bar A and sideways-R; *Senacus presbiter hic iacit cum multitudinem fratrum* 'Senacus, a priest, here lies, with a multitude of the brethren'. As *cum* 'with' takes the ablative, this should read *cum multitudine*, not -*dinem*, but this is no unlearned error. Analysis gives:

		W	S	LD	LM
1	S E N A C V S	1	3	7	7
2	P R̄ S̄ B (= presbiter)	1	3	3	9
3	H I C I A C I T	2	3	8	8
4	C VM MVL T I T V	2	4	7	10
5	D INEM		2	3	5
6	F R A T R VM	1	2	6	7
		7	17	34	46

As well as the four ligatures, shown in *Fig.31* and calling for very careful transcription, the letters R S overlined count as single. The first thing we might notice is that *S* is *17*, *LD* at 34 is twice *17*, and the word initials S P H I C M F, 17.14.8.9.3.11.6, make 68, four times *17*. This is the LaN total for *Adam* (1.4.1.11), 'Man, as God's creation', as well as the base for the triangular 153.[20] The corresponding (Greek) LaN total for ΑΔΑΜ, as we have just seen, is 46; in the analysis, *LM* is 46 and the last letters of the six (model) lines add to 92, twice 46. Is this a coincidence? No; a signpost.

If we look for any LNu reading, 21 of the 34 display letter are numerals; MMMM (4000), D(500), CCCC (400), L (50), VVVVV (25) and IIIIII (6). They total 4981; not surprisingly, this too is a multiple of *17* (=17 x 293). We can list all the significant numbers. The gap between *LD*, 34 and *LM*, 46, is *twelve*. The six line initials make 52, their last letters (display, not model, with PRSB in line 2) make 78; *thirteen by four*, *thirteen by six*. The sum of *W*,7, *S*,17 and *LM*, 46 is *seventy*. In the *model* text, the line initials with 52 and last letters with 92 give us *a hundred and forty-four*. The only sum that contemporaries would have had to tot up on a piece of slate is that for all 46 (model) letters; it is *five hundred and one*.

The name 'Senacus' is not Roman, but Celtic (*sen-* + *aco-*); so for that matter is (392) *Veracius* along with it.[21] They could both be Gaulish, as could also have been the unknown composer; the Gaulish character of the memorial is implied by its wording, its epigraphy (and, to a limited extent, the isolated and sea-accessible location). The computus of 391 *Senacus* makes no use of squares, grids (34 and 46 are only two-divisible), or triangular totals. Its character closely resembles what we saw earlier in the Vulgate, and one assumes readers were expected to interpret the signalled numbers in Biblical terms. In fact there is a clear pointer. If 17 = ADAM, it is also, as elsewhere, an implication of 153, $\Delta 17$, symbolising God's redeeming Net, from John 21 (*cf*.p. 189 later). There is another Gospel version of the Miraculous Draught of Fishes story, with Christ not yet crucified. In Luke, 5, we read how the disciples' net enclosed *piscium multitudinem copiosam* 'a plentiful swarm of fishes'. It is the MULTITUDINEM, carried over into the inscription, that alerts readers; giving both the second meaning for *seventeen* and the indication that the New Testament contains all the allusions.

What, then, *are* these? In line 5 the display was designed and cut (*Fig.31*) so that the <u>INE</u> ligature, with the D before it (and the I doubling up as the first vertical of the N) looks like 'DNE', a conventional abbreviation = DOMINE 'O Lord'. *Twelve* stands for the Disciples, as in Matthew 10, 2-5 (*duodecim … apostolorum*, and *hos duodecim misit Iesus*) — the complete catalogue of their names, as we have just seen, takes up 36 words in Jerome's Latin — and *thirteen*, for the same, around their Lord. If his friends thought Senacus worthy to be so associated, what could he (and any other members of his little community, buried before him) have been doing here in an extremity of Wales? In Luke 10, 1-18, we read how Jesus appointed another *seventy* people over and above the band of disciples and sent them out 'before his face, into every city and place'. Capel Anelog becomes one such location. Could Senacus rest in hope of the Resurrection? Had Christ indeed arisen? Paul offered proof in 1 Corinthians, 15.6. 'He [Christ] was seen of *above five hundred brethren at once* '(*plus quam quingentis fratribus*) 'of whom the greater part' (*multi*) 'remain unto this present'. Note how the Latin *fratribus, multi* is echoed by the text with its **FRATR**(um), **MULTI**(tudinem). If the overall LaN total of all the letters is 501, 'Above five hundred', the 'one' is Senacus himself.

At this point, remembering that among the signalled numbers have been 13, 34(=*LD*) and 144, someone might have noticed that these occur in the first Fibonacci set, 1.2.3.5.8.*13*.21.*34*.55.89.*144*... Because 391 *Senacus* is relatively early, it is unlikely that its text contains the fully-developed sort of precession-and-interval reading, probably reversed, to be found in Welsh inscriptions of the seventh century; but it is worth seeing if anything is there. Taking this first Fibonacci number-set as supplying potential intervals, from the complete text we could discover:

s **E** na **C** usp **R** esbit **E** rhiciaci **T** cummultitudine **E** mfratrum / (*ends*)
   1   2   3   5   8   13   (8)

(which offers better sense than trying to use the set to indicate letters:

     S E N a **C** us **P** resb **I** terhici **A** citcummultit **U** dinemfratrum /
      1 2 3   5   8   13   21   34

—giving a meaningless SENCPIAU.) What the first attempt offers is **E C R E T E**. If one allows, irregularly, the initial **S**, this is SECRETE, *secrete* 'concealed, secretly (written)', which is apposite even if it does not tell us what is secretly written here. Or we might read **EC RETE**, *ec(ce) rete* 'Behold, the Net', i.e. of God's redemption, referring back to 17, 153 and John 21.11.[22]

ab aquilone

	17										17	
S	E	N	A	C	U	S
P	R	e	S	B	i	t	e	r
H	I	C	I	A	C	I	T
C	U	M	M	U	L	T	I	T	U
D	I	N	E	M
F	R	A	T	R	U	M

6   11
52   92

ab austro

32   391 *Senacus.   The image, generated mentally from the 6-line inscription and here
elaborated graphically; a display plan of the Heavenly City, Apocalypsis chap.21,
containing the souls of Senacus and the* fratrum. *Initial (=52) and last (=92) letters of
the lines denote, as 144, the height of the enclosing wall in cubits. North, ab aquilone,
and south, ab austro (21.19) are marked by each sharing 4 letters with lines 1 and 6 –*
AqUiloNE/ sENAcUs, AUsTRo/ fRATrUm. *The City has 12 gates; the six, N
and S, are marked by E A U / R T U, total of 78, six by 13. Four corners, as might
have been envisaged by a composer who knew Late Gallo-Roman walled towns, seem to
be 'manned' by 17, 17, 6 + 11 (from ADAM = 17). Finally central letters, lines 1,2,5
and 6 only, A B N T = 33, years of King David's reign in the real Jerusalem, 1 Kings,
2.11.*

Finally, where is the soul of Senacus? We are told, by *one hundred and forty-four*. Apocalypsis, 21,16-17; the Heavenly City is square, each side 12,000 *stadia* ('furlongs') in length, the enclosing wall 144 cubits high. Its inhabitants (7.4), 12,000 from each of the Twelve Tribes, total 14,000. Look again at the inscription, *Fig.31*. An approximate rectangle would contain the lettering. The initials of the lines add to 52. Expanding PRSB mentally to PRESBITER, final -R, the last letters total 92; and 52 + 92 = 144.[23] Within the display, the dead priest's name becomes the dominant exhibit.

It appears that, at a simple level — much as for Corellia Optata's earlier and longer memorial — this inscription generates a mental image, a *display plan* of the Heavenly City. Two sides adding to 144 (cubits, the wall-height) and four corners 'manned' by the combinations of 17 (=AΔAM, Man) are the start. *Fig.32* shows how. There is a long and specific description of the City in Apocalypsis. It stands four-square to the compass-points. In the top line the central A of sen)**A**(cus marks *Aquilo* 'north'. The Vulgate here has for 'south' not the usual *Meridies*, but *ab Austro*; and the **AU** s **TR** o is matched by line 6, fr **ATRU** m. Each side has three gates, 12 in all. For the *six* on the north and south, line 1, E A U and line 6, R T U, add to 78, *six* times thirteen; on the two sides, the pairs of central (lines 3,4) letters, H C T U, give 48, *six* times eight. The author's own idea of any city, real or Apocalyptic, would be coloured by that of Late Roman walled towns and fortresses; hence, perhaps, the corners.

Clearly this little inscription is potentially far richer, more closely linked to the Vulgate and more obviously focused on the life and Christian death of Senacus than a first glance could indicate. If the precession-and-interval reading (S)ECRETE can be accepted as present, there may even be a second reading *backward* (not necessarily introduced by a RURSUS split-anagram); like this, m **V** rt **A** rfm **E** nidut **I** tlummuct **I** (caicihretibse R psucanes) / *ends* — where the first five letters at any rate, V A E I I, might be read *Vae ! ii* 'Woe! I have departed [from you]' — almost as if Senacus were being allowed to record a farewell.

What we must surely read into 391 *Senacus* is its witness to an enlargement of the repertoire for the composition of such texts, continuation of the display-plan device (which we meet again, in fifth-century Britain, in the next chapter), and adherence to the Vulgate marked by a suite of widely-recognised symbolic numbers; this in addition, of course, to a general exploitation of 20-letter LaN. There is sufficient reason to present *Senacus* from various epigraphic features as intrusive, i.e. the work of clerics from Gaul (or the Continent). If so, it could be expected that post-400 Continental Christian inscriptions should exhibit at least some of these features stemming from a common source in Late Roman teaching and practice. The last section of this chapter can address the point.

A common inheritance

At a future time the huge corpus of Christian inscriptions from most parts of France will have to be examined. There are obstacles. Many stones are broken and their texts incomplete; transcripts to the requisite standard of accuracy (absolutely correct recording of all ligatures and internalised letters, for instance) are not yet available except for a few

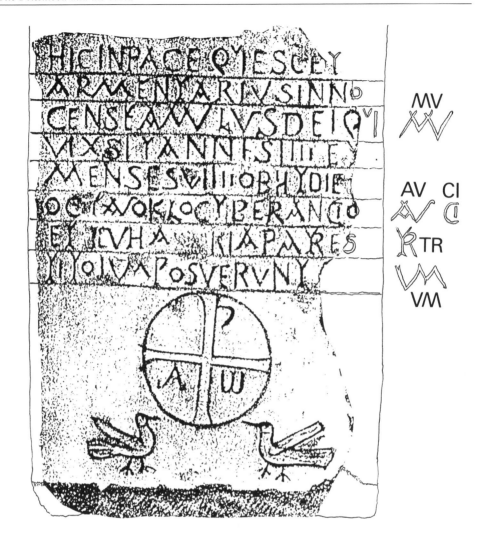

Fig.33   *The memorial Boppert 125* Armentarius, *which appears to have been trimmed (as a building-stone?), restored. On the right, four ligatures (MV, AV, TR, VM) and the internalised* I *within* C; *all these count as singles for computus purposes.*

regions; and a particular problem arises from other features. These are citation of age at death in years, months and days, and of absolute dates (equivalent of dates AD) as consular years. Both are ferociously abbreviated, giving large gaps between *LD* and *LM*, the display and model letter totals; and correct expansion can pose difficulties.

However, moving a little further afield, Vives' corpus of the Spanish inscriptions, and Walburg Boppert's short but meticulous study of some from the Middle Rhine, begin to provide enlightenment. We can look at Boppert's 125 *Armentarius* from Boppard, south of Koblenz, in an enlarged form *(Fig.33)* and, given that the top and right edge were not too badly trimmed, restore the original. The stone should be not later than the early sixth century. It was set up by Berancio and Eu(c)haria — these are German, presumably Frankish, names — for their little son Armentarius (a Roman name)[24] aged 4 years and 9 months who died, year not specified, on the eighth of the kalends of October, in our system 24th September. Our impression might be of a devout well-off family of converted Franks, within an educated community; the father Berancio may have composed this himself. Note at the start that within the ruled guides we have *eight* lines using familiar ligatures (and one case of an internalised letter); and that, as in the Vulgate, the initial K (Kalendas) is counted in the 20-letter LaN as if it were C=3. Here is the analysis; see *Fig.33* for the ligatures and the CI internalised.

		W	S	LD	LM
1	HIC IN PACE QVIESCET	4	7	17	17
2	ARMENTARIVS INN[O]	5	7	15	15
3	CENS FAMVLVS DEI Q [VI]		7	16	17
4	VIXSIT ANNIS IIII (=quatuor) E[T]	4	8	17	20
5	MENSES VIIII (=novem) OBIIT DIE	4	9	19	19
6	OCTAVO KL(=kalendas)OCT (obres) BERANCIO	4	13	17	30
7	ET EVHARIA PATRE [S]	3	7	14	15
8	TITOLVM POSVERVNT	2	7	15	16
		26	65	130	149

Three observations arise. First, the text is susceptible to just the same kind of tell-tale analysis as any of the Insular ones. Second, the various abbreviations are there to reduce *LM*, which happens to be 149, to the desired *LD* at 130. Third, we see potential structure at once by mean-ratio division — the sections of *W*, 26, at 13.13, and of *LD*, 130, at 65.65, coincide at the end of the line 4 with the mid-point of the whole inscription.

If readers care to turn back to William Hanks, and *Rostece*, they will see that *Armentarius* is another case where 4 (years) plus 9 (months) makes 13; from then on, we are on familiar ground, with 'thirteen' for the child's age being repeated by immediate totals, LaN, and LNu. The totals 26, 65 and 130 are all *thirteen*-divisible. First and last letters overall, H T, 8.18 = 26; the eight initials of the lines make *thirteen* times six (78). The system is not unlike the Corellia Optata text (p. 44). Even by LNu, taking the higher numerals, the model text has five M's (5000), seven C's (700) and three L's (150); total, 5850, *thirteen* times 450.

There is a second of these key numbers; *eight*. It is from the initials of the three names in the family; *A*(rmentarius), *B*(erancio), *E*(uharia), A B E, 1.2.5 = 8. Note, too, that the names contain 26 letters; this is because of *Euharia*, which could equally well have been written 'Eucharia' (cf.p. 66). The initials of all 26 words (model) add to *eight* times 31 (248); by LNu, letter 'I' (*unus*) occurs *eight* times 3 (24) times in the display, *16* in the model.

As a memorial, this is a standard Latin piece with only two Late spellings (*vixsit, titolum*). It has four semantic divisions:

1   Hic in pace quiescet Armentarius innocens famulus Dei[25]

2   qui vixsit annis quatuor et menses novem

3   obiit die octavo kalendas Octobres

4   Berancio et Euharia patres titolum posuerunt

('Here in peace lies at rest Armentarius, an innocent, servant-of-God; who lived four years and nine months; he died on the eighth day of the kalends of October; Berancio and Euharia, the parents, have set up the memorial.') It has some neat structural details, as David Howlett points out. Recourse to 1,2,5, 8 and 13 might recall the first Fibonacci set *1.2.3.5.8.13.21.34.55.* Word (8+13=) 21 is *Berancio*, father and possible author. Of the four clauses above, the first has *eight* words; in the second, the *fourth* word is '*quatuor*' and there are *nine* syllables before 'menses *novem*'; the third and fourth have *eight* words following '*octavo*', and also *twenty-four* syllables appropriate to a death on the twenty-fourth day of a month.

Another of the Rhineland memorials shown in *Fig. 25*, 72 *Panto* from Mainz (of *circa* 700?) has a simpler but related computus, not analysed here. It stresses throughout the age at death (25 years), and readers might like to find this in the transcript of the rather odd lettering as: + IN HAC TOMVLO / REQVIISCIT BO/NE MEMORIE / PANTO QVI VI/XIT ANNV/S FIGNITI (*sic*: = viginti, 20) ET / IIII (= quinque, 5) OBIET IN P/ACE FE[LI]/CIT[ER] — nine lines, framed and ruled. There are others, less impressive than *Armentarius*, in the collection. What 125 *Armentarius*, a Latin monument of approximately the same date as 391 *Senacus*, must surely tell us is this. It is a structured Christian Latin text composed with much care. It uses 20-letter LaN, LNu, display/model differentiation, the equivalent of two key numbers tied to age-at-death and the personal names, quartering of the text, mean ratio, a hint of the first set of Fibonacci numbers, and the usual additions of internal totals, initial and last letters and other aspects (mainly to emphasise *thirteen* and *eight*). It does not seem to use acrostics/telestichs, or to generate any mental image; there is no triangularisation, nor use of precession-and-interval.

Implausibly, a sceptic might see this as a case of independent invention, within a Christian community on some other frontier-spot of the Late Empire in the West. Rather more acceptably, it shows an undeveloped branching-off from a common Western and Latin usage earlier represented by *RIB 684 Corellia Optata*; a Rhineland parallel of sorts to 421 *Rostece* (and, less so, to 391 *Senacus*). But if that be the case, we could indeed postulate 'a common inheritance' from, presumably, a world of secular Latin composition; earlier than the Vulgate, where many devices were so obviously deployed. And what has so far been analysed and illustrated suggests that, in the Christian Celtic milieu of post-Roman Britain, this inscriptional style then underwent developments (including the generation of images) not found elsewhere. We need to see further examples, preferably well within the fifth century. A prize specimen awaits us in the next chapter.

Notes to Chapter 4

1.   See my *Christianity in Roman Britain*, chap.2, listing this minimal evidence.
2.   See under *Further Reading*.
3.   This idea was developed by Wendy Davies, within her *Patterns of Power in Early Wales* (Oxford 1990), noting the importance of royal courts as foci of religious and secular

power.

4. *Cf.* the maps, figs.32 and 38, in Wendy Davies, *Wales in the Early Middle Ages* (Leicester 1982); subsidiary kingdoms certainly existed but are sometimes known only from passing references.

5. *H.E.*,II.2; the place is still unidentified.

6. In *De Excidio Britonum*, cap.66 onward.

7. *DEB*, 67 (end), Michael Winterbottom's translation.

8. *Vita Prima Sancti Samsonis*, cap.37.

9. There is another IVSTI on a Welsh stone (344); Justus, bishop of Lyon in the late fourth century (who became a hermit), was the subject of a widespread cult during the fifth.

10. Conceivably, the 14 letters were deliberately cut as *four* lines; INGEN/VI/MEM/ORIA gives, by LaN, initials adding to *four* by *thirteen* (52) and last letters adding to 33.

11. The opening of his letter to the soldiers of Coroticus; Howlett, *Saint Patrick*, 26-7.

12. Likely dates are discussed by Jeremy Knight, 'The Early Christian Latin inscriptions of Britain and Gaul; chronology and context', in: Nancy Edwards and Alan Lane, eds., *The Early Church in Wales and the West* (Oxford 1992), 45-50.

13. See my *Mute Stones*, map, fig.7.5, and 99.

14. For closer definitions, see *Glossary* at end.

15. The principal feature here is that the 'loop' of the rho is open, or hooked (contrast the closed P-loop of 393 *Carausius* in *Fig.*); further discussion, Chap.5, at p. 115.

16. An extended treatment, with numerous examples, of literary figures like these occurs in Howlett, *Celtic Latin Tradition*, part I, also covering Hebrew and Greek.

17. Though the Vulgate uses K, Y and Z, the examples cited (and many others) employ 20-letter LaN as a *convention* (with K = C = 3, and Z = S = 17; Y is probably treated as I = 9).

18. The ordinary numerical values of the Greek alphabet, employed for counting since the 6th century BC, had to be used; there was no separation between LaN (values) and LNu (numerals) as in Latin. In the full, archaic, 27-letter range the first nine were 1 to 9, the second nine, 10 to 90, and the third, 100 to 900. See, e.g., O.A.W. Dilke, *Mathematics and Measurement* ('Reading The Past' ser., British Museum 1987), for a clear account. The fewer Roman numerals, most not originally letters at all, had a completely different origin. For the Greek New Testament (used by Jerome) Greek LaN was certainly applicable; though possibly not so widely used as in the Latin version.

19. The site: *RCAMW Caernarvonshire Inventory, III (West)* (1964), 3, no.1460. Some kind of building is implied, but is undated.

20. First and last letters overall, S M, 17.11 = 28, which is Δ7. The extreme section of 46 (*LM*) falls at 18:28. It is worth noting that if the *last* 28 letters(C IACIT…FRATRUM) are triangularised the inverted (only) repeats the key number. Apicals are C C M = 17, and the sides are 86 and 84 (= 170). Presumably the composer noticed, if not arranged, this result.

21. The element *sen-* means 'old, senior, venerable?' (Latin *sen-ex*); *-aco-* is an adjectival

ending. Veracius may be from *＊uer-* 'kind, gentle, amiable', plus *ac(i)o-*, *cf.* Old Breton *Uueroc*. The names are certainly not Roman ones.

22. Vulgate (John, 21.11), 'and he pulled in the net to land', is *et traxit* rete *in terram*.

23. Apart from the impossibility of conveying any number as large as 12,000 (or 48,000) by LaN totals, note that 52 + 92 = 144 is supplied by, visually, verticals, like the side elevations of the city wall.

24. Gregory of Tours' mother's name Armentaria would suggest a grandfather Armentarius; earlier the fourth-century emperor Galerius Maximianus, son of a shepherd, is said to have had a cognomen 'Armentarius' (*armentum* = herd of cattle, flock of sheep, goats).

25. Famulus = an immediate servant; post-Classical *famulus Dei* meant primarily 'a Christian'. *Cf.* (Anglesey, early sixth) 325, with FAMVLVS DI on the memorial to (Au)diva, wife of the *sacerdos* Bivatisus; this must have long passed into Insular usage.

5 Scotland and Ireland

Modern Scotland, less the northern archipelagoes of Orkney and Shetland, is 250 miles (400km) from north to south. The population is about five million, of whom fifty per cent can be found in the central Forth-Clyde corridor; (Greater) Edinburgh, Stirling and Falkirk, (Greater) Glasgow. Large parts of the country are still sparsely peopled. Substantial tracts are, agriculturally, uninhabitable.

Scotland might well be described as Scottish, rather than firmly Celtic. It has been pointed out that R. Burns, the national bard, wrote in a northern offshoot of English and that an earlier form of the same language-family (Anglian), and then its descendants, has been the main speech of the nation's capital since about 640 — the capture by the Northumbrians of Edinburgh's Castle Rock fortress. In AD 500, when the country's population was probably at most one-tenth of today's, the South — the Borders, land between the lines of the Antonine Wall and Hadrian's Wall — was home to various groupings or tribes, some certainly organised as native kingdoms, representing a pre-Roman Iron Age population and speaking British; perhaps a northern dialect of it, in the post-Roman period called Cumbric. Much of Scotland north of this, or north of the Highland Line, contained (more densely on the eastern side) other peoples, a mixture of tribes that may have consolidated their territories earlier in the Iron Age with still older Bronze Age remnants. Historically these became the Picts, *Picti* in Latin, people well beyond the Roman frontier; differentiated from the North British of the Borders, whom the later Welsh knew as *Gwyr y Gogledd* ('men-of-the-North'). Insofar as remnants of place- and personal names allow this, we assume that some or most Picts spoke 'Pictish P-Celtic', probably an earlier form of British. By 500, and thereafter increasingly so, a third ethnic component appeared. Permanent settlers under what became their ruling families crossed from the northern part of Ireland, first to the coastal belt of Argyll with its bridgehead citadels like Dunollie and Dunadd, and then across the southern or inner Isles and north-east across the Great Glen. We are less concerned here with two more injections of peoples, both Germanic-speaking; a later sixth- and seventh-century spread of the Northumbrian Angles up into the Lothians and to the Forth basin, and later still, at numerous separate points, the first settlements of the Scandinavian Norse.

The progress of Christian conversion was geographically fragmented and, against Scotland as a whole, at an uneven pace. (It is in fact possible to think of at least four 'conversions'.) A religion like Christianity, so closely bound to a single non-vernacular written language for all its instructive and liturgical text, can make very limited headway within a rural populace unequipped to receive its teachings. The only part of Scotland where there could have been a degree of familiarisation with Rome, her ways and speech, was the South. This is not only the scenario for the first Christians (on the Galloway coast) but the restricted setting of the dozen or so inscribed memorials of the same sort as those in Wales and the South-west, and their date-range is from the early fifth to the seventh century.[1] For the Irish, or Dalriadic, settlements in Argyll the assumption is that at the ruling level there may have been some Christians, the outcome of earlier labour by Patrick and others in the north of Ireland. The landmark of this, as a second and separate conversion or rather consolidation of a first Christian hierarchy, remains the AD 563 establishment of a monastery on Iona under Columcille or Columba.[2] Irish-originating Christianity, from the evidence we have emphatically monastic in tone, was a prime agency in the gradual conversion of the Picts. That story remains impossible to delineate in convincing detail. Over a huge area there were too many scattered settlements, probably too complex an internal political structure, to allow any single horizon for a Pictish Christianisation. There is a further complication, if we approach the evidence for definite Christian burials and commemoration of Christian dead, because the Picts — possibly inspired by an element of time-distant Roman models — had adopted their own commemorative style; displays on stone, not of words and letters but of a range of highly distinctive symbols. It remains no more than an assumption that these are the equivalent of individual grave-markers and (cryptographically, as it were) there is not enough material to allow any agreed interpretation of what the symbols meant.[3] Then, moving south again, in the seventh century by which time the Northumbrian Angles were themselves largely Christian, we find their regional ecclesiastical domination in south-east Scotland, extending briefly (from their short-lived see at Abercorn) to the southernmost Picts in Fife.

Whithorn, Ninian and Christian beginnings

The inscribed stones of Southern Scotland, few as they are, constitute the earliest and arguably the only early evidence for the introduction of Christianity to these particular Celts; Cumbric-speaking North Britons whose most prominent and certainly longest-surviving kingdom we have to call 'Strathclyde', a major centre being a citadel on Dumbarton Rock. For that accessible, agricultural, coastal belt with its various low promontories stretching west from Roman Carlisle and the end of Hadrian's Wall — the coastlands of Dumfries and Galloway — the focus of interest is the small burgh of Whithorn. But not until the 730s do we have Bede's too-short statement[4] that here, a place he knew in Latin as *Ad Candidam Casam*, there had long ago been a bishop's seat, distinguished by the name (and a church) of the Bishop Saint Martin (i.e., of Tours; died 397). Here, a most revered and holy man of the nation of Britons, by name *Nynia* 'Ninian', who had been *Romae regulariter fidem et mysteria veritatis edoctus* 'brought up at Rome in Faith and mystery of the Truth' (i.e., total orthodoxy), would appear to be the first-known bishop, *episcopus*. When Bede wrote this, not long before 731, his own *Anglorum gens*, the English of Northumbria, had extended their conquests into Galloway and had set up their own see at Whithorn (*iam nunc* 'just now'; some time after 700).[5] It was reported that the place was already called *Ad Candidam Casam* 'At the White House' — Whithorn is simply an Old English translation of this name — because there Nynia had built a church of stone, noteworthy because he did so *insolito Brettonibus more* 'in a way to which the Britons were unaccustomed'. (It is not clear if this means that the British built only in timber — incorrect — or if this church differed from all other known British-built churches.) Nynia, it was believed, had been buried in his church at Whithorn.

This tertiary source, as it must be seen, also mentions Columba of Iona and his part, or the part played from Iona, in converting the northern Picts; more controversially, a tradition that Nynia had preached to and converted at least some of the southern Picts. We cannot pursue this; the emphasis rests with Whithorn. Today (it is fair to say) there is a body of opinion that would hold what follows. Bede's account, which simply brings together snippets of information from several (oral) sources, contains a factual element. The man he calls Nynia very probably existed; was a bishop, in this instance a territorial *episcopus*, to a sub-Roman Christian community at or around what is now Whithorn; built, or caused to be built, an actual church, though it is very doubtful that it still stood when the Anglian see was inaugurated there; and was buried there in some distinctive fashion. The most acceptable period for this is sub-Roman, say 400 to 450. A limited degree of Romanisation, even some currency of Latin, in fifth-century coastal Galloway is not improbable given easy contact by sea, as well as overland, with *Luguvalium*, Roman Carlisle, centre of the civitas of the Carvetii. Nynia's Christian and Roman background (Bede's *Romae* 'at Rome' need imply nothing more) could well have been Carlisle and its purlieus, a setting that has in fact also been put forward for that slightly better-evidenced British sub-Roman bishop, Patrick, his Roman citizen father Calpornius (deacon, *decurio*, owner of an estate) and his grandfather Potitus (*presbyter*), let alone whatever school taught Patrick both Latin and Biblical-style skills.[6]

The complete religious history of Scotland can be almost as fascinating to the social as to the strictly ecclesiastical historian. In the many mysteries always cloaking the Picts, it is quite likely that some communities were never really converted; a minor theme of heathenism persisting, as the Auld Religion (or witchcraft), until a scandalously late date has long attracted Scotia's pious sons (*cf.* John Buchan's *Witch Wood* (1927), with I Kings,15.11-14 on the title page). In the last two centuries, St Ninian (whose present name comes from an early misreading, *Ninianus*, of a medieval Latinisation of Bede's Nynia as *Niniauus*) could be elevated as the original Father of the (Protestant) Kirk to counter the unwanted fame of Columba of Iona, undeniably an Irish Papist.[7] What is both new, and welcome, is the publication of a long campaign of excavations at Whithorn; and (I am convinced, not unnaturally) the proper interpretation at last of the oldest and most significant inscription, 520 *Latinus*. Whithorn stands in the Machars peninsula (*Fig.34*). Scarcely less significant may be three (or four) more inscriptions, the Kirkmadrine group, from the final peninsula, the Rhinns. Not only may their location be a parallel (as a small Gaulish mission?) to Capel Anelog in Wales, with 391, 392 *Senacus* and *Veracius*; their elaborate texts can propose one explanation why Bede had been told that Nynia's see and church were traditionally linked to Martin of Tours. This is the primary evidence, alone, for Scotland's earliest Christianity.

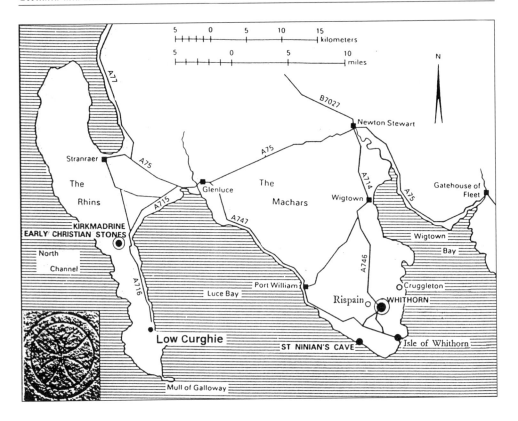

Fig.34   South-West Scotland (Dumfries and Galloway). Location map for principal inscriptions, modified from an HMSO guidebook map, Crown Copyright reserved.

A temple-building family

We now have in print, thanks to Derek Craig, a proper account[8] of the contextual history of these Galloway stones, correcting all previous statements (mine included). The *Latinus* stone, a slab of local rock about 1.3m high, was found shortly before 1888 during William Galloway's excavations at a point just north-east of the medieval Priory church and therefore within the central focus of the whole site-complex. Dr Craig has shown that, at the time and until 1891 at least, the presence of an incised Constantinian chi-rho motif, the X and P monogram (see *Fig. 35*), above the top line of lettering was observed and recorded. Incredibly, because this is still just detectable in many older photographs, its existence was then ignored by everyone for about a century.

The text is cut in small capitals, twelve lines in all, with both ligatures and the deliberate omission of a few letters (cf. the PA(ce) of *Rostece*, p. 16). Complete accuracy in transcription is vital because every detail of this inscription was planned. Despite erosion, especially on the right margin, this can be made out:

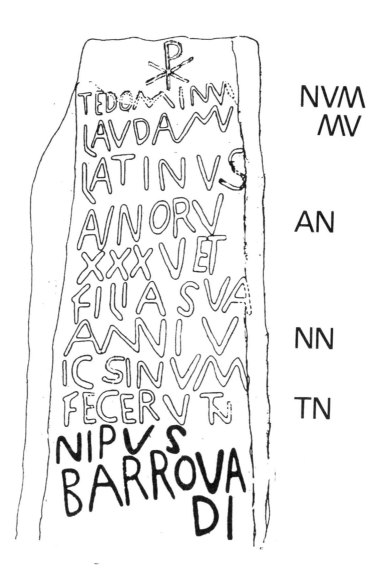

NVM
MV

AN

NN

TN

Fig. 35   *520 Latinus ('The Whithorn Stone'), now displayed at Whithorn. With slight corrections drawn in situ, 1992, and the rediscovered chi-rho added, this is Dr C.A. Ralegh Radford's version (the best). On the right, five ligatures (note TN, for textual NT); the bottom lines, shown black, were added to the original display and, even if this happened a week/month/year later, they fall outside the planned model composition and its corresponding display.*

	(chi-rho)	LD (only)
1	T E D O M I N V M	7
2	L A V D A M V (s)	6
3	L A T I N V S	7
4	A N N O R V (m)	5
5	X X X V E T	6
6	F I L I A S V A	8
7	A N N I V	4
8	I C S I N V M	7
9	F E C E R V T N	7
10	N I P V S	5
11	B A R R O V A	7
12	D I	2

The full expanded model is: *Te Dominum laudamus Latinus annorum XXXV* (= *triginta quinque*) *et filia sua annorum* IV (= *quatuor*) *ic sinum fecerunt nipus Barrovadi* ('Thee Lord we praise. Latinus, of years 35, and his daughter, of years 4, here a *sinus* made. Descendant of Barrovad(us)').

Except for TN (= NT reversed) the ligatures are normal; the sole post-Classical element is the common *ic*, for *hic* 'here' (silent H). *Sinum* is the accusative of *sinus* (of which more, in a moment). Only R.A.S. Macalister saw that lines 10-12, the gratuitous information that, presumably, Latinus was 'a descendant of Barrovadus', do not form part of the original; he thought a second cutter had added them. They may have been appended very soon afterwards, as what was felt to be a desirable social comment. We can add that not only was Macalister demonstrably right; whoever cut lines 10-12 fully understood the main computus. The *LD* total for *nipus Barrovadi* is 14; for the preceding text, 57 (or 14 times 4, with 1 over).

This is not a memorial and all previous interpretations are wrong.[9] No-one is said to have died. Latinus and daughter form the plural subject of the plural verb *fecerunt*. To adjust *ic sinum fecerunt* to *ic signum fecerunt*, even *hoc signum fecerunt* (or *fecit*) and to read 'here made a sign = put up this memorial-stone', with 'a descendant' (or grandson) 'of B.' as the subject and agent, is just insupportable. *Sinus*, originally 'fold in a garment, gown, toga', then 'hiding-place in the bosom, safekeeping place', has a further figurative meaning of 'refuge'. If, as here, it must imply a Christian building of sorts, 'church' is permissible. *Signum* can mean 'sign' (as, coincidentally, for the chi-rho) but not 'a memorial' and the reading is anyhow *sinum*.

We have here a building-stone. The verb *facere* means 'to build'; Bede wrote that Nynia himself *ecclesiam fecerit*. The early form of chi-rho, the capital lettering, correct Latin and use of *fecerunt* link 520 *Latinus* to Late Roman Britain and suggest a pre-450 date. *RIB* 658, York, is another building-stone, a *serapeum* (temple to Serapis) set up by some wealthy army officer (*Fig.36*). Ignoring the oddity of ages 35 and 4, we can see the closeness of the parallel texts:

Fig.36 *RIB 658, from Roman York; building-stone for a Serapeum or temple to Serapis, perhaps early 3rd century and in many ways a parallel to 520 Latinus as another building-stone, 200 years later.*

	RIB 658	*520*
Invocation	DEO SANCTO SERAPI	TE DOMINUM LAUDAMUS
Object	TEMPLUM	SINUM
Adverbial	A SOLO ('from the ground')	IC ('in this place, here')
Facere (perf.)	FECIT	FECERUNT
Subject	CLAUDIUS HIERONYMIANUS	LATINUS et FILIA SUA
Qualifier	LEGATUS LEGIONIS VI VIC.	(NIPUS BARROVADI)

The Whithorn stone is wholly Christian, even if the phrase *Te Dominum laudamus* eludes attribution. It is also native, rather than potentially Gaulish in the 391 *Senacus* sense. To a limited extent its computus recalls that of Corellia Optata, but it possesses a direct allusive quality (and a further potential) that moves it into the special world of post-Roman Insular inscriptional style. Now we may go back to a proper analysis:

		(chi-rho)	*W*	*S*	*LD*	*LM*
(A)	1	T E D O M I N U̲M̲	2	4	7	9
	2	L A V D A M̲V̲ (s)	1	3	6	8
			3	7	13	17
(B)	3	L A T I N V S	1	3	7	7
	4	A̲ N̲ N O R V (m)	1	3	5	7
	5	X X X V (triginta quinque) ET	3	5	6	17
	6	F I L I A S V A	2	5	8	8
	7	A N̲ N̲ (orum) I V (quatuor)	2	6	4	14
	8	I C S I N V M	2	3	7	7
	9	F E C E R V T̲N̲ (= NT)	1	3	7	8
			12	28	44	68
		(Totals, (A) plus (B) =	15	35	57	85)

(c)	10	N I P V S		1	2	5	5
	11	B A R R O V A	{	1	3	7	7
	12	D I	{	_	1	2	2
				2	6	14	14

(Totals, (A) plus (B) plus (C) = 17 41 71 99)

Line 5 has *five*, not six syllables because, in quinquĕ-ĕt, the two short e's must be elided into one syllable. The immediate fact is that between parts (A) and (B) we have a consistent ratio:

	(A: 1-2)	(B: 3-9)	
Words	3	12	1:4
Syllables	7	28	1:4
Letters, *model*	17	68	1:4

The display letter totals are less relevant but note how we can see

| *LD*, of A + B | 57 | (of C) 14 | 1:407 (=1:4) |

and this must have been arranged when (C), *nipus Barrovadi*, was added. If quadruple ratio, 1:4, is the first pointer — bearing in mind that the *four* is also symbolic of the basic 'square', as well as being one of the two stated numerals IV, XXXV — the others emerge rapidly. By LNu, part (A) has: tedom **I** n **V** m la **V** dam **V** s, giving I (1), VVV (15) = 16, *square* of *four*. Part (B) manages to provide: latin **V** sannor **V** mxxx **V** etfilias **V** aanni **V** icsin **V** mfecer **V** nt, or **V** (five) times 7 = *thirty-five*.

Note, then, the following. In (A), **T** edominumlaudamu **S** has T S, 18.17 = 35. Ignoring (C) from now on, there are *thirty-five* syllables. The span *Te Dominum laudamus Latinus annorum XXXV* has *thirty-five* letters. The word FILIA, 6.9.10.9.1, happens to add to *thirty-five*. First and last letters (of (A) and (B)), T T, make 36, the *square* of 6. Initials of line 1 to 9, T L L A X F A I F, add to 81, *square* of nine lines and also *square* of a *square*. There are more LaN results on similar lines but these can suffice. It seems clear that the original composition (in which one begins to entertain suspicions; *was* Latinus really aged 35? *Was* his un-named daughter really 4 and did she in fact exist?) has three firm numerical clues. One is one-to-four ratio; the next, 35; the third, a square. Without any recourse to acrostics, triangulars, hidden readings or anything save basic LaN, LNu and immediate totals, this has been plainly conveyed.

The composer, and it may have been 'Latinus', based this text recording the building of a *sinus* on a detailed descriptive account of the building of the greatest of all Houses of God; the Temple of Solomon, in David's city of Jerusalem. This was *Domini Domus*, the House of the Lord, and the shared letters in /te **DOMIN**um lau**D**a**MUS**/ advertise the link at once. The account used was not the primary one of 1 Kings, 6 and 7, but the later and secondary version found in 2 Chronicles, 3 to 5. Early as 520 *Latinus* is, there is every indication that the text employed for it was Jerome's Vulgate (and that might constrict the likely date to not before *c*.420).

It is completely immaterial whether or not this huge Late Bronze Age edifice, something like an Egyptian temple, was ever built and completed.[10] The composer's model was what he read. The Temple was aligned east-west, the smaller front part (*porticus*) at the east, opening into the major portion or body (*maior domus*), at the end of which stood the Holy of Holies, *sanctum sanctorum*, the permanent Tabernacle for the Ark of the Covenant. Before the east entrance stood two tall pillars (like the pylons of an Egyptian temple?) and, in a courtyard, a separate large external sacrificial altar. There were many other details but these are the relevant ones.

The *maior domus* measured 60 cubits long, 20 across. In 1 Kings, the *porticus* is 10 cubits long and 20 across; but in 2 Chronicles, where it is described differently, the length is 'according to the breadth of the House', i.e., 20, not 10, cubits. On any reading, that makes a ground plan of (60+20=) 80, by 20. *That is the 1:4 ratio of the text*, whose roughly rectangular disposition contains a suggestion of 20 to 80 cubits. The two *columnae*, the columns *Booz* (north, left) and *Iachin* (south, right), sheathed in metal, were 35 cubits high. *That is the thirty-five*. The internal Holy of Holies, occupying the west part of the main building, was in plan 20 by 20 cubits, as was also the *altare aeneum*, the external bronze or brass altar. *That is the four, and the squares, of the text*.

We cannot expect that any church, any *sinus* (of stone; for this would be the prototype for *Candida Casa*) at Whithorn necessarily approached these dimensions. Nor is it clear where 520 *Latinus* stood; in a wall? a main doorway jamb? outside the entrance? It has been the recital of the, not wholly believable, ages (reminiscent of Rostece, ANI XIII; or poor little Armentarius, also ANNIS IIII) that understandably misled us into thinking that this had to be a tombstone (of sorts), and into traducing the competence of the Latin. But another obvious thought will be that if here, in sub-Roman North Britain not far outside the (collapsing) frontier of Empire, someone among relatively recent converts — even putatively a bishop — could choose this model from the Latin Old Testament to such good effect, did anyone else do the same elsewhere?

There is a combined memorial and building-stone from Vildé, near Burgos, in north-east Spain, probably sixth century (=Vives 505 *Anduires*).[11] Another tall slab with 14 lines of capitals including ligatures and abbreviations, it was (medievally) trimmed into an arch stone, but not beyond the point where the text cannot be fairly confidently completed. Expanding the text to the full model, we have the following analysis: semantically, it is in five sections.[12] Omitting the details of the lines and the actual display we can look at the totals, the important feature, by section:

	W	*S*	*LM*
(a) +IN NOMINE DOMINE			
LOCUS ANDUIRES INLUSTRIS FEMINAE	7	18	44
(b) QUI HANC ECLESIAM CUM VIRO SUO			
ANDUIRO INLUSTRE HOMINE FECERUNT	10	23	54
(c) FUERUNT PARTICIPES ANNOS XXXV (as letters, read			
TRIGINTA QUINQUE) QUATER			
NUTRIERANT FILIOS	7	22	59

(d) (et) RECESSIT SUPRADICTA MATRONA IN PACE	5	13	31
(e) ET IN SUMMA CASTITATE CUM CERTITUDINE	<u>6</u>	<u>14</u>	<u>32</u>

Totals, (b) to (e)	<u>28</u>	<u>72</u>	<u>176</u>
Totals, overall	35	90	220

This means: '+ In the name of the Lord! The grave of Anduires, a noblewoman; who built this church with her husband Anduirus, nobleman. They were partners [in marriage] 35 years and four times they reared children. The above-named lady has departed [this life] in peace; and in the highest steadfast faith, with assurance [of her resurrection].' (In (d), the clear computus shows that the, stylistically superfluous, opening (et) was somehow inserted in error and has to be discounted.)

Again we can harbour doubts. *Were* these two married exactly 35 years? Did they *really* raise four children? But the pattern overall is by now familiar, and remarkably close to 520 *Latinus*. Here, from the (expanded) model text, are the proportions;

	(a)	(b) to (e)	
Words	7	28	=1:4
Syllables	18	72	=1:4
Letters	44	176	=1:4

(Note that the years-together, text XXXV, seems to be treated as one word, but (tri.gint.a.quin.que) 5 syllables and — model as above — 15 letters; and that while ECLESIAM, through Vulgar Latin the Spanish *iglesia*, remains 4 syllables, FILIOS in (c), Spansh *hijo*, counts as only 2 syllables because of synizesis of the second -i-.) This time, we have *thirty-five* as the word total. Totals *W* 35, plus *S* 90, make 125; divided as 25:100 this gives the 1:4 ratio, of five *squared*. As well as four children, we see that (taking the initial + as letter no.1) letter no.*35* is R = 16, *square* of *four*. Extreme section of the words at 22:13 → 35 (from 4.9.*13*.22.*35*.57...) emphasises ...QUATER / *nutrierant*, and of 90 syllables at 56:35 → 90,...QUA/ter. Observe, too, that the first four words end with DOMINI LOCUS and that, like te **DOMIN**um lau**D**a**MUS** earlier, this picks up the Temple's description; **DOMINI l0cUS = DOMINI DOMUS**. We are specifically told that 'they built a church', *eclesiam fecerunt*. Thirty-five, one-to-four, four, and squares are clearly signalled.

The Temple, depicted (*Fig. 37*)

Shortly before presenting these analyses to Scottish academic audiences (April 1997) it occurred to me that in the top line of Vives 505 *Anduires* the placing of the two I's (+ **I**. NNOMINEDOMIN. **I**) might suggest the two tall columns, Booz and Iachin, *in vestibulo Templi unam a dextris et alteram a sinistris* (2 Chron., 3.17). Then, looking at 520 *Latinus*, I

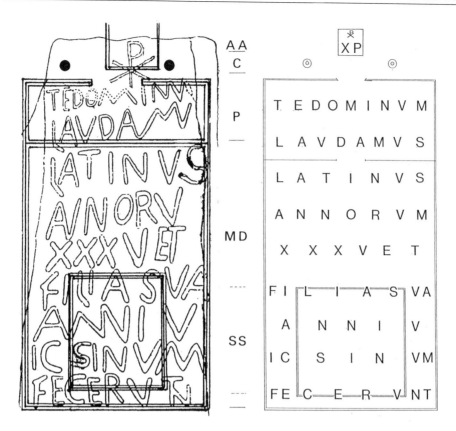

Fig. 37   *520 Latinus; introductory form of the image, a display plan of the Temple of Solomon at Jerusalem described in 2 Chronicles, 3 & 4. Left, a first reconciliation of the visible lines and letters with the Biblical components of the Temple; right, much clearer when the display text is expanded to a model form. AA, altare aeneum, large forecourt altar (= the chi-rho). C, two columns, mentally supplied. P, porticus, front part of the temple. MD, maior domus, the main body, containing SS, the square (domus) Sancti Sanctorum or Holy of Holies. From here onwards, the image calls for a very close knowledge of the Vulgate descriptions with its dimensions and details.*

suddenly realised that the whole tall inscription, less the NIPVS / BARROVA / DI, was, and was meant to be, a *display plan* — a complete, elaborately labelled ground plan — of the Temple. *Fig. 38* shows how, by using those letters (mostly vowels) in common between the textual lines and the Vulgate description, this author has provided what still seems to be the earliest and among the more comprehensive examples of *labelling* — using deliberately-placed words and letters to label and to coincide with elements of the image.

The top of the inscription represents the Temple's façade, at *oriens* (East), two other points being included, and the divisions into *porticus, domus maior* and *sanctum sanctorum* are shown; the last, not spatially coincident with the western end as in the Vulgate but reduced inside it to pick up the items denoting 'a square' and, by using V V V V, 20 cubits. *Fig. 39*

Fig. 38   *Immediate labelling of the image. The external altar (the chi-rho) is 20 cubits square, 10 high; X = 20 (LaN), and 10 (LNu). Lines 1-2 contain part of pOrtIcUs and most of **DOMIN**i **DoMUS**, lines 3-4 part of dom**US** mai**OR**, lines 7-8 part of s**AN**ct**U**m Sa**N**ctor**UM**. The Temple's facade, columns and portal face east; Oriens, Aquilo and Meridies are all correctly placed. The Holy of Holies was 20 cubits square; on its right, we have **V** a . **V** . **V** m . **V** n t, VVVV = 20 (LNu). Note that, in the image, the square is formed by 14 letters; the corners, L S C V, 10.17.3.19 = 49, square of seven.*

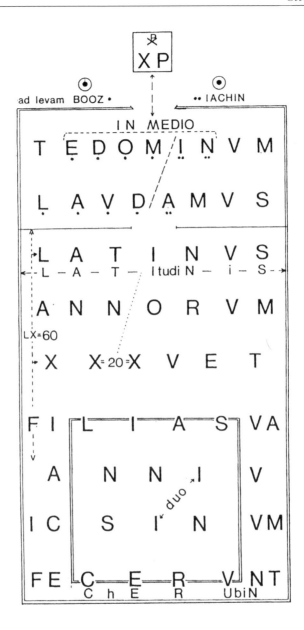

shows how the given dimensions are introduced, LX and XX, the 60 and 20 cubits; and how *Latinus* and *fecerunt* coincide with *latitudinis* and the two *Cherubin*. Of particular interest is the treatment of the chi-rho at the top of the stone. First, this represents the external *altare aeneum*. Because the Greek *chi* of the chi-rho is the Latin X, its LaN value = 20 is the horizontal dimension (20 by 20 cubits) and its LNu value as *decem*, 10, the height of ten cubits (2 Chron., 4.1; *et decem cubitorum altitudinis*). But there is more. As Greek *chi*, *rho*, CH.R, the symbol must be *Christos*, Christ. In the depiction, of course He could not be shown physically within a Temple built so many centuries before the New Testament story (in which Christ's earthly life, 33 years, fulfilled the 33 years of David's reign in (Late Bronze Age) Jerusalem, 1 Kings, 2.11). Nevertheless, Christ is placed 'in the middle' at the summit of the picture. Apocalypsis, 1.12-13, and 2.1, 'I saw seven golden candlesticks' (*candelabra*) 'and *in the midst* of the seven candlesticks, one like unto the Son of Man...These things saith he, that holdeth the seven stars in his right hand, Who walketh *in the midst* of the seven golden candlesticks'.

Our author had read this enigmatic passage (by Rufinus ?), which has an *arithmetica* based on 7, and probably noticed that in the first part *medio* is word no.18, in the second no.17 (18+17 = 35(!)). Look now first back at *Fig. 35*, and see how in the top line the central 'M' was deliberately cut extra-wide; it represents the great doorway or main entrance in the middle of the East facade. Next, in *Fig. 39*, line 1 is (T) (*seven* letters) (M); those seven, with M central, EDOMINV, contain anagrams of both IN and MEDIO. (So too, remarkably, coincidence or not, the top line of 505 *Anduires* — with (cross plus) 14 letters, twice *seven* — could be partitioned as: (+) I N N O) **M I N.E D O** (M I N I, the central M I N E D O also containing IN MEDIO by anagram.) The Temple belonged, as *Domini Domus*, to the OT God, Jahweh, Jehovah, The Lord. Because the NT was the fulfilment of the OT, The Lord manifest as Christ is thus included in the image; part of it, yet spatially (and also verbally) distinguished.

What can we say about this astonishing opening to the whole tale of Christianity in Scotland? There is no need to appeal to external (Gaulish or other) inspiration. The display plan extends what we saw in *Corellia Optata*, the additions are first-order, the use of LaN actually quite elementary. The stone remains sub-Roman and North British, quite probably set up in 420-450 (not later) and as a building-stone harking back to Roman Britain. Intellectually, even theologically, the evidence of Biblical learning and the degree of ingenuity must lead us to wonder, first, what the associated *sinus* was like — did it conceivably contain painted wall-plaster on Roman lines, even with texts on the interior? And, second, what if anything this may have to do with Bede's Nynia? Did he, as a British *episcopus reverentissimus*, compose this to accompany a first small church? Is it conceivable that 'Latinus' was none other than Nynia?[13]

Kirkmadrine; a second mission-station?

The three inscribed stones, 516-517-518, now preserved in the porch of the old burial-chapel at Kirkmadrine (graveyard) in the Rhinns peninsula (map, *Fig. 34*) must be considered as a group. Various dates have been proposed for them, some far too late[14] on any count. Derek Craig and the present writer would argue, independently, that they probably belong to the same century, and I propose outside brackets from about 500 (for 516 *Viventius*) to, at the latest, about 600. To them must be added a lost stone, not in *CIIC*, seen and noted early in the last century as a slate grave-cover(?) at Low Curghie, 7 miles (12 km) south from Kirkmadrine. It contained the name Ventidius and the information 'that he was a subdeacon of the Church', probably implying all or part of SVBDIACONVS.[15]

The primary monument is to two *sacerdotes*; priests, and insofar as this is relevant, perhaps in episcopal orders.[16] *Fig. 40* shows it. In this case, the encircled second-type chi-rho with its 'open' rho, flanked by *alpha et* and *omega*, ranks as a line of the text. A capital 'A' marks the *alpha*. The W-shaped *omega* is recorded but has flaked off. The upper reverse of this slab, now concealed, repeats the encircled chi-rho on its own (shown in *Fig. 30*, bottom left). The epigraphic features to note apart from ligatures are: inclusion of HIC IACENT, overlining of SCI (=sancti) and the use of both angle-bar A and sideways R. In these respects 516 *Viventius* is a close match to 391 *Senacus*, *Fig. 31*, and the same comments as to origin apply. In the analysis it transpires that a first line must be treated with *alpha et omega* verbalised as /ah-et-o/, 3 words, 3 syllables and , with ET ligatured, 3 letters. The S C I here counts as three letters.

		W	S	LD	LM
1	A E T (chi-rho) O	3	3	3	4
2	H I C I A C E N T	2	3	8	9
3	S C I (= sancti) E T P R A E		4	9	12
4	C I P V I S A C E R	6	5	10	10
5	D O T E S I D E S [T]		4	10	10
6	V I V E N T I V S	1	4	8	9
7	E T M A V O R I V S	2	5	8	10
		14	28	56	64

We read: *Hic iacent sancti et praecipui sacerdotes, id est, Viventius et Mavorius*, 'here lie the holy and excellent bishops, that is, Viventius and Mavorius'. This is in two semantic parts:

		W	S
(a)	A et O Hic iacent sancti et praecipui sacerdotes	9	17
(b)	id est Viventius et Mavorius	5	11
		14	28

Both totals exhibit extreme ratio, from 1.4.5.9.14.23...and from 1.5.6.11.17.28.43..., the purpose being to lay special emphasis on SACERDOTES. This inscription has a very full computus, carefully planned to discernible ends, using a wide range of devices. There are two fairly obvious key numbers, but not of equal importance. We can deal first with *nineteen*; it is there to validate or confirm the inclusion and spelling of the two names, Viventius the more important.

Note that the initial V(iventius) = 19, and that there are *nineteen* letters in VIVENTIUSETMAVORIUS. The line initials are A H S C D V E, 1.8.17.3.4.19.5 =

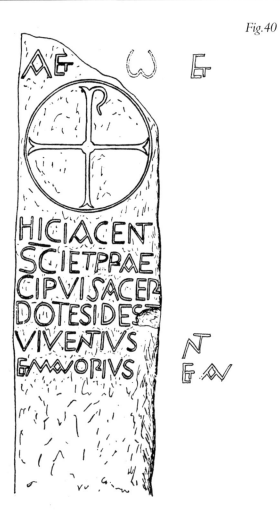

Fig.40   *516* Viventius et Mavorius, *from Kirkmadrine; by Macalister, slightly amended. The now-lost, W-shaped, omega top right may have been more central. Ligatures are indicated right. The upper reverse face (inaccessible) bears an encircled chi-rho only.*

nineteen times 3, 57. The expanded model has 64 letters, indicating a letter square:

```
A E T O H I C I
A C E N T S A N
C T I E T P R A
E C I P U I S A
C E R D O T E S
I D E S T V I V
E N T I V S E T
M A V O R I V S
```

It has no acrostics (in col.6, ISPITUS is neither a word or name!) and is entirely LaN-based. The left column adds to 38, *19* times 2. The corners, A I M S, 1.9.11.17 = 38 likewise. The combined total of the top line (66) and bottom line (105), at 171, is *nineteen* by 9. Lastly, in the full text of 64 letters, those at places numbered 19, 38 and 57 are I, T and M; 9.18.11, making 38 yet again.

The vital number is *seven*. Totals *W*, *S* and *LD* as 14, 28 and 56 are all divisible by seven; their sum (98), twice *seven* squared. In the display, using LNu, we find five C's (500), six V's (30) and nine I's (9); total, 539, or *seven* squared, times 11. Omitting the A ET O, the initials of the remaining eleven words (as H I S E P S I E V E M) make 119, or *seven* times 17. In the full 64-letter text every *seventh* letter adds up to 112; *seven* times 16.

There may yet be, even at this point, those who still think this could have happened fortuitously, or that it still requires to be 'proved' statistically. Let us continue to the bitter end. We had the letter square, 64, 8 by 8. From $N^2 = \Delta N + \Delta(N-1)$, this will contain the triangulars from 8 and 7; 36 and 28. In fact that is indicated already by V(iventiu)S, M(avoriu)S; V S = 36, M S = 28, and we then triangularise just the first 36 letters of the 64:

1	A	1	1	A E T O H I C I	9
5	E T	18	1	A C E N T S A	1
13	O H I	9	12	N C T I E T	18
3	C I A C	3	14	P R A E C	3
5	E N T S A	1	9	I P U I	9
12	N C T I E T	18	17	S A C	3
14	P R A E C I P	14	5	E R	16
19	U I S A C E R D	4	4	D	4
72		68	63		63

Cleverly, the results are all multiples of seven. In the pyramid, left, 72+68=*seven* times 20. In the inverted, right, each side is *seven* times 9, and the apicals A I D, 1.9.4 = *seven* times 2. The base of the pyramid (74) and top of the inverted (66) make 140, *seven* times 20 again. The *seventh* lines; of the inverted, E R, 5.16 = *seven* times 3, of the pyramid, P (raeci) P, 14.14 = 28.

We can move on (with relief) to what this means. 516 is a memorial to two *sacerdotes*. 517 names two more men, no parentage; perhaps also clerics. The lost Low Curghie stone, if it is roughly contemporary, supposedly names a fifth, a *subdiaconus*.[17] What if we picture Kirkmadrine, at any rate, as the locale of a small band of incoming priests — from Gaul — around or shortly before 500, some of whose burials are thus recorded on stone?[18] What if the original band, excluding or including lay followers or any native converts, helpers or servants, had happened to number *seven*? Is this what we are being told, and seemingly told not too obliquely either?

A context or meaningful allusion for almost any low figure can be found in the Vulgate; but let us assume that the composer of 516 *Viventius* (whose name is apparently not concealed anywhere) knew his Bible well enough to think of a passage in the synoptic Gospels, the tale of Christ confounding the Saducees. Members of this strict sect disbelieved any doctrine of the Resurrection. They posed the case of a man dying without issue; under Mosaic law the next available brother would have to marry the widow. If six more did so, and all died, to which of the seven could the woman possibly be the wife in the next world? (The answer; in Heaven, all will be as the angels and there will be no marriages, past present or future.) The opening premise 'There were seven brothers' appears thrice as:

Mark, 12.20	*septem ergo fratres erant*
Luke, 20.29	*septem ergo fratres erant*

but in Matthew, at 22.25 we read:

erant autem apud nos septem fratres

'There were with us seven brothers', ignoring all that follows, is a statement easily lifted from this context and applicable elsewhere. We can look at it, as others must have done around 500, and rapidly see:

> *Six* words, concerning *seven* brothers; *six* by 5 (30) letters
> Initials E A A N S F, 5.1.1.12.17.6 = *six* by *seven* (42)
> Last letters T M D S M S = 78, *six* by (*six*-plus-*seven*)
> As a *six*-across, five-down, grid, left column E U U E R = 64,
> right A P S F S = 55; total 119, *seven* by 17.
> *Six* times 2 vowels used; *six* times 3 consonants.

Not all of this was taken up. But let us read on, using the favoured Matthew text. Jesus's second conclusion (22.32) is 'He is not the God of the dead, but of the living'. In Latin, it provides a surprisingly apt conclusion, if we entertain the idea of this as a source: *non est Deus mortuorum, sed* **viventium**.

The other two Kirkmadrine inscriptions (*Fig. 41*) are shorter, and one is now defective. Do they give any support to a hypothesis about an original mission-party of seven brothers, *fratres*, a fact to be incorporated in any memorials? In 517, which repeats the encircled chi-rho, part of name no.1 has flaked off. Macalister, in an off-moment, wanted to read ISTIS 'with-them, with-these', i.e. Viventius and Mavorius. But a careful look at the stone, and at older photographs, shows (a) space for five letters at the most, and (b) just a stub of letter no.2 escaping the flake that is certainly not the base curve of an S; it is vertical, for T or I. The name is lost. *Titus* is one possibility; a greater probability is that this name was only two syllables. Here is the analysis:

		W	*S*	*LD*	*LM*
1	. (T, I?) . . S <u>E T</u>	2	3	6	7
2	F L O R E N	1	2	6	6
3	T I V S	—	2	4	4
		3	7	16	17

This at least shows *seven* syllables; expanding ET, line 1 may have had *seven* letters. W, 3, plus S, 7, confirms the *ten* letters of Florentius. (If the missing name *was* 'Titus', line initials would be T F T, or 18.6.18 = *seven* times 6.) We go on to stone 518. This is not a memorial. It might be construed as dedicatory, another way of marking God's presence or protection by *initium* (=*alpha*) and *finis* (=*omega*).[19] Here, the letters of ET are, strictly,

518

517

Fig.41 *517 and 518, both from Kirkmadrine; based on Macalister's drawings but (for 517) amended from early photographs showing details of first-line flaking. ET is ligatured in 517, but not in 518.*

conjoined, not ligatured.

	W	S	L
1 INITIVM	1	4	7
2 ET FINIS	2	3	7
	3	7	14

This tiny text, whatever its liturgical function (? to mark a new or expanded cemetery), takes us firmly back to the key number. We see *seven* syllables; each line has *seven* letters. Line initials, I E, 9.5 = twice *seven*, last letters M S, 11.17 = *seven* times 4. All the letters of INITIUM = 87, of FINIS = 53: total, *seven* times twenty. Now we might see why this particular formula was selected. If *seven* had anything to do with the start of the Kirkmadrine episode, stone 518 — the latest of the three — brings it in again at the finish.

An archaeological peculiarity of the Kirkmadrine site, which is a disused ecclesiastical one in Stoneykirk parish and in fairly open agricultural countryside, is that neither repeated fieldwork nor air photography has given the slightest sign of buried structures, an enclosure, a small (monastic) settlement or anything one would have associated with a Christian focus of the date of the stones. Derek Craig points out that all the evidence is that 516, 517 and 518 were found very close to where they are now housed. My own belief, which puts two and two together hoping to find four, is that such absence of expected material could suggest that, perhaps before 600 even, any Kirkmadrine clerical community — successors to the *septem fratres* — removed themselves from the Rhinns peninsula to the Machars; to Whithorn. From that, three things might have followed. First, if Kirkmadrine represented a Gaulish incursion, this (not Nynia's own lifetime) was when the cult of Martin of Tours, introduced from its extensive Gaulish popularity, was connected with Whithorn; if so, probably with a 'genuine' representative relic of St Martin being placed in a new altar, or even in some new small Whithorn church.[20] Second, just as 'Whithorn', Old English *hwit aern(e)*, is a calque, a direct word-for-word translation, of *Candida Casa*, did the latter when somehow transferred to, or applied to, Whithorn arise as an earlier calque on a Gaulish-Latin place-name *★Louco-tegia* (*louco-*, *leuco-* 'white, fair'; *-tegia*, *-tigia* 'hut, small building'), which had been that of St Martin's first monastic attempt and church, now Ligugé, dept. Vienne?[21] Third, though Bede never stated that *Candida Casa* under bishop Nynia was a monastic establishment (only *locus*, *sedes episcopatus*, and *ecclesia*), the retrospective evidence points otherwise. It seems likely that a Whithorn monastery existed at the time when the Northumbrians acquired the see (and, archaeologically, considerably altered it) and our next literary source, the late eighth-century *Miracula* poems, appear to describe a monastic setting, anachronistically taking it back to Nynia's time.[22]

Without digressing into the topic of Insular monastic origins it can be said that, while the influence of Martin's pioneer Gaulish monasteries may have been largely responsible in Late Roman Britain, as in Gaul, for a few 'gentleman's monasteries' around 400 and later on villa estates — Llanilltud Fawr and Lullingstone have been noted as potential instances (p. 61) — it remains highly unlikely that any such existed by *c*.450 at Whithorn; which is better seen as provision of an episcopate, accompanied by church-building, for a sub-Roman Christian community in Galloway, Carlisle being the place behind this. What *can* be suggested is that any Kirkmadrine station of incomers was basically monastic, a rural community of clerics (and followers) in a remote but sea-accessible spot living under a monastic rule. If from Gaul, and if then responsible for bringing the cult of Martin to sixth-century Whithorn, we might see this also as primarily of Martinian inspiration. There can be no certainty. But the character of 516 and 517, the possibility that the surviving male names point to Gaul, even the odd record of a *subdiaconus* [23], could support such a reading. In terms of the sequence of Insular inscriptions in general, particularly those in Biblical style, an identification of at least two entry-points of Continental ideas — Capel Anelog, and Kirkmadrine, both around the end of the fifth century — fits well with

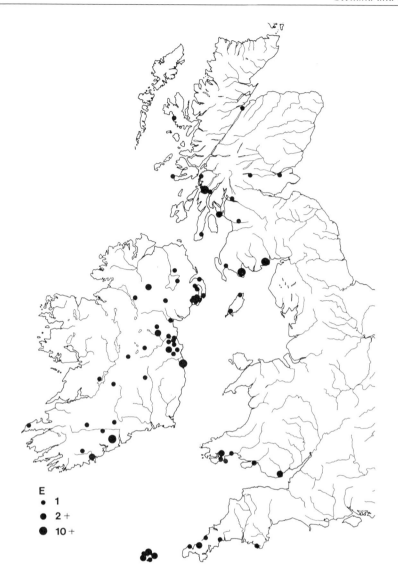

Fig. 42   *One minor material indication of Insular maritime contact, involving trade and*
passengers, with (probably) Atlantic Gaul during the late 6th and 7th centuries; discovery
of sherds, with numbers of likely vessels represented, of 'Class E ware', wheelmade
containers of Gaulish origin. (Map is 1990; subsequent finds do not alter pattern.)

(even if, strictly, it gains no support directly from) a known pattern of transmarine contact
(see map, *Fig. 42*) that has been built up from archaeological finds.

Some further implications

When the slab, 520 *Latinus*, was unearthed by William Galloway it had probably been re-cycled into buildings several times; the chance is that this happened first in the Northumbrian period but, most unusually, we seem to have slight evidence that it was standing, visible, legible, *and properly understood*, for some considerable time after *c.* 450. It has been supposed that a now-lost Latin *Vita*, a book of the life and posthumous miracles of Nynia, existed; and that it was probably written in pre-Anglian Whithorn (seventh century, perhaps after any Kirkmadrine reinforcement). Ailred of Rievaulx's twelfth-century *Vita* tells us that its author drew on a *liber de vita et miraculis* of the saint, *barbario scripta* (i.e., to this Norman, written in an archaic and uncouth Latin style; perhaps also a very ancient copy). It is clear that the authors of the eighth-century set of poems *Miracula Nyrie Episcopi* drew on both Bede and presumably this same Life. In both (poem 4 of the *Miracula*, cap.ii of Ailred diverted to describe Martin's church at Tours) the extent of direct obvious quotation from 2 Chron., 3 and 4 implies that, in the lost Whithorn life, Nynia's building of his first church was couched in Temple of Solomon terms. It multiplies hypotheses beyond necessity to find an explanation for this, other than that 520 *Latinus* was still on view, and its allusive and image-generation content publicly known.[24]

The other comment concerns the handful of memorial inscriptions, beyond Kirkmadrine and Whithorn, known in an approximate south-to-north belt up to the Forth. There are five, possibly six, of these. None can be shown to be in Biblical style. On the other hand they have certain features marking them off from the general run in Wales. One certainly, 511 *Coninie*, and a second possibly (slight damage: 515 Yarrow Stone), commence with line-height initial cross, rather like the + as 'letter no.1' on 505 *Anduires*. The Yarrow Stone has IN LOCO; a lost stone from Peebles apparently began LOCUS. This post-Classical memorial term (*locus*, originally 'place', meaning 'grave, grave-plot, tomb') occurs only on Scottish stones. There are examples of sideways R (511, 515). A late stone from Peebles, not in *CIIC*, has NE ITANO / SACER DOS around a central cross (*Fig. 30*), *Neitano sacerdos* 'bishop Neitan'. The considerable hint of a Continental element in these stones, from the late sixth century, may point to mixed influences in the northward spread of the Faith through the Borders; not wholly Insular, Kirkmadrine as well as Whithorn. By 600 or so Strathclyde, where the comparable founding saint was Kentigern (Mungo), and several native principalities around the Forth, had embraced Christianity but we need not follow the story further.

If 391 *Senacus* brings into the picture the possibility of Gaulish clerics whose Latin style included , from a common pre-400 base, advanced Biblical-style composition and a suggestion of presenting a text as a simple display plan, what 520 *Latinus* must show is a particular development — by a master-hand, with access to the Vulgate OT — of devices, LaN, LNu, ordinary quadruple ratio, current in Romano-British teaching; and a development with extremely clever labelling of a ground-plan image, earlier found in *RIB* 684 *Corellia Optata*. In a way, 520 *Latinus* opens the special and innovative character of purely Insular inscriptional construction and we can pursue that in Chapter 6. And, when talking of the conversion of the Celts of southern Scotland, these Men of the North, we see that it is proper to suggest *two* localised conversions, both probably before 500; with bishop Nynia at Whithorn, a place still admissible as the Cradle of the Kirk and, slightly west of them (introducing monasticism as well?), these putative *septem fratres* of Kirkmadrine and district.

Ireland: a nil return?

From circumstances and necessity, certainly not from choice, this concluding section will be short. The theme of this book, its centrality and claim to originality, is the light shed upon the Christian Celts (undifferentiated) and their particular Roman-originating culture by one class of surviving contemporary evidence, that of selected memorial inscriptions. Ireland participated to a very large degree in the same culture. Some knowledge of spoken and then written Latin, with the capitals, cursive hands and numerals, had been passing from Britannia to the east and south of Ireland in the Roman centuries — trading-stations, returning mercenaries, plain adventurers and apparently some Late Roman Christians form likely channels. Patrick, who wrote Latin (and in Biblical style) and learnt some Irish, must have taught Latin to his Northern converts. In 431 when Bishop Palladius and his entourage arrived in Leinster it is more than likely that their baggage contained Latin Christian writings beyond the Vulgate, and that they encountered groups who could read these. As David Howlett has shown, by 600 we find Irish clerics engaged in advanced Latin composition; start of an impressive Hiberno-Latin (and Christian) output.

Somewhere, at a time that is not known but has been guessed as anything from the early third to the fifth century, a person or a learned committee invented a completely new script, a short and long strokes system; ogam. An adjusted density-distribution map (*Fig. 43*) implies that this began in the south-west, Cos. Kerry and (west) Cork; one scenario might locate this at a coastal or estuarine trade post, where details like the incremental Roman numerals (I II III IIII) and characters of particular letters in, e.g., wax tablet script provide much of the idea. Ogam, like the 20-letter ABC, has five vowels and fifteen consonants. Its prototype grouping is lost, and (putting what Damian McManus shows were the original intended sounds) there may once have been a four-set system like this:

A O U E I . B L W S N . H(?Y) D T K Q(=kw) . M G GW ST(?) R

With some sound-value changes, it was however later presented as:

B L F S N . H D T C Q . M G NG Z R . A O U E I

the vowels coming last. These are not the Latin letters, and ogam must have been tailored to reflect the different phonology of Irish in Roman times (Ogam Irish, Primitive Irish).

Its disposition (*Fig. 44*) requires a base- or stem-line, with strokes to left, to right and diagonally through. Ogam was also written *upwards*, reading vertically bottom to top. The nature of many rocks in Ireland that break along bedding-planes (like limestone) meant that an arris, an angle between planes or faces, could act as the line (*Fig. 45* is a good example). Again our view must be distorted because the earliest corpus of ogam is preserved on stone, the Great Survivor; it may also have been written on wood, bone, wax, and prepared skins, and there are a few later instances of such.

This writer's view, if it reads like over-simplification of a most complex problem, is that

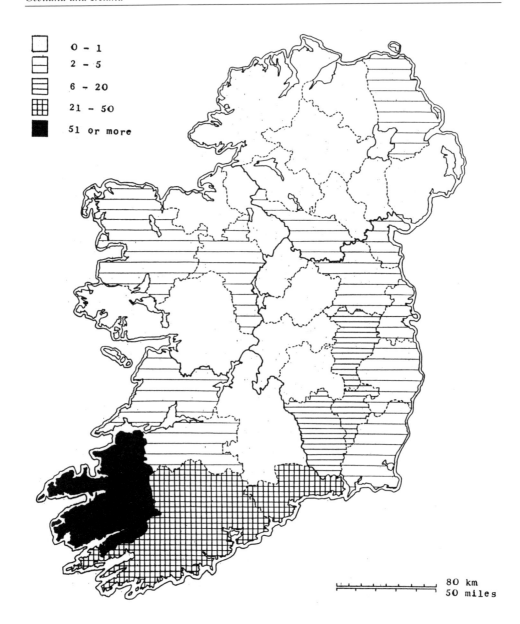

Fig. 43   Ireland; ogam-inscribed memorial stone, shown as a density-distribution (total
occurrences per county adjusted to median area of all counties). On this showing,
Co.Kerry has the greatest concentration followed by Cos.Cork and Waterford; can this
mean both the invention and primary use of ogam for memorials must be placed in south
Munster?

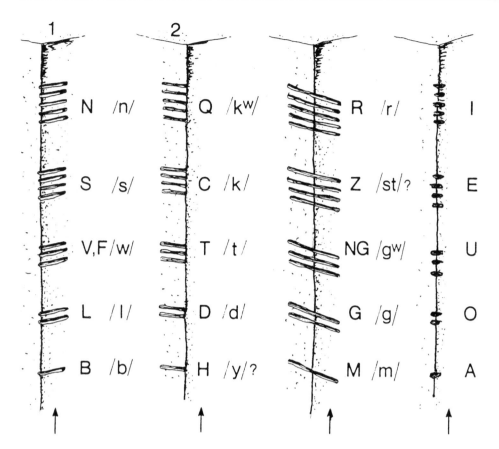

Fig. 44   The ogam script, a 20-letter 'BLF' or 'AOU' (not 'ABC') system as cut on the arris or angle of stones. Capitals, the medieval written values; lower-case between slashes, the likely Primitive Irish phonetic values argued by MacManus, Ogam. Face 1 is sometimes called 'the B-surface' and face 2 'the H-surface'.

ogam was invented (about 300-plus?) specifically to write short, not particularly cryptic, memorials in the 'Of A; of the son of B' category on unprepared stone surfaces, that it avoided the obstacle of curved Roman capitals (BCDGOPQRS), was easily copied and cut by illiterates, and was inspired by the shorter Roman tombstone inscriptions of Britain (or some on the Continent). The oldest ogam stones — fourth and fifth centuries? — need not even be for Christians but, again, were mainly for prominent or aristocratic people. Consider the very simplest of Roman memorials; *RIB* 1180 at Corbridge, D . M / AHTEHE /FIL.NOBILIS /VIXIT ANIS / V, *Dis Manibus Ahtehe filiae Nobilis vixit anis V* 'To the Gods, to the shades — To Ahteha, to the daughter of Nobilis; she lived years 5'; or (Spain)[25] 6184 AEMILIVS MA/TERNVS FLORI /FILIVS ANNO / XX 'Aemilius Maternus, son of Florius, of 20 years' — and, among post-Roman Insular texts, 472 VLCAGNI FILI / SEVERI 'Of Ulcagnus; of the son of Severus'. The irreducible nucleus, *A, son/daughter of B*, or *To/of A, of a son of B*, is found in dozens of ogams like 119 *DALAGNI*

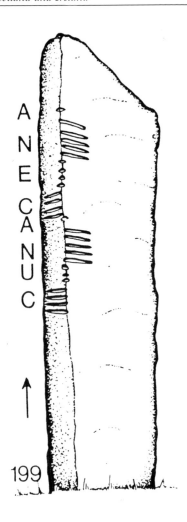

Fig. 45   An example (CIIC 199) of a single-name ogam inscription, Co.Kerry; gritstone with sharp angle, CUNACENA reading upwards.

MAQI DALI, or 147 *MOINENA MAQI OLACON*, or 449, from Wales, a 'bilingual', in Roman capitals SAGRANI FILI CVNOTAMI ('Of Sagranus; of a son of Cunotamus') with ogam *SAGRAGNI MAQI CUNATAMI* — both names are in fact Irish; settlers here. *Maqi*, replacing *fili*, is for Irish **maqqas* 'of a son'; a conventional and probably imitative distortion to end in the epitaphic-I (p. 211), and by the same token though the ogam spellings can reflect the far-reaching spoken sound-changes in Irish between the fourth and seventh centuries, some names are patently archaic in form. They must be seen, just as in Britain (p. 69) as deliberate use of IOC.

This is not to say that the several hundreds of Irish ogam memorials run exactly parallel to those in Wales (and Cornwall). They do not; in both areas, up to the sixth century, where families of Irish-originating settlers are commemorated, a few stones use both scripts and both Latin/neo-Brittonic (names) and Primitive Irish, but one profound distinction exists. There is no evidence that 20-character ogam, either starting A O U E I or B L W S N, used the 1-to-20 values of Latin's 20-letter LaN scheme. It is not possible

Fig.46   *CIIC no.1, Inchagoill,*
           Lough Corrib; two small
           crosses, two lines of book
           hand, lie luguaedon
           macci menueh
           (photo: author).

yet, and one suspects never will be, to show a computus structure in a purely ogam text. The British system simply did not apply, even though half-a-dozen ogams in the south (*Fig. 47*) contain Roman names, whether of Roman merchants dying there or returning Irish legionaries; 16 (Co. Carlow) *DUNAIDONAS MAQI MARIANI* 'Of Dunaido, of the son of *Marianus*', 166 (Co. Kerry) *COIMAGNI MAQI WITALIN* 'of Coimagnas, of a son of *Vitalinus*' (two epigraphic-I's here), and 188 *MARIANI* (solo).

Certainly Christian both from their ecclesiastic contexts and the associated art of developed post-650/700 forms of ornate crosses, a later class of Irish inscribed recumbent cross-slab memorials gives us texts in a Latin bookhand, Irish names and formulae (OR(ait) DO, AR 'a prayer for', etc.) and a few Latin words. Macalister's *CIIC* ii, 597 to 850, lists the huge range from Clonmacnois, Co. Offaly.[26] At almost no point do the Irish and British memorial-stone series seem to come together, and in Ireland — specifically, working on stone — the rich verbal development of British memorials was replaced by the visual and artistic elaborations; eventually the didactic Biblical-scene panels of Irish High Crosses, a separate unique achievement. The oldest Irish memorial inscription not in ogam is *CIIC* 1, from Inchagoill (island, Lough Corrib), Co. Galway — *Fig. 46*. Of late seventh century date, it employs an insular bookhand that could have been used for at least

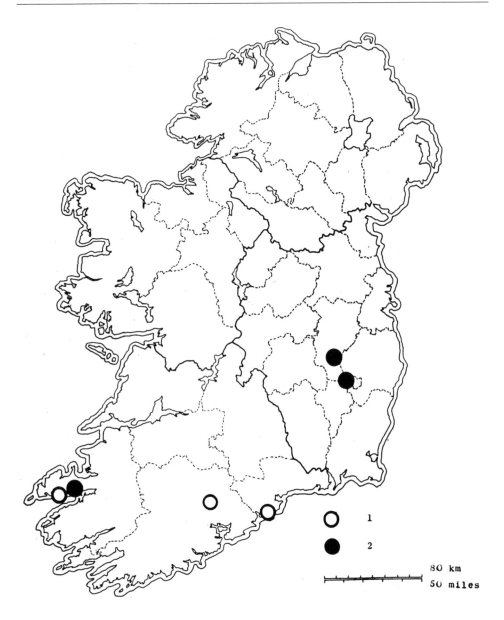

Fig. 47   *Ireland: southern Leinster, southern Munster, six instances of ogam stones bearing Irish names (of the type MARIANI, WITALIN = Vitalinus, AMADU = Amatus). 1, single Roman name; 2, Irish-named son, Roman-named father, as* COIMAGNI MAQI WITALIN.

a century in Irish (Latin) manuscript writings. Below two crosses, two lines read, using capitals: LIE LUGUAEDON / MACCI MENUEH, 'Stone of L., of a son of M'. The first name, in Primitive Irish *Luguaidonas* (gen.), can be regarded as a kind of IOC spelling (LUGAIDON would be expected).[27] If we analyse this, so:

		W	*S*	*L*
1	l i e l u g u a e d o n	2	5	12
2	m a c c i m e n u e h	2	5	11
		4	10	23

at least it exhibits symmetry, mean ratio, division 1.1, throughout. (In the first name, the second (old compositional) vowel -u- is /w/, which reduces the syllable count in line 1 to five.) If, and it must be a big 'if', 20-letter LaN applies, the *eleven* (letters, line 2) is repeated; initials, line 2, M M = 22; the sum of *S*, 10 and L, 23 = 33, but (one might say), so what? If the deceased, (Old Irish) *Lugáed*, nom., was a priest this bipartite character might allude to one who lived by the two-fold (OT, NT) Word of God. Eleven is not so explicable. What we have to conclude is that in *CIIC* 1 *Luguaedon*, itself an odd and isolated inscription, we do not find the intricate developed Biblical style of broadly contemporary British texts like 986 *Ioruert*, 970 *Catamanus* (with 6 words).

Only a rash person would rule out a remote possibility that ogam memorials, a few of which do run to six or more words, contain some separate inner secret structure; but if so it remains a secret. No amount of squaring, gridding and triangularising ogam texts whose letter-totals are squares, four-multiples and triangular numbers gives anything approaching acrostics or telestichs in any language. Nor as yet is there really sufficient academic consensus about the origin and range of uses of ogam, let alone firm dates and the precise connection with a Christian faith that entered and spread through Ireland within the ogam-cutting period, to pursue the subject here. It is unsatisfactory to argue mainly from inferences (e.g., that the invention of ogam presupposes an Irish currency of Latin, probably before Christanity) because so much evidence is missing. In another area, that of the introduction of monasticism to Ireland — first, in 431, by Palladius and his circle, and through relevant literature?— similar inferences have the support of place-name elements[28] but the problem of ogam stands very much on its own. From later and longer Christian Latin writings we cannot doubt the existence of Irish scholars as much as home with the scriptures, the rules of Biblical style and the necessary literary skills as their British fellows (with whom, in fact, they were in constant touch). Not wholly because *Hibernia* had lain outside the Roman Empire, and apparently not because Christianisation there proceeded at its own pace, the early personal memorials of Ireland were entirely Irish. Using neither the language nor the script of Rome in the West their creators were unable or unwilling to echo the corresponding British inscriptions. When, rarely, the two traditions met — on a few dozen Welsh and Cornish memorials of *c.*450 to 600 — common ground went no further than bare essentials: (This is the stone) of A; of a son of B.

Notes to chapter 5

1   My 'The Early Christian Inscriptions of Southern Scotland', *Glasgow Archaeol. Journal*, 17 (1991-92), 1-10, is a discursive catalogue of all thirteen, including three not in *CIIC*.

2   See Richard Sharpe, *Adomnán of Iona. Life of St Columba* (Penguin, Harmondsworth 1995) with its very full discussion and notes.

3   For those genuinely interested, Eric H. Nicoll, ed., *A Pictish Panorama. The Story of the Picts and A Pictish Bibliography* (Pinkfoot Press, Balgavies 1995) is the essential starting-point.

4   Bede, *H.E* iii.4 (also briefly in v.23); text and translation in *St Nynia* (2nd rev. edn., Polygon, Edinburgh 1990), by John MacQueen, with translations of the *Miracula* poems and Ailred's *Vita* by Winifred MacQueen.

5   On this chronologically difficult subject, see Rosemary Cramp's Third (1994) Whithorn Lecture, *Whithorn and the Northumbrian Expansion Westwards* (Whithorn 1995).

6   See my *Christianity in Roman Britain to AD 500*, chap.13 — this 'North British' background is by no means universally accepted.

7   Amusingly outlined in Sharpe, *Adomnán*

9   They are listed in my First (1992) Whithorn Lecture, *Whithorn's Christian Beginnings* (Whithorn 1992), which introduced the interpretation as a building stone, not a funerary monument.

10 The original Temple, its site not archaeologically accessible, now has a wealth of expert literature; a classic account remains that by Professor Archibald Kennedy, *Encyclopaedia Britannica*, 11th edn., 1911, with reconstructions, using both Biblical accounts.

11 See note 23 to Chap.3.

12 The restoration slightly modifies that by Vives (e.g., *feminae* for his *femine*); in (d) the opening *et*, stylistically clumsy and redundant, appears to have crept into the eventual display. Its excision must be right because all totals are then in 1:4 ratio.

13 Bede's written Nynia should stand for a Celtic-Latin, or neo-Brittonic, *∗Nini-a,-au, an*. Was this itself a hypocoristic name developed from by-forms of the attested (*RIB* 2491.101,*CIIC* 470) *Latinus*, as *Latinianus, Latininus*? The former occurs also on *RIB* 2491.101, graffiti on a tile from Caves Inn, Warwicks.

14 Notably for 518 *Initium et Finis* ('seventh century', '700 or later') but all its letter forms can be found on inscriptions or of mid- or late sixth century dates (CIIC nos.334, 342, 470,477, and 492).

15 Details in Hill, *Whithorn*, at 619 (Derek Craig).

16 (Bishop) John Dowden's paper 'Observations and Conjectures on the Kirkmadrine Epitaphs', *Proc.Soc. Antiquaries Scotland*, 32 (1897-98), 247-74, remains a classic analysis of what *sacerdos* meant; he also pointed out that Rufinus of Aquileia's translation of Eusebius, *Hist. Eccles.*, vii, cap.24, with *praecipuus sacerdos*, may have prompted the wording of 516.

17 Sub-deacons were a clerical order, usually in some large centre where the full range

of (seven or eight) major and minor orders existed.

18 Mavorius and Ventidius seem Celtic (Gaulish?) rather than Roman; Florentius was common in Gaul (Florentius, a consul (West), 515; Gregory of Tours, b.538, was actually Georgius Florentius); *vivens* 'living' (in the Christian sense of *vita Christiana*) and *viventia* 'Life' underline (Christian) Viventius. Lyon, 5th-century, has a memorial to VIVENTI PRBI (*presbyteri*) EGLISIAE LUGD. None of this is conclusive, but it could be consistent with a Gaulish origin.

19 Apocalypsis, 21.6 *et dixit mihi…ego sum A et W initium et finis.*

20 Professor Owen Chadwick, 'The Evidence of Dedications in the Early History of the Welsh Church', at p.181 in: Nora K.Chadwick, ed., *Studies in Early British History* (Cambridge 1959) firmly dismissed an idea of 'a personal influence of Martin on Ninian at Whithorn'.

21 This is *monasterium Locotigia (censim)* in Gregory of Tours, *De Virtut. S. Martini*, iv.30; for the site, see my *Christianity in Roman Britain to AD 500*, 166, fig.22 and refs.

22 See W. MacQueen's translation in MacQueen, *St Nynia*, 88 ff.; I now follow Dr Andy Orchard's analysis of this as a set of poems by up to fourteen different pupils of Alcuin, but using the lost Vita.

23 At Trier (an Imperial centre), memorials contain the rare entries BASILIVS SVBDIACONVS and VRSINIANO SVBDIACONO; from Spain, Vives records only *diaconus* (a very few examples). Was Ventidius as a junior cleric sent to man some small outstation at Low Curghie?

24 The full references and quotations are set out in my John Jamieson Lecture (see Further Reading).

25 José Vives, *Inscripciones latinas de la España romana* (Barcelona 1971).

26 See, too, P. Lionard's illustrated discussion, 'Early Irish Grave-Slabs', *Proc. Royal Irish Academy*, 61C (1961), 95-169.

27 McManus, *Ogam*, 120-3 ('our earliest contemporary Irish text in the Latin alphabet'); it is difficult to date it closely but the various small crosses suggest a date in the 7th rather than 6th century, and perhaps towards the end of that century.

28 As shown in my paper (prelude to a full study of the origins of Insular monasticism), 'Cellular Meanings, Monastic Beginnings', *Peritia*, 13 (1995), 51-68.

6   Mental Images

In working time 'Lewis Carroll' was Charles Lutwidge Dodgson, an Oxford lecturer and professional mathematician to whom everything in this book would have seemed elementary and obvious and, in respect of letter-games and codes, very much the kind of thing with which he relaxed.[1] Both the first version of *Alice's Adventures Under Ground* (1862) and its printed revision *Alice's Adventures in Wonderland* (1865) contain the story of Alice meeting a Mouse who, saying 'Mine is a long and sad tale!' ('It is a long tail, certainly,' said Alice, looking down with wonder), then recites it ('Fury said to a mouse, That he met in the house' and so on). In Dodgson's MS and then in all revised printed versions this tale/tail is printed in the form of a long and sinuous caudal appendage (*Fig. 48*). The author is realising the image visually from his own knowledge — Christ Church, Oxford, was probably swarming with well-fed mice — then reproducing it on a two-dimensional surface; from which, prompted by the story's context, readers generate their personal perceptions of what an actual mouse-tail would look like.

Mental images differ from conventional pictures because they require the exercise of a human viewer's mind and imagination to raise them to the equivalent of a direct representation, and solely in the direction intended, suggested by surrounding clues. *Alice Through The Looking-Glass* (1871) opens with a real chess-problem and in its chap.ii we have another mental image; from a little hill Alice sees the countryside divided up into squares by brooks and hedges and this, brilliantly realised by Sir John Tenniel (*Fig. 49*), generates the, actually greater than 8-by-8, 'chess-board' inherent in the story.

With the ten or more Insular inscriptions that can be said to generate mental images, *pictures* of any kind because they transcend the verbal information carried by words, names, letters and numerals, we soon find that there is a fourfold division. Some images are there already in the display, in what any viewer sees, but have to be spotted or detected; have to be recognised through the prompting of a text's allusions, or because of appropriate labelling (520 *Latinus* was a good instance). These are all *display* images. They still exist in books for small children or the intellectually unstretched, where joining up in the right order all the numbered dots printed on a flat page results in a picture of Mickey Mouse, Winston Churchill, Marilyn Monroe, even (1997) Tony Blair. But what we are about to encounter is something different (already presaged in the first chapter, *Figs. 2, 8* and *9*, referring to 421 *Rostece* of about 500, and 350 *Idnert* a good three centuries later).

We call them *devised images* because, never apparent as part of a surface image, they are created through the use of one or more computus *devices*; re-arranging the letters, usually *LM* and not *LD*, into a square or a grid, equalising lines and columns by their LaN totals,

'Mine is a long and a sad tale!' said the Mouse, turning to Alice and sighing.

'It *is* a long tail, certainly,' said Alice, looking down with wonder at the Mouse's tail; 'but why do you call it sad?' And she kept on puzzling about it while the Mouse was speaking, so that her idea of the tale was something like this:

```
          " Fury said to a
              mouse, That
            he met in the
              house, 'Let
                us both go
                 to law: I
                  will prose-
                  cute you.—
                  Come, I'll
                 take no de-
                 nial: We
              must have
            the trial ;
         For really
        this morn-
        ing I've
        nothing
        to do.'
        Said the
         mouse to
          the cur,
           'Such a
            trial, dear
              sir, With
               no jury
                or judge,
                 would
                  be wast-
                 ing our
               breath.'
             'I'll be
            judge,
          I'll be
        jury,'
        said
        cun-
        ning
        old
         Fury;
          'I'll
            try
             the
              whole
              cause,
              and
              con-
             demn
            you to
          death'."
```

Fig.48   *'The Mouse's Tale/Tail', from the first printed version of* Alice's Adventures in
Wonderland *(Macmillan & Co., 1865, similarly printed in all subsequent editions).*
Since Alice is 'looking down' at the tail, the image must be classified as a display plan.

Fig. 49   *Another mental image, drawn by Tenniel for Lewis Carroll's* Alice Through the
Looking-glass; *from the little hill, the countryside is disposed to suggest the massive
chess-board on which the books characters move. As this is detectable, suggested by
features of what we would see looking along a horizontal plane, the generated image
would have to be classed as a display profile.*

even triangularisation. If these have more recent equivalents, I have not encountered
them. But display and devised images come in two kinds. If display/devised is a *horizontal*
bar across a corpus of images, we must add a second, *vertical*, division (*Fig. 50*).

What was discovered in *RIB* 684 *Corellia Optata*, 520 *Latinus* and 391 *Senacus* was in each
case a ground-plan; as images, *display plans* of a little funerary temple or shrine, the (2
Chronicles) Temple of the earthly Jerusalem and the (Apocalypsis) Heavenly City of the
celestial Jerusalem. All are depictions that the Romans, the Christian Celts and we
ourselves would expect to lie flat; to be seen from *above*, looking near-vertically down. In
this they are at one with a builder's ground-plan, a map on a table-top or floor, the
inscribed surface of a horizontal tomb-cover. There was a prolonged Roman familiarity
with the surveyor's plan, the graphic model for military installations; even larger or world
maps (lettered, or labelled) reproduced as mosaic floors.[2] It is understandable, surely, that
the earliest inscriptional images (despite appearing on vertically-set surfaces?) would come
to us as display plans; from Late and sub-Roman Britain, from Gaul.

Radically different must be those images that present pictures of anything that, in
reality, would normally be seen *sideways-on*; by viewers looking at them along a near-
horizontal plane (a tree, a mound, a standing Cross, people, animals, complete structures).

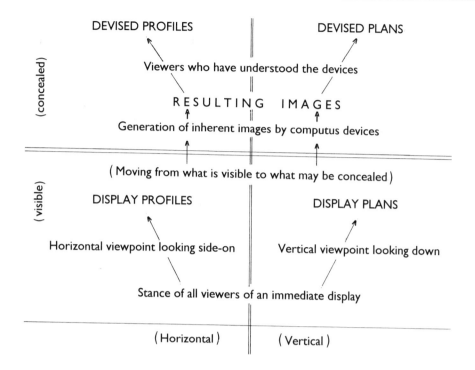

Fig.50   *An attempted classification of mental images generated by inscriptional (and other ?) texts. The practical distinction between profiles viewed horizontally and plans viewed vertically is then intersected by a boundary between the supposedly perceptible, the displays; and inherent or deeper images revealed only by devices.*

These are mental images presented to us as *profiles,* and they too may come in either a devised or display guise. Both kinds occur. The evidence rehearsed below marks profiles as an invention, an Insular invention that seems to have taken place by the sixth century, and in Wales. ('Profile' is preferable to *perspective,* the usual term for all sideways-viewed representations in, say, Roman wall-painting or flattish pictorial sculpture-panels. Leaving aside the limited Roman progress towards showing true perspective, inscriptional mental images by definition cannot contain this.) How it arose remains a puzzle. In the early fourth century at Rome the poet Optatian[3] built into his 35-by-35 letter squares of Latin verse the craziest kind of horizontally-viewed images; obvious because he drew attention to them in his commentary and because, in the circulated originals, they were almost certainly picked out in colour. To Romans these were real *figurae* 'pictures'; hence *carmina figurata, scriptura figurata,* for poems and writings that (uncommonly) contained such tricks. Again, in Britain after 500 the addition of small pictorial elements to manuscripts (of the Bible?), notably initial capitals, and the chance that on a few stones a heading (chi-rho-derived cross) was construed as a basic picture of the Cross (*Fig. 51*), offers a hint of new profile depictions — they are certainly in no sense plans of anything. Alternatively, the Insular profile images really were Insular inventions and nothing else.

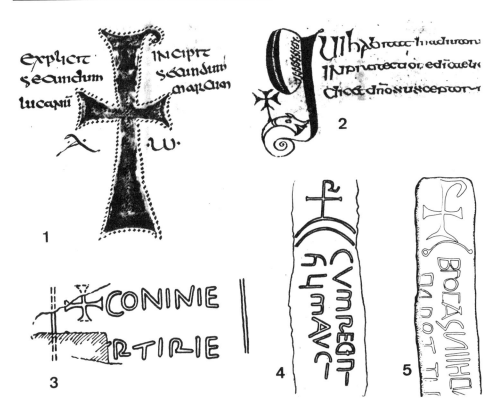

Fig. 51   Possible minor factors in the development, 6th-7th centuries, of profile images; depictions of anything seen sideways ? Top, details from Dublin, T.C.D. MS A.4.15 and Dublin, R.I.A. MS S.n. (the 'Cathach'), both after 600; below left, line-height initial cross, 511 Coninie (SW Scotland); below right, both from Cornwall, 486 Cumrecini, 478 Brocagni. Are these rho-hooked crosses surmounting curves inspired from some early detail of the crucifixion scene?

Conceivably there had been Romano-British wall painting on plaster (most are unfortunately fragmentary), where scenes in profile contained extra or symbolic meanings; but those would be pictures within pictures, not potential pictures within lines or blocks of writing. At the moment, generation of any images by Insular inscriptions cannot be shown later than the ninth century, with 350 *Idnert*, and it may be that so exotic a practice petered out. The only partial parallel from later centuries that occurs to me might be recent claims that Nicolas Poussin's seventeenth-century paintings Les Bergers d'Arcadie I and II contain hidden geometric images, clues to the nature of the Rennes-le-Château treasure, burial (in France) of Jesus as ancestor of the royal Merovingian line and further exciting mysteries; but extraction of points, line and angles from geometrically-constructed scenes is not confined to Poussin's enigmatic oils.[4] Actually more exciting, to many, would be the serious suggestion that in parallel with a construction of image-generating inscriptional texts (all necessarily short), post-Roman Wales occasionally produced something similar in longer writings preserved in subsequent manuscripts. Imagine an account of a journey, uphill and down-dale, from A via B,C,D, and E to F with letter, word and *sectio* totals so arranged that one could draw out a linear profile from a text (using triangles) corresponding to the spatial contoured profile of the journey, the named spots A to F being in their correct places. Imagine an elegant Latin poem about the interior of the Temple of Solomon (as in 520 *Latinus*), focused on the Holy of Holies and using familiar language (*Templi, lapides sanctuarii, duae columnae, duo Chirubin* and so on), allegorical in content and purpose — with the author's original, a tall rectangle of 25 lines, physically written so that it generates a kind of labelled, *display-profile* image of that interior. (The 'image' of the journey would be a *devised* profile.) Could such extraordinary compositions exist? Why not? It is logical to suppose that those who could compress image-generation into brief memorials would have exercised their skills on a larger canvas.[5]

Venedotia, and the first devised images

Back to the world of William Hanks (p. 13). You are Neil once more and, after that challenging visit to Much Binding, you go back to the cramped cottage in Tewkesbury that you share with Joan. It is supper-time. Space is short, you both like a civilised drink but you have to store the wine in a cupboard under the stairs, in those square plastic containers (bins). You get out a tall thin bottle of an obscure German hock. It tastes a bit, well, ancient; and Joan says to you, I've not seen this before — where is this kept? Your answer is: *This is in a wine bin.* Your reply is verbal, linear and brief because life is too short to allow communication by cutting letters on stone. However your answer has 16 letters. If written, as a 4-by-4 letter square, you would be astonished (would you?) to see that the device of squaring your text produces an image (*Fig. 52*). It has turned into a *devised profile*; a sideways-on, see-through, X-ray profile of the tall thin bottle standing in its square-section bin, and it even has another, S-for-S(horter), S(quare-face) bottle of gin alongside it. The tattered label, to your alarm, say '1958'. But that is apparent from the image; in 26-letter LaN, the corner letters are T S E N, or 20.19.5.14 = 58.

In sub-Roman Wales, a powerful kingdom arose in the north-west. Later it was supposed that it originated at the end of Roman times with an Imperially-organised transfer of Cunedag, or Cunedda (in IOC, *Cune-dagos*)[6] and eight sons from their kingdom of Manau (Guotodin) around the upper Firth of Forth, implanted to stiffen resistance to would-be Irish raiders and settlers. Gwynedd is the medieval and the revived postal-and-administrative name; its British forerunner can be restored as **Veneda* (/we:neda/), with an adjectival stem **Venedot-*.[7] 'Venedotia' and 'Venedotian' are antiquarian but acceptable labels. Its pre-600 Christian history is obscure in the extreme. One reason for this is that no major and dominant ecclesiastical centres can yet be clearly pinpointed in Gwynedd, unlike quite a few in the south of Wales. For secular royal centres, one apparently lay on Anglesey; it has been suggested, in the south-east part, at

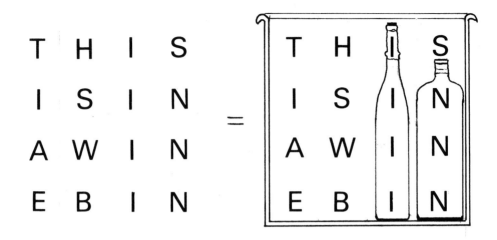

Fig.52   *How to generate a devised profile image from 16 letters; the square is a cross-section of the wine bin, containing the tall bottle of w**IIII**ne and the Squareface gi**NNN** beside it.*

Aberffraw. When around 540 Gildas addressed himself to *Maglocune* (vocative), the king Mailgun (Maelgwn) five generations in supposed descent from Cunedda, he called him *insularis draco* 'Dragon of the Isle', i.e., of Anglesey.[8] Near Aberffraw is the church of Llangadwaladr, named for and presumably re-founded by Cadwaladr, grandson of the Cadfan or 970 CATAMANUS (p. 162) who was Mailgun's great-great-grandson. This is a long dynastic run for Gwynedd — early fifth to eighth centuries — ruling from one small district.

Gildas is specific that Mailgun had 'pondered on the godly life, and the Rule, of the monks' (*monachorum decretis*); had publicly vowed to become a monk and may briefly have been one,[9] and had as a boy benefited from having had 'as your teacher, the most refined Master of almost all Britain' (*paene totius Britanniae magistrum elegantem*). If it is right to suppose the *magister* had been Illtud with his school down south at Llanilltud Fawr in Glamorgan (p. 58), indeed that Gildas and the backsliding king had been fellow-pupils, is there an implication that around 500-525 no such intellectual centre existed in the north-west? We cannot be sure.

The immediate interest of the 30-plus north-western and northern Welsh inscriptions lies in the sheer range of their Latin wording and high proportion of continuing-Roman names.[10] Most stones have come from what are now isolated churches and villages in Veneditian valleys or upland trackways. This could warn us against projecting a present, depopulated and post-industrial, rural landscape into what must have been a very different pattern of the fifth to eight centuries. For example, Penmachno, a small Snowdonia village up a side-valley off the higher reach of the river Conway, had some importance as a Christian centre of a district with stones 393, 394, 395 and 396; one person so mentioned, 394 *Cantiori* in a nine-word text that cannot be shown as being in Biblical style, was

VENEDOTIS CIVE — still, after 500, a latter-day, Roman-type, Venedotian citizen. The extent of a real if dispersed heritage of *romanitas* in Gwynedd is hidden from us and comes in tiny packets. Outside the Late Roman auxiliary fort at *Segontium*, Caernarvon, the Llanbeblig church early cemetery could have been a civilian one adopted for use by post-400 Christians. At Holyhead on Anglesey itself another Late Roman fortified naval base at Caer Gybi contains a church that probably began as a small monastic foundation for St Kebius (Cybi); the medieval Life of this saint names the king Mailgun as the donor.[11]

In the previous chapter, we looked at the likely role of the *ecclesia* represented by the Kirkmadrine stones in the Christian story of Galloway. The accomplishments shown in what may be a second Gaulish mission-post at Capel Anelog by the 391 *Senacus* memorial — its stylistic economy, computus, Biblical allusiveness and display plan — might, one would think, have had some overspill into the nascent inscriptional style of north-west Wales. What we can observe is a group of comparative short memorial texts that, Capel Anelog influence or not, exhibit from the late fifth and sixth centuries some very simple mental images as plans (both display and devised). The common plan is small-scale, local, and probably not just of the deceased's grave but also of a grave-plot. Archaeologically, this would only exceptionally survive. We can assume a kind of surround or delineated small area (square, rectangular, ?curvilinear; bounded by stones, a little bank, a ditch?) that in open county or within a Christian cemetery marked off a particular burial.[12]

The instance of the wine-bin and Neil's 16-letter reply (*Fig. 52*) was not completely frivolous because it demonstrates how these texts work. The tall pillar, 399, at Clochaenog, Denbigh, has two lines of capitals, SIMILINI / TOVISACI (and, assuming some Irish family background, ogam SIBILINI TOWISACI.[13] This too has 16 letters. As a display (*Fig. 53*), readers could see two pairs of vertical I's; and devised into a letter square, a column of four I's which, as I I I I, 9 9 9 9 = 36, affirms the square notion. In Fig. 53, (2) does that column look like a linear grave inside a squareish plot? In (1), is the text's rectangle itself the grave? In that case, the pairs of I's might be two upright stones, one the actual inscribed pillar. Is this a little more acceptable in the light of Edward Lhuyd's report, just before 1700, that the detectable grave was within a hollow eight feet in diameter (shape not stated), and that there were indeed 'two stones at each end…4 feet asunder', one of them the pillar?

The second stone (with *Senacus*) at Capel Anelog, 392 *Veracius*, for another *presbiter*, shows a model of 25 letters. Set out square (*Fig. 53*, (3)) it is the corners, V C I T, that give 49, square of seven; in this tiny devised plan, the column of I I I would mark the burial. Closely similar is 402 from Caerwys, Flint, at the eastern edge of Gwynedd (4). Its two lines are HIC IACIT MVLI/ER BONA NOBILI(s), 'Here lies the good wife of Nobilis', reading *bona* as 'good' rather than her name. Note, for its model, that line initials H E = 13 would be doubled by the last letters I S, 9.17 = 26, and that omission (in *LD*) of final -s makes the lines equal with 12 letters in each. Squared, as 25 (= its *LM*), it too contains a column of I I I. The acrostic as H C L O B, 8.3.10.13.2, repeats a square (36); and the corners as H A B S, 8.1.2.17, give the good lady a perfect 28.

Introductory forays along these lines could have arisen anywhere in Wales. Superficially a close parallel to 399 *Similini* stands at Nevern in north Pembroke, an ancient and important Christian foundation. A second tall pillar also with two lines of small capitals

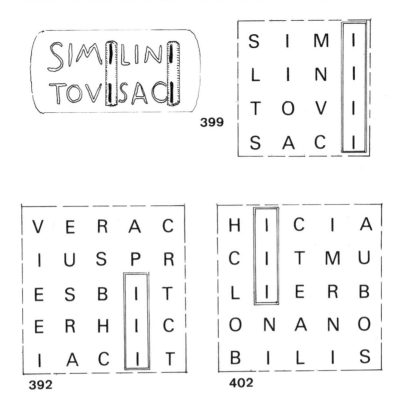

Fig.53   North Wales, 6th century; preliminary stage of devised images? 399 Similini, left, may be a very simple display plan of a grave with two upright slabs. The rest, squared from 16 and 25 letters, would count as equally simple devised plans denoting a grave (column of I's) within a formal plot or individual burial-area.

(*Fig.54*), 445 (=*ECMW* 354) *Vitaliani* reads VITALIANI / EMERETO, the AL ligatured and N reversed. *Emeritus*, an army term for legionaries rewarded for having served out their full time, is used in a spiritual sense (for a priest, most probably) and the spelling *emereto* for *emeriti* is deliberate. This, too, has an accompanying ogam, *WITALIANI*.

There is a surprising amount in this little memorial. Initial and last letter of his name, V I = perfect 28. From both words, we have V I E O, 19.9.5.13 = 46; the Man as God's Creation, from the Greek AΔAM = 46 again (p. 92)? Squaring the letters, col.2 might denote Vitalianus's grave, and I I E E repeats the figure of 28; and once more the corners, V A R O, 19.1.16.13, are a square (=49). The bottom line R E T O is an anagram of *oret* 'let [any reader] pray [for V's soul]', which might explain the deliberate spelling. Nor can one rule out a partial orientation in the devised-plan image; A(*quilo*), north, and O(*riens*), east, align the grave itself, as the I I E E column, correctly east-west.

Returning northwards, 387 (= ECMW 95) is of special relevance because this sixth-century stone is from Llannor, in the Llyn peninsula and only 14 miles from 391, 392, *Senacus* and *Veracius*. In three lines of less expert lettering (*Fig.55*) we read it as FIGVLINI

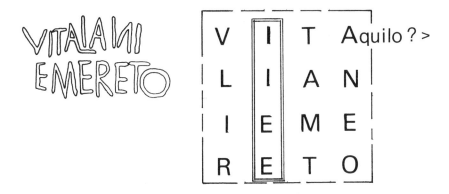

Fig. 54   South-west Wales, 6th century; 445 Vitaliani, at Nevern. Left, actual text (drawn from photographs); right, 16 letters squared, with another 'grave in plot' devised plan (as Fig. 53).

FILI / LOCVLITI HIC IACIT; precisely rendering the tiresome epitaphic-I genitives, 'Of-Figulinus, of-the-son of-Loculitus, here he lies'. These are both odd continuing-Roman names, extended from *figulus* 'potter, maker of earthenware' and *loculus* 'small space, spot'.

It is, however, textually a vehicle for recognisable use of Biblical style and another rudimentary image. A slight semantic re-arranging as:

		W	*S*	*L*
(a)	Figulini hic iacit	3	7	16
(b)	fili Loculiti	2	6	12
		5	13	28

gives all three totals as (a):(b) in extreme ratio, *W* from 1.2.3.5.8.13, S from 1.6.7.13.20… and *L* (times 4) from 1.3.4.7.11. There is even an obvious key number, *six*. Letter F = 6. In the actual display, *Fig.55*, initial and last letters F T = *six* by 4. Line 1 (display) has *six* syllables; *W*, 5 plus *S*, 13 = *six* times 3. A plausible reason would be a death, aged 36, of someone whose name began with F = 6. Line initials F L H make *six* times 4. For 36, last letters of the lines I I T = *36*; all the letters in (nom.) FIGULINUS = 108, or *36* times 3; and triangularising the 28 letters as Δ7, the apicals of the inverted are F N T, 6.12.18 = *36* again. (The two sides of the inverted, 70 + 68, make 138; *six* times 23.)

The text is not ostensibly Christian beyond the inclusion of HIC IACIT, but triangularisation of the pyramid provides us with:

```
  6                     F                    6
  9                   I   G                  7
 19                 U   L   I                9
 12               N   I   F   I              9
 10             L   I   L   O   C            3
 19           U   L   I   T   I   H          8
  9         I   C   I   A   C   I   T        18
 84                                          60
```

Fig.55   *387 Figulini, Llannor, NW Wales; unimpressive, maltreated as a gate-post (the four holes) but textually intricate. Drawing based on ECMW, by permission of the National Museum of Wales.*

— and a statement of a Christian death (apicals F I T = 33) and a soul in that Heavenly City, proclaimed on the nearby 391 *Senacus* (the sides, 84 + 60 = **144**). Finally, since we have both this 6/36 emphasis and *L* as 28, 4 times 7, what about suitable grids?

F	I	G	U	L	I		F	I	G	U	L	I	N
N	**I**	F	I	L	I		**I**	F	I	L	I	L	O
L	O	**C**	U	L	I		**C**	U	L	I	T	I	H
T	I	H	I	**C**	I		**I**	C	I	A	C	I	T
A	C	I	**T**	.	.								

(1) (lines of 6)   *(2)* (7 by 4)

If we expect another basic devised plan of a grave-plot, then (*1*) with its telestich I I I I column provides it. But in (*2*) note the acrostic FICI, also there in (*1*), reading diagonally and down from the upper left corner F. As an example of ordinary neo-Brittonic orthography in 500-plus, medial Roman C stands for /g/. I wonder if, in a memorial that seems very closely keyed to the man commemorated, we now have 'Figi', the hypocoristic (pet, family) name that replaced in life the formal Figulinus. No-one could call this stone (*Fig.55*) a particularly impressive monument but a little attention shows that it represents an established style; ER, LaN, adding of totals, a triangular, acrostics from gridding. It gives allusive 33 and 144. If we wanted Christ and His Disciples, *13*, and the Gospels as the Word, *4*, we could discover LNu in the text; f **I** g **VLI** n **I** f **ILI L** o **CVLI** t **I** h **ICI** a **CI** t = CCCLLLL VV I I I I I I I I I I - and add 300, 200, 10 and 10 to get 520 (= ten times *13* by *4*). And finally, taking this as the product of a Christian family, look at the grid (1) again — column 4, acrostic UIUIT, *vivit* 'he lives!'

A clever girl and a lost betrothed

The handful of smaller Welsh memorials, above, to be dated loosely between 500 and 600,

appears to illustrate a continued use of reduced mental images, generated as (unlabelled) *plans* and now *devised*, by using a single device of squaring or gridding; in contrast to the earlier and much more proficient *display* plans of *Corellia Optata*, *Latinus* and *Senacus*. It sets the stage for the next step, images in the shape of *profiles*, which we could expect to be both present in displays, and devised in various ways. We have actually encountered one already in the first chapter, 421 *Rostece* with its devised profile of her grave at the foot of the Cross; again, to be dated 500 x 550 and, for what that may signify, as a text with continuing-Roman names *Rostece* (= Rustica) and *Paterninus*. The probability is that profile images were invented after 500 at several localities. We go now to the vicinity of Penmachno, back to Veneda or Gwynedd, to examine 393 (= ECMW 101) *Carausius*.

    The inscription, five lines of capitals (*Fig. 56*), is topped by the second (fifth-sixth century) pattern of chi-rho, combined + and P with closed loop. The stem of the motif is a pointer; not right above line 1's central letter, but intentionally between R and A (*cf.* later and similarly, 427 *Catuoconi*, p. 169). We can read: CARAVSIVS / HIC IACIT / IN HOC CON/GERIES LA/PIDVM. This does *not* read *Carausius hic iacit in hoc congeries lapidum*, 'C. here lies in this pile of stones', uninterrupted. 'In this pile of stones' would be *in hac congerie*; a (masc.) noun, probably *tumulus* ('grave') is understood, with *Carausius hic iacit in hoc [tumulo]; congeries lapidum*, 'a pile of stones' being separate and descriptive. Without more ado we meet the composer, whose use of a letter grid and telestich name goes back to Lullingstone, and Avitus's fact-packed mosaic inscription:

```
      c   a   r   u   s   i   V
      s   h   i   c   i   a   c   I
5     t   i   n   h   o   c   c   O
      n   g   e   r   i   e   s   L
      a   p   i   d   u m / c   A = (starting again)
                  8
```

Viola's place in the recital of Insular inscriptional inventiveness is assured because of her extraordinary range of generated images. This text has two key numbers, *seven* and *seventeen* (the latter at once literally pointed out, with the chi-rho foot between R A, 16.1 = 17). The analysis of 393 *Carausius* shows us:

		W	S	LD	LM
1	C A R A V S I V S (ligatured AV)	1	4	8	9
2	H I C I A C I T	2	3	8	8
3	I N H O C C O N		3	8	8
4	G E R I E S L A	4	4	8	8
5	P I D V M		2	5	5
		7	16	37	38

with a semantic division —

(a) Carausius hic iacit in hoc (?)	5	9		22
(b) Congeries lapidum	2	7		16
	7	16		38

There are *seven* words here; part (b) has *seven* syllables; by LNu the text shows I I I I I I I = *seven*; first and last letters overall are C M, 3.11 = *seven* by 2. The name CARAUSIUS adds to 120; *seventeen* by six. Every *seventh* letter (display), V C C E V, makes *seven* squared, 49.

With chi-rho and HIC IACIT this is a patently Christian memorial, but allusive piety goes a step further. Extreme section of 38 (*LM*) letters, taken from 1.7.8.*15.23.38*..., falls either at 15:23 or 23:15, hic ia**C**/it in, hoc **C**/ongeries, both stressing letter C. Why? We find that five line-initials C H I G P (=40), and five last letters, as S T N A M (=59), give 99. But C is also (LNu) 100. Carausius, in death, is the lost sheep saved; sheep no. 100, the sheep that the shepherd, leaving his 99 other, sought when astray and brought rejoicing home (Matthew, 18.12; Luke 15,4 — see the later examination of this, p. 152).

Viola put *hoc* and *congeries* together, giving O C C O, because her first image, a display profile, was quite new and wholly remarkable. The stone is small (about 65cm high), a little upright grave-marker. To claim that '*in hoc congeries lapidum* is more probably a figure of speech than a literal reference to a cairn', apart from misreading the Latin, is nonsense.[14] We can picture here a formal burial below a (shaped?) cairn or stone-heap, part of which

Fig.57   *393* Carausius; *the first display profile in which the stone (the upper chi-rho cross) effectively becomes 'a picture of itself', atop the* congeries *or* cairn *whose pebbles are indicated by the rounded parts and interiors of the letters.*

may have comprised glacial or river-worn large pebbles and small boulders. And the stone's display is *a picture of itself*; the inscribed stone on this cairn (*Fig. 57*). The large chi-rho is the whole, chi-rho-topped, inscribed slab. The five-line block of letters is the cairn. When all those letters with rounding are blacked-in, they become the constituent stones.

The text contains split or diffused anagrams (beyond the opening telestich for Viola's name) and they are now used to make further small images, display profiles, confined to the text. The letters of CARAVSIVS are contained in an outline of the dead man, shown within his burial-mound in a seated position (*Fig. 58*). This is even partially labelled. His head, *caput*; line 1, C A AV V. The body, *corpus*; line 3, C O; and the feet, *pedes*, line 5, P D (*cf.*p. 166 later). Next, the grieving Viola shows herself in the tomb, alongside Carausius (*Fig. 59*). The nature of her attachment is specified. A third diffused word, again using this 'seated person' shape and reading bottom-to-top, appears in *Fig. 60*. The assumed British spoken Latin *privatus*, literally 'belonging to one's self', perhaps the Roman legionaries' word for 'sweetheart, boy-friend' (and of course *privata*, fem.), by this time / priwat, priwad/ in speech, lies behind Middle Welsh *priawt*, Old Cornish *priot*, Welsh *priod* ('a betrothed, a spouse'.) Here, most unexpectedly, the source itself may be attested.

In the text the final letters of the words, S C T N C S M, make 81, a *square*; the display itself has two prospective squares (16 graphs) in C A R <u>AV</u> S I V S H I C I A C I T, C O N G E R I E S L A P I D V M. There is another potential 'grave-plot' devised plan lurking

Fig.58 *395* Carausius; *the second display profile, with the constituent letters of the name discerned in an approximately human outline.*

here (*Fig. 61*), where the inner square — ? area of the actual burial — has 3 letters from the name, R I A (=36, a *square* again) and the 12 letters around it add to 119, product of *seven* and *seventeen*. (Unless this alludes obliquely to 17, 153 and God's Net, was seventeen Carausius's age at death?) Finally, subtracting the core of the epitaph, *Carausius hic iacit*, a 17-letter sentence on its own, from *LM*, 38, the remainder as 21 letters is a triangular, Δ6:

9			I			9
12		N	H			8
13		O	C	C		3
13		O	N	G	E	5
16	R	I	E	S	L	10
1	A	P	I	D	U M	11
64			**(58)**			**46**

Now this looks to be intended, because apicals A I M = *seven* by 3, and sides and base, 64 + 46 + 58 = *seven* by 24 (168). This could generate yet another image, a devised *profile* this time; the pyramid is used as a lateral 'see-through' image of the cairn, ridged, with Carausius again within it (as the pyramid derives from 6, appropriately *six* of the name's 9 letters are employed; Fig. *62*).

The memorial is in every way sub-Roman. *Carausius* was the usurper, would-be

Fig.59 *393 Carausius; Viola's own name , as a kind of irregular telestich, adjoins the outline of dead Carausius.*

Fig.60 *393 Carausius; if the word* PRIVATUS, *reading upwards, denotes the relationship of Carausius to Viola (as 'betrothed' ?), note how most of its letters approximate to the Carausius outline.*

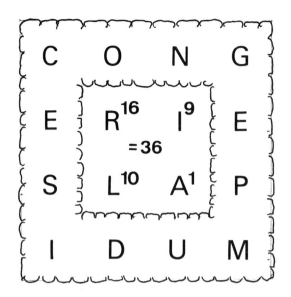

Fig.61 A devised plan *this time, exploiting the fact that the words* CONGERIES LAPIDUM *have 16 letters. It conveys an idea of a ground plan of the burial cairn (real or imagined), with the deceased centrally contained. Internally, three of the four letters occur in his name (c* **A R** *a u s* **I** *u s); all four add, as* R I L A *, 16.9.10.1, to 36, a constant letter-square total. The twelve peripheral letters, as 3.13.12.7.5.14.11 19.4.9.17.5, make 119, product of the two key numbers (7 x 17); we are informed that this validated 'square' is intentional.*

emperor, of the late third century, and Viola (still in use) a rare but recorded cognomen. The capitals are regular, and the form of chi-rho probably first appeared in Britain around 400. If this is slightly earlier than 421 *Rostece* (whose author we do not know), Viola should be credited with drawing on the recent Welsh circulation of simple devised plans but, at the same time, introducing images as profiles. We have four display profiles, a devised plan and a devised profile; six at least. Our author was educated. The text is mainstream; *congeries lapidum*, found only here, may be from Pliny.[15] For *in hoc* ('tomb?') *cf.* Vives 172, *Eustadia…pausavit in hoc tumulo*, and there may even be a slight parallelism as

A	Carausius	**C** (7 letters) **S**
B	hic iacit	i **A** c **I** t
	in hoc	
A'	congeries	**C** (7 letters) **S**
B'	lapidum	l **A** p **I** dum

There is certainly a metrical aspect, as David Howlett has found.[16] It is a great pity that we have almost no information about the context of the grave itself.[17]

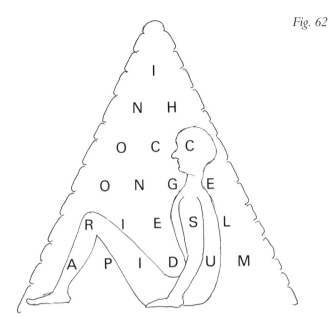

Fig. 62 *393 Carausius; a devised ('see-through') profile, the cairn with Carausius in it. The last 21 letters are triangularised, as from Δ6 (and apicals I A M = 21). Six of the name's 9 letters, **C S U I R A**, hint at the dead man's sitting profile.*

Early Cornwall; a name, an age and more allusive numbers

By the sixth century a native kingdom we know as *Dumnonia* or *Damnonia* in Insular Latin comprised Cornwall, Devon and parts of Somerset. There is no evidence of Roman-period Christianity west of the river Exe. In Cornwall (west of the river Tamar) the Faith was introduced gradually, not before about 500, and then seemingly as an aspect of small-scale settlement entering North Cornwall, with incoming families from south and south-west Wales.[18] The main evidence for this comprises some forty inscribed stones (others, in west and south Devon, imply a spread of these settlements and a native adoption of the memorial-stone custom.) Certain place-name elements offer secondary evidence.

Nevertheless we find an isolated instance of Christianity in west Cornwall, by Hayle, in St Ives Bay, not long before 500. Slight indication that this could have been another arrival from Gaul, like the postulated Capel Anelog and Kirkmadrine sites and memorials, starts with a cut-down fragment of granite with a first type of chi-rho, the rho being the (Gaulish?) open-looped kind, now built into the mother church of Hayle, Phillack (*Fig. 63*) and, nearby, the anomalous *479 Cunaide* stone, unearthed alongside a mounded cist-grave in 1843 just outside the (unexcavated) coastal fortlet at Carnsew, Hayle.[19] The inscription is eroded. The granite pillar, now cemented into a wall, has suffered many indignities, but the text is just legible. Eleven lines of small shallow-cut capitals with ligatures contain the formulaic *Hic…pace requievit* and *Hic in tumulo iacit*, unlikely to have spread from the Continent before about 470. What can be made out (*Fig. 64*) is to be analysed as below:

Fig.63   *Phillack church, now built into gable over south porch, and found in the fabric in the
1860s; small, fine granite stone, probably cut down (in medieval times?) from a larger
memorial, leaving a slightly raised boss and a chi-rho with a definitely 'open' loop
(drawn in situ by Carl Thorpe).*

		W	S	LD	LM
1	H I C P A		2	5	5
2	C E <u>N</u> V P (er) (=nuper)	3	3	3	7
3	R E Q V I E V I T	1	4	9	9
4	C V N A I D E	1	3	7	7
5	H I C I N	2	2	5	5
6	T V <u>M V</u> L O	1	3	5	6
7	I A C I T	1	2	5	5
8	V I X I T	1	2	5	5
9	A N N O S	1	2	5	5
10	X X X (=triginta)	1	3	3	8
11	I I I (=tres)	1	1	3	4
		13	**27**	**55**	**66**

Several letters are damaged or near-totally eroded but as a Biblical-style composition of
some complexity this text is restorable. It falls naturally into three parts:

Fig.64   *479* Cunaide, *Carnsew, Hayle, in west Cornwall (drawn by Carl Thorpe). In line 2, ligatured* NVP *can scarcely be traced now but must be indicated; line 5,* IN *(eroded) is obvious; line 6,* MV *is ligatured; lines 9 and 10,* AN *and* XX *are conjoined, not ligatured. The granite pillar has suffered three transverse breaks since 1843. The seeming 'cross' among the top three lines is natural, a crossing of mineralised veins.*

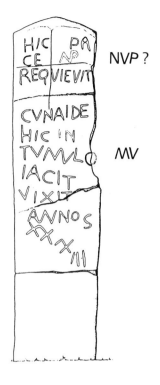

	W	*S*	*LM*
(a) Hic pace nuper requievit Cunaide	5	12	28
(b) Hic in tumulo iacit	4	7	16
(c) Vixit annos triginta tres	4	8	22
	13	**27**	**66**

('Here in pace lately went to rest Cunaide. Here in the tomb she lies; she lived years thirty-three.') We notice that *W* and *S*, putting (a) as the lesser part, (b) plus (c) as the greater, show extreme ratio, 5:8 → 13, and 12:15 → 27 (4:5 → 9, from 1.4.5.9.14…) and that extreme section at CUNAIDE /Hic emphasises the name. Earlier it was shown (p. 88) that parts (a) and (b) contain a parallelism; the whole text is also chiastic —

a	Hic pace nuper	3 words; time general, **I A E N R**
b	requievit	Verb perf.ind., **V I I T**
c	Cunaide	Subject of verb in c'
d	hic	Place, general
d'	in tumulo	Place, specific
c'	iacit	Verb for subject in c
b'	vixit	Verb perf.ind., **V I I T**
a'	annos triginta tres	3 words; time specific, **N R I A E**

— and a good example of this odd 'inscriptional chiasmus'.

The composer was concerned with a computus that validates two things; the *exact* spelling here of the name as CUNAIDE (where a nominative CUNAIDA might have been used)[20] and the reality of the stated age. CUNAIDE, 3.19.12.1.9.4.5 = (LaN) **53**; this is what he proceeded to incorporate. The display contains, as LNu, four X's and thirteen I's or XXXX = 40, plus 13, making *fifty-three*. In the model, totals *W*, 13, *S*, 27 and *LM*, 66, make 106; *fifty-three*, twice. The five initials of the words in (a) above, H P N R C, 8.14.12.16.3 = *fifty-three*. Because LM as 66 is a triangular, $\Delta 11$, triangularisation gives an inverted (not set out) whose sides are 124 and 141; they add to 265, or *fifty-three* times five.

Possibly because the whole text is so plainly in *three* clauses (each a separate sentence), and age 33 = 3 times *11*, the computus otherwise makes great play of key number *eleven*, alone and in numerous multiples. *LD* is 55, *LM* is 66; there are *eleven* lines; part (a) has 28 letters which, when triangularised as $\Delta 7$, give us side-totals of *66* (pyramid) and *77* (inverted), and the sum of the initials of the *eleven* (model) lines is 121, square of *eleven*. An explanation could be that Cunaide was genuinely aged 33 at death; the emphasis is to confirm her age as real, not just an imitative allusion to Christ's earthly years.

The Biblical allusions are conveyed in this pattern:

(a)	8	H	i	C	3
	14	P	a c	E	5
	12	N	u p e	R	16
	16	R	e q u i e v i	T	18
	3 = **53**	C	u n a i d	E	5 = **47**
(b)	8	H	i	C	3
	9	I		N	12
	18	T	u m u l	O	13
	9	I	a c i	T	18
(c)	19	V	i x i	T	18
	1	A	n n o	S	17
	18	T	r i g i n t	A	1
	18 = **100**	T	r e	S	17 = **99**

This is readily interpreted, wholly in terms of the New Testament. *Initials* and *last letters* in (a) total **100**, and mark Cunaide (like Carausius) as a Lost Sheep, saved; that total is affirmed by the *initials* of (b) and (c). The *last letters* of (b) and (c), wording that does not contain her name, mark the **99** Sheep who were not astray, the righteous souls among whom she is now at rest; the total of *all* initials, **153**, takes us to John, 21.11, the Fishes (p. 189) and the Net of God's redeeming Grace. All of this is familiar. It might be difficult to explain the sudden appearance of this quite ornate text, unrelated to anything in the Roman south-west or to any other early Cornish inscription, without appealing to outside inspiration.[21]

One does not have to exclude the first Christian Celts of Cornwall and part of Devon, several of whose sixth-century memorials otherwise exhibit things like angle-bar A, devolved chi-rho motifs, final horizontal I, epitaphic-I, and IOC spellings (458 *Dunocati*,

Bodmin, is a good illustration), from the intellectual character of that much larger Celtic Christian, British, bastion in Wales; but Cornwall's next inscription of real interest, the (1051) Penzance Market Cross (p. 186), belongs to the early eleventh century, a long period ahead. If Cunaide's name is both feminine and Irish, the second feature is probably explicable by this date; but was she an aristocratic convert and, if so, who converted her so early? Was the composer of this isolated memorial a maritime incomer? We have to leave these and other questions. What we do see here is an inscription that must establish a geographical spread of this, the foundation-course of Insular inscriptional style, all the way from Cornwall to Galloway.

Notes to Chapter 6

1   See, in Alexander Woollcott, intro, *The Complete Works of Lewis Carroll* (Nonesuch, London 1939), his Double Acrostic (p. 833) and pt.VII, all his mathematical puzzles and games.
2   Notably the lettered topographical mosaic of the 6th-century basilica, Madaba, Jordan, of the Mediterranean and Levant; Dilke, *Greek and Roman Maps*, 151-3.
3   The best assessment is W.Levitan's 'Dancing at the End of the Rope: Optatian Porfyry and the Field of Roman Verse', *Trans.American Philological Assoc.*, 115 (1985), 245 69; for an amusing revival in the age of Charlemagne see Howlett, *Celtic Latin Tradition*, 213-6.
4   The fullest example is Richard Andrews and Paul Schellenberger, *The Tomb of God* (Little, Brown & Co., 1996), chaps.9 to 12.
5   This is not quite fair to readers; both have recently been found. For the image generating poem, the exquisite Oratio II of Moucan or Maucannus, see D.R.Howlett, *Cambro-Latin Compositions* (Four Courts, Dublin, at pp. 65-6); for the profile of the (90-miles) journey, also later 7th century, my forthcoming *The Land of Brecheniauc; a critical analysis of the Brychan Documents*.
6   If so, 'Good-Hound, Good-Wolf'; the most recent assessment of the episode is R.Geraint Gruffydd, 'From Gododdin to Gwynedd; reflections on the story of Cunedda', *Studia Celtica*, 24/25 (1989-90), 1-14.
7   *LHEB*, 655; medieval *Guenedotia* was formed from the adjectival stem.
8   *DEB*, cap.33.
9   If true, might this have been at Capel Anelog (with Senacus, etc.)? It is only a 20-mile sail from Aberffraw to the Llyn peninsula; sites for new church and monastic foundations (deserted forts or marginal land) were traditionally granted by local kings.
10 Comparative lists are given in my 'The Early Christian Inscriptions of Southern Scotland'; see n.1 to Chap.5.
11 Wade-Evans, *VSBG*, 246-7; these and related sites, conveniently in Frances Lynch, *Gwynedd* (=*A Guide to Ancient & Historic Wales* ser.) (CADW/H.M.S.O., 1995).
12 Actual examples; my *The Early Christian Archaeology of North Britain* (Oxford 1971), 139-45 illus.

13 From **touisacos* 'prince', Welsh *tywysog*, OIr *toísech* ('Taoiseach'). The *B* in ogam *SIBILINI* represents /ṽ/, lenited m, in *Similini*.

14 RCAMW *Caernarvonshire Inventory*, vol.III, at p.cxiii.

15 Nat.Hist., 18,31.74; the Vulgate, OT, uses *acervus* 'heap, body of' (Joshua, 7.26 *acervum magnum lapidum*, 2 Samuel 18.17 *acervum lapidum magnum*). Viola's source was almost certainly secular.

16 For this and other Welsh inscriptions as metrical productions, see his *Cambro-Latin Compositions*. Viola's text, he finds, scans perfectly (a.a.b.a.a.b, a dactylic hexameter) when syllabic feet are re-sorted *backward* (um lapid/es geri/con hoc/, etc.). It could be noted that this anticipates the subsequent backward readings of the texts, indicated by *rursus-retrorsum* split anagrams. We seem to have just about everything except an absolute date; one hesitates to suggest, from the text by LNu, re-arranging letters CCCCC L VVV to give 565 (later than suggested, but not impossible).

17 Dr Nancy Edwards, Bangor, kindly tells me the stone may have been found a mile or so outside Penmachno itself.

18 For the detailed background to sub- and post-Roman Dumnonia and its earliest Christianity, not repeated here, see my *Mute Stones*, chaps.12 to 18.

19 *Mute Stones,* chap.12, maps and all background details.

20 *LHEB*, 188, 329 n.l; the belief is that the fem. version of an Irish **Cunaedo* (not recorded) might appear as *Cunaeda* (nom.), of which a Latinised genitive (*-ae*, from *-a*) could be written *-e*. However here the name is plainly nominative and one can only think that its contemporary written form was agreed as CVNAIDE.

21 Note that *requievit* (perfect) is much rarer than (Gaulish) forms of *requiescet, -cit, quiescet, -cit* (present); but Vives records for Spain about 20 instances of *requievit* (*in pace*). Citation of age (as for 421 *Rostece*) is virtually absent on British memorials, but usual on the Continent. A north Spanish incoming or returning cleric does not have to be ruled out.

7 Culminations in Wales

For this we remain in Wales, looking at three inscriptions whose likely dates fall between 640 and 740. They are from Anglesey; the inland basin of the upper Wye; and Caldey, off the Pembrokeshire coast. What they show is the fullest development of inscriptional style, drawing upon everything we have already found back to Roman times, but now including purely Insular novelties and elaborations. All three appear to name native kings (for different reasons!). The texts are ostensibly Christian Latin and each stone is ornamented with at least one incised cross. We shall see they hold allusions to the Vulgate and to secular sources; that their computistic elements range from simple acrostics to an advanced use of non-Fibonacci numbers; and they all conclude with reversed precession-and-interval readings, signposted by split anagrams of *rursus* and/or *retrorsum*, revealing their composer's names (and, in one case, status as well). Two generate mental images, display and devised, and these are accompanied by schemes of *labelling* somewhat like the scheme in 520 *Latinus*. Our survey begins with the earliest, 986 *Ioruert Ruallaunque*. Again, it happens that all three stones seem to be overtly or implicitly linked to larger (Christian) archaeological monuments of one sort or another, but 986 is probably the only one for which the monument — an exterior tomb, partly surviving today — could actually be reconstructed on paper.

Silent in the shroud; a kinsman's tribute?

When in the 1690s the antiquary Edward Lhuyd enquired about the church of Llanlleonfel or (better) Llanllywenfel, then in a poor state and largely rebuilt in 1870, he was told of a massive inscribed slab. It was standing upright in this once sub-circular churchyard, just east of the church, and 'had another stone 8 feet off opposite to it'. Of these two stones, one is still there, and at the right distance from it is a second slab. It is hard to tell which is which, but one of those now visible is apparently a replacement for the inscribed stone, which about 1939 was moved into the church and clamped near the inner south wall. On its reverse face are traces of three (pocked) ring crosses, like that on 358 *Voteporigis* (*Fig. 78*). They must suggest that the stone first stood the other way up, and may mark Llanllywenfel as the site of a Christian burial-ground a century or so earlier than the inscription.

The memorial (*Fig. 65*) shows five lines of text in letters that combine a few capitals and a tall stilted bookhand, giving an impression of a composer's idiosyncratic model, accurately reproduced by a skilled mason-cutter. There is a central, higher-than-line,

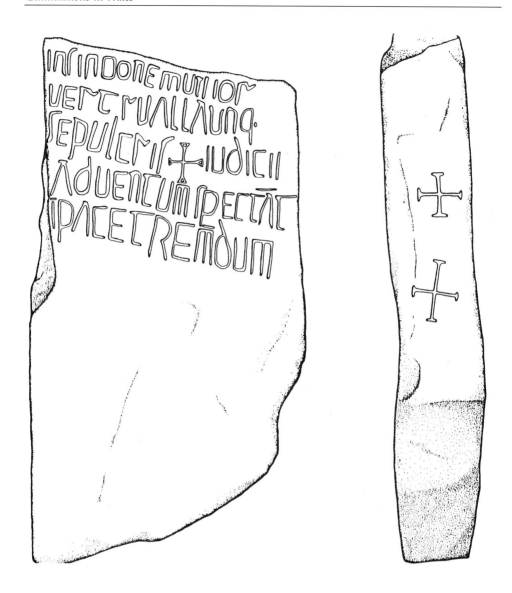

Fig.65   986 Ioruert (Ruallaunque), *now in Llanlleonfel church; heavy slab 62in (1.57m) high. The inscription, drawn* in situ *and from many detailed photographs; right, the thicker edge, showing two pocked crosses (there may have been a third at the top).*

expanded-terminals cross (and two, if not three, smaller barred-terminals crosses on the upper part of the thin right side of the slab, as one looks at it). The display revives that use of overlining for abbreviations, widespread in Insular MSS, that we found in 391 *Senacus*, 516 *Viventius*; and *que* 'and' is curtailed to Q followed by a dot(?).[1] What can be read is this: IN SINDONE MUTI IOR/UERT RUALLAUNQ(ue) / SEPULCRIS + IUDICII / ADVENTUM SPECTĀT (=spectant) / Ī(=in) PACE TREM̄DUM (tremendum). 'In

156

the shroud, silent — Ioruert and Ruallaun, in the graves, await in peace the dreadful coming of the Judgement.'

Because we are here concerned with this unique, majestic and in its way beautiful memorial I give no more than historical conclusions that must be explained fully elsewhere. It marks the open-air double tomb, a large slab construction above ground and above a double burial, of Riuallaun or Riuallon, a king of *Brecheniauc* (Brycheiniog) in the seventh century, and his son Ioruerth. We are in border country, the broken valley-system of the Irfon running into the upper Wye, probably between Brecheniauc and Demetia (Dyfed); one guesses that the two fell in some battle and were interred and commemorated *in situ*. The composer, who names himself, may have been a priest if not court bishop for this royal line and quite possibly of the same family. Ioruerth does not figure in later genealogies; Riuallaun does,[2] and when on his death his daughter Keindrech, 'Fair-of-face', was married to the son of the Demetian king, Brecheniauc became and remained a subordinate smaller kingdom under the shadow of Demetia. On this interpretation, 986 was composed in approximately 640 x 660.

The inscription has twelve words — *six* and *six*, around its central cross — and the abbreviations are there to reduce a model 78 letters (78 is the triangular from twelve) to 72, twelve by *six*. That is our opening into a computus whose key elements are *six, five*, and the concept of a *square*. Twelve words around one Cross symbolise, first and foremost, Christ and His Disciples. On my sixth or seventh visit to this stone the lectern Bible lay open at Matthew, chap.10; I have given up wondering why, though the late M.R.James would not have hesitated to offer a reason. Reading the Disciples' names as that Gospel lists them, and trying to remember how Jerome gave them in the Vulgate, I glanced at the slab (which stands right beside the lectern) and saw the obvious:

The stone		*(Vulgate, Matthew 10)*
I N	2	I o h a N n e s (son of Zebedee)
S I n d O N E	5	S I m O N . . p E t r u s ('Peter')
M U T I	4	M a T t h e U s p u b l I c a n u s
S E p U l C r I S	6	S I m o n C a n a n E U S
I U D I C I I	6	I U D a s I s C a r I o t e s
A D v E N t u m	4	A N D r E a s
S p E C t A n t	4	i A C o b u S a l p h E i
I n	1	I a c o b u s (son of Zebedee)
P a c e	1	P h i l i p p u s
T r e M e n D U M	5	T h o M a s D i d y M U s
i O R U E r T	5	b a R T h O l o m E U s
r u A L L a U n q u e	2	t h A D D E U s
	46	

Not counting that enforced doubled-letters match, ruaLLaun, thaDDeus, the text's words now comprise 76 letters, 46 of which (60 percent) appear in the names mostly in the right sequences — and see how Judas Iscariot is paired with 'the Judgement', *iudicii*. If this is a literary, allusive, starting-point we can postpone *arithmetica* and find, first, that the whole memorial constitutes a proper double hexameter, two lines of six feet each, as shown by

David Howlett. Next, it also constitutes a piece of inscriptional chiasmus:

a	IN SINDONE MUTI	3 words, In + 'silent'	**D NE MU**
b	IORUERT RUALLAUNQUE	2 words, subj. of b'	**U E T A N E**
c	SEPULCRIS	1 word, 'graves'	**U C I**
c'	IUDICII	1 word, 'judgement'	**U C I**
b'	ADVENTUM SPECTANT	2 words, verb for b	**E T U E A N**
a'	IN PACE TREMENDUM	3 words, In + 'peace'	**END UM**

Third, leaving the five-lines display, the words can be re-arranged like this (a textual quartering, 12 as 3.3.3.3) and we can start to apply (20-letter) LaN configurations.

I	n sindone mut	I	13 letters	I as /i/
I	oruert Ruallaunque sepulcri	S	27	I as /y/
I	udicii adventum spectan	T	23	I as /y/
I	n pace tremendu	M	15	I as /i/
=36		=55	=78	

The quartering was meant to be noticed (and it will prove to have another aspect; p. 179). Already we saw *LM*, 78, as a triangular; here are two more, 55 as $\Delta 10$ and 36 as $\Delta 8$ — the special '36' *also* there as the *square* of 6, and the product of the *square* of 2 and the *square* of 3.

Fourth, the text is Biblically allusive; it continues with Matthew, to so many of Jerome's admirers, new and apparently old, one of his stylistic masterpieces. Given the combination of Christ and the 12 Disciples, the Cross, and a joint burial *in sepulcris*, one might expect it to refer to the death on the Cross and its aftermath. In Matthew, 27.59, Joseph of Arimathia wraps the body of Christ in a clean winding-sheet or cloth; **IN**volvit Illud **SINDONE MU**nda. The text's IN SINDONE MUTI picks this up, and the last six words seem to paraphrase things like 2 Peter, 3.12, *exspectantes…in adventum*, and Hebrews, 10.27, *terribilis expectatio Iudicii*. But the text of 986 remains primarily one man's original composition.

Lastly, given the scope of 78 letters there are various inner readings as anagrams — they include Divine Names; DEUS, IESUS, and DNE (=DomiNE 'O, Lord') — but we must notice one in particular, a validated split anagram. Its placing is supported by the favoured convention 5.7.12.19.31.50…, initially suggested anyhow by 5 and 12 in the display. It comes in the first *five* words with *twelve* syllables, as a span of *nineteen* letters in a total of *thirty-one*; and it reads

in / **S** ind **O** n **EMUT** i io **R** ue **R** t **R** / uallaunque = S O EMUT R R R
2   19   10   (=12 +19 = 31)

supplying **retrorsum**, 'backward', which is needed subsequently.

The computus, the total *arithmetica*, is so elaborate and has so extended an array of virtually every known device that it would swamp this chapter to set it out in full. There are constant appearances of squares, especially 36, and constant pointers to triangularisation. The 78-letter model, as $\Delta 12$, gives in its inverted-triangle form the usual side-totals of 144 (the Heavenly City). What we need to carry forward is key number *five*, *retrorsum* and certain extreme-ratio sets to find the composer's name; and the *square*, notably as 36 made up I I I I, 9.9.9.9, to generate the culminating mental image.

The author was *Elri*. This is not recorded as an Archaic Old Welsh name, but it would comprise *el*-'much, many' plus *-ri* (*<rigi*) 'king', both widely used in name-compounds.[3] He seems to have included his name four times, twice forward, twice *retrorsum*. Here is one of the reversed inclusions, for which we write out the first *five* words in reverse, divide 31 by extreme ratio as 19:12, and use precession-and-interval with key number *five* as a *regular* interval:

$$
\begin{array}{ccccccc}
& 5 & & 5 & & 5 & \\
\textbf{E} & \text{uqnua} & \textbf{L} & \text{laurt} & \textbf{R} & \text{euroi} & \textbf{I} \; / \; \text{tum enodnis ni} \qquad = \textbf{ELRI} \\
& & & 19 & & & 12 \qquad\qquad\qquad (= 31)
\end{array}
$$

It is also 'buried' in the word SEPULCRIS, using extreme ratio from the set 1.*4*.*5*.*9*.14…, like this:

$$
\text{s}\,\textbf{E}\,\text{p}\,\text{u}\,\textbf{L}\,\text{c}\,\textbf{R}\,\textbf{I}\,\text{s} = \text{spucs}\;(5) + \textbf{ELRI}\;(4),\; 5{:}4 \rightarrow 9
$$

— and, involving what he probably would have regarded as two other symbolic numbers, *three* (Triune God), and *seventeen* (ADAM, 1.4.1.11; and basis of Δ17, 153, God's Net) in the set (x 3) 1.8.9.17.26.43, there is a forward reading contained in the text as a whole. The intervals as key number *five* and the Christ-and-Disciples *thirteen* hardly rank as arbitrary:

in sindone muti Ior		17
E rtrua **L** launquesepulc **R** isiud **I** = ELRI		27, span
5 13 5		
cii adventum spectant in pace tremendum		<u>34</u> __
		51 **27** = **78**

— where 27:51 → 78 is of course 1.8.*9*.*17*.26.43…, times three.

The sepulchre revealed

In Jerome's version of the Matthew story of the burial of Jesus, the rock-cut Jewish tomb of square or rectangular internal shape, its entrance to be closed by a large discoidal slab (*saxum*) rolling in a groove, is called a *monumentum*. But the internal niche where the body was laid, probably one of several, is *sepulchrum*. Elri had his reasons why the combined, two-in-one, grave and tomb superstructure for Riuallaun and Iouerth was not *in sepulc(h)ro*, singular, but as *sepulcris*, plural. Look now at a further presentation of our stone, *Fig. 66*, in which the five lines occupy a rhomboidal space, a tilted square of sorts, and within which the central Cross *is* Jesus. Do we have here an introductory image, a *display plan*; in fact, is this another schematic ground-plan in the idiom of a funerary-shrine, Solomon's Temple, the Holy City, those early Welsh grave-plots, but this time of the very Tomb of Christ? Is the middle line 3 the interior where Christ lay? Consider the wording. Initial S blocks the entrance (Matthew, 27.60, *advolvit* **S***axum magnum ad ostium* 'he rolled the great stone at the entrance'). Consider the hard-worked SEPULCRIS, now as (4:5 → 9)

Fig.66   986 Ioruert. *Immediate image as a simplified display plan, irregular outline of the Holy Sepulchre (*monumentum*) with interior (*sepulchrum*), closed by a large stone (*saxum: the 'S' of line 3). Within the interior, the Cross is Christ's Body.*

S E p U l c r I S, with **SEUIS** = IESUS by anagram.

When we followed Elri's hint to quarter the text, its first and third quarters encapsulate the sense of his memorial — Silent in the shroud, they await the coming of the Judgement — and they have (13 + 23) 36 letters. Set out as a square, thus,

I	N	S	I	N	D
O	N	E	M	U	T
I	I	U	D	I	C
I	I	A	D	V	E
N	T	U	M	S	P
E	C	T	A	N	T

suddenly it has become rather *special*. This square of perfect 6 uses perfect-6 words. Its corners I D E T, 9.4.5.18, also make 36; so does that left-central block I I I I (= 9.9.9.9) and, reading those letters as LNu, IIII = *quatuor*, we get 'four', the square.

This would go somewhat beyond my recognition, *in situ*, of the twelve words as twelve names; but in theory a reader as clever as the composer and trained in the same way might muse at length in front of the slab, discern the quartering, pick out lines 1 and 3, add the letters and thereby perceive Elri's eventual goal. In practice I do not think this happened. There is a point beyond which only a *written* exploration can give the full result, and we have probably reached it. To assert as much, we take into account the likelihood that Elri, and then others, pointed out the details to selected viewers; and another likelihood, that far more people than we may have supposed habitually walked around carrying writing-materials (p. 183).

Fig. 67 expands the chosen letters into the full image (a devised plan), to which most of the computus clues are directed. It is the Holy Sepulchre, from Matthew's account.

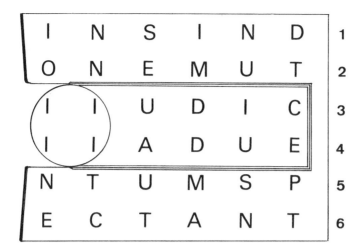

I	N	S	I	N	D	1
O	N	E	M	U	T	2
I	I	U	D	I	C	3
I	I	A	D	U	E	4
N	T	U	M	S	P	5
E	C	T	A	N	T	6

Fig.67   *986 Ioruert. Elri's annotated* devised plan *of the Holy Sepulchre, containing the bodies of Christ, Ioruert and Ruallaun; produced (as directed) by a 36-letter square from IN SINDONE MUTI.IUDICII ADVENTUM SPECTANT. The corners I D E T, 9.4.5.18, also = 36. The blocking-stone of four I's (I,9 = 36) repeats the square. In the upper and lower parts, over 70 percent of the relevant words from Matthew, 27 & 28, are contained as part-anagrams. Within the tomb, the same system tells readers what the chamber contains.*

Within a *monumentum* is a *sepulchrum*, containing the body of Our Lord *and* those of the two men. The entrance-blocking stone (I I I I) is there because neither the Resurrection nor Last Judgement has taken place. And this unprecedented elevation in death of Ruallaun and Ioruert has been preluded by matching their names with those of Thaddeus and of Bartholomeus, two of the lesser Disciples. The image is labelled, remarkably so, by part-words throughout. In lines 1 and 2 we have (Matthew 27.60) *Ioseph…posuit…in monumento suo novo*, ' Joseph placed (Christ's body) in his new tomb-chamber'. Here are the letters of lines 1 and 2 in the image:

I N S I N D
O N E M U T

and here the part-readings as labelling, with the letters in common:

I	.	S	.	.	.	
O	.	E	.	.	.	Ioseph (4)
I	.	S	.	.	.	
O	.	.	.	U	T	posuit (5)
I	N	.	I	N	.	
.	.	.	.	.	.	in(2)

.	N	.	.	.	.	
O	N	E	M	U	T	monumento (7)
.	.	S	.	.	.	
O	.	.	.	U	.	suo (3)
.	N	.	.	.	.	
O	.	.	.	U	.	nouo/novo (3)

In lines 5 and 6, we move into the start of Matthew 28, with the words (post tres dies) *resurgam* 'after three days I shall arise' *sepulchrum, angelus* (Domini), the angel in the Tomb and, of Joseph's making his tomb, (exciderat in) *petra* 'he had cut it out of the rock'. The two lines give us the letters:

N T U M S P

E C T A N T

.	.	U	M	S	.				.	T	.	.	.	P	
E	.	.	A	.	.	resurgam (5)			E	.	.	A	.	.	petra (4)
.	.	U	M	S	P										
E	.	.	.	.	.	sepulchrum (5)			—and the closing word						
N	.	.	.	S	.				N	.	.	M	.	.	
E	.	.	A	.	.	angelus (4)			E	.	.	A	.	.	amen (4)

In the earlier twelve words, twelve names, the coincidence of letters was 60 per cent; more than sufficient to dispel any idea that the words were not chosen to match. Here, in the top two and bottom two lines, we have eleven Vulgate words using 64 letters, of which 46 (=72 per cent) occur in the textual setting. We are left with lines 3 and 4, which read

I I   U D I C

(=stone)

I I   A D U E

On the right, the four corners (U C A E, 19.3.1.5) make 28; as in 350 *Idnert*, a (perfect) attribute of God, or the Body of Christ? The *D I C* suggests *Dominus Iesus Christus*; *D C*, or *D D C*, *deposita corpora* 'the bodies placed within' and, given the tenor of the memorial, U A and U E must represent r)**UA**(llaun, ior)**UE**(rt.

The devised-plan image is spatially not very complicated; its impact is in the labelling, which harks back two centuries to the precedent of 520 *Latinus*, Whithorn — LATINUS/**LATItU**di**NiS**, FECERUNT/**ChERUbiN** are much the same as MONUMENTO/i**N**sind**ONEMUT**, POSUIT/**InSindOnemUT**, indeed rather less anagrammatic — and serves to bind specific words from a Vulgate passage to a generated image of its subject. Those who go to forlorn little Llanllywenfel, up the track across sheep-pastures, passing the remains of the royal tomb-structure[4] as they reach the church's south door, can gaze on Elri's composition; a seventh-century manuscript so fortunately frozen on stone, and in a most powerful sense a page of early British history. If it can now be read, unravelled, understood and admired, that is wholly because its composition in full Biblical style was perfected to guarantee an understanding of it; at any future time, and so long as the lettering persists.

The House of Gwynedd slighted

The fourth king of Gwynedd after *Mailcun*, Maelgwn (who, *per* Gildas, had been reigning for at least a decade before 540) is named in later genealogies as *Catman*,[5] Cadfan (in correct IOC spelling CATUMAN(N)US < *Catu-mandos*), and is represented as the mighty Maelgwn's great-great-grandson. Cadfan appears to have died around 625. In the parish church of Llangadwaladr, Anglesey, built into a wall there is a slab incised with an

Fig. 68   Catamanus; *Llangadwaladr church, Anglesey; drawing from ECMW, modified slightly from photographs, by permission of the National Museum of Wales.*

ornate cross, heading four-and-a-bit lines of unevenly-sized letters, almost all recognisable as an Insular book hand (half-uncial). The slab is now 1.2m long and some 50cm wide. We cannot by the nature of things know this, but I suggest it may have been secondarily trimmed, was originally longer, and may have lain flat over a grave. It commemorates CATAMANUS REX, king Cadfan (*Fig. 68*). The Cadwaladr of the place-name (OW *lann* 'Christian location, cemetery with church, church'[6] — the word meant many things through time) has been identified as Cadfan's grandson, whose death is recorded in 682. If the first consecrated burial-plot or church here was the work of Cadwaladr, the place could have been named for him as donor (or, additionally, from his own burial, though no inscription has survived). But a proposed date of *c.*660-680 would imply that his grandfather Cadfan was formally re-buried at the time, a new slab being then commissioned. That is indeed proposed. The question will arise as to whether the memorial was quite what the Venedotian ruling family had in mind.

The six-word text is arranged, it would seem unnecessarily splitting three words, as CATAMANUS / REX SAPIENTISI/MUS OPINATISIM/US OMNIUM REG/UM; 'Catamanus, king — wisest, most renowned, of all kings'. In a Latin epitaph, *opinatus* is unusual, but perhaps from the Vulgate (Judith, 2.13). Both superlatives are as *-isimus*, not *-issimus*. Given the instances of (Anglesey) 325 SANCTISSIMA, AMATISSIMA, (Carmarthen) 360 PIENTISIMUS, (Scotland) 515 INSIGNISIMI this may be the composer's choice from alternative Insular spellings. Short as it is, the text seems to show an (inscriptional) chiasmus:

a	CATAMANUS REX	2 words, 'king'	**M NU REX**
b	SAPIENTISIMUS	superlative:	**PI NTISIMUS**
b'	OPINATISIMUS	superlative:	**PIN TISIMUS**
a'	OMNIUM REGUM	2 words 'of kings'	**MN U REG**

Do we have any initial indication of a computus? From *four* chiastic terms, *nine* letters in the name, *thirteen* in the longest word, *twenty-two* syllables, the convention

4.9.13.22.35.57.92... might be borne in mind. But — and this is where doubt creeps in — is the whole statement not excessive? Cadfan cannot have been as renowned as his own son Cadwallon[7] who, joining forces with Penda of Mercia, slew king Edwin of Northumbria and ravaged his lands; nor, surely, as famous as his great ancestor Maelgwn. Elsewhere we find *sapientissimus* used for King Solomon or reserved accurately to reflect contemporary assessment of Gildas as a towering intellectual and sage. *Omnium regum* is not Biblical. It is an inverted borrowing from *DEB* cap.33, where Gildas catalogues the sins of his *Maglocune* and, most inappropriately borrowed, *regum omnium (regi)* there refers to God. 970 *Catamanus* taken at face-value has been described thus, by Nash-Williams in *ECMW* (p.57); 'The magniloquent phraseology of the inscriptions plainly echoes the formal language of the imperial Byzantine court', and others have repeated this (e.g., 'reflects the far-flung European contacts, the ambition, and indeed the standards of elegance and learning, at the court of Gwynedd in the 7th century').

We must examine the display very closely. The various A's are strange, not the conventional half-uncial A, and in lines 3/4 the 'A' of OPINATISIMUS has been cut as twice line-height and straddles both lines, as if it had some separate function. In line 2, 'EX' of REX is not ligatured, or conjoined. The bar of E has become a fifth limb of X, which itself is now almost humanoid (and, one has to say, looks for all the world as if it is engaged in penetrating the cringing 'E'). There is a second Anglesey inscription, *ECMW* 35 (not in *CIIC*) from somewhere near Llangadwaladr, now in Llangaffo church, unfortunately defective but interestingly-worded — ERE/XIT / HUNC / LAPI/DEM 'put up this stone' — which shows some quite similar letters, but its solitary 'A' is line-height and the 'X' is more normal.

Given that there are 48 letters, a good many grids could arise; 16 by 3, 12 by 4 (or 4 by 12), 6 by 8, 8 by 6. As there are also *four* chiastic terms, and as it looks as if the inscription (*Fig. 68*) could (given the available surface-space) have been set out in *four* rows, not as four with the stub -UM, we may try a disposition using *four* lines of 12 letters each:

C	A	T	A	M	A	N	U	S	R	E	X
S	A	P	I	E	N	T	I	S	I	M	U
S	O	P	I	N	A	T	I	S	I	M	U
S	O	M	N	I	U	M	R	E	G	U	M

It cannot be accidental that, counting all the vertical pairs of letters, triple columns of S S S (twice) and a diagonal row of N N N N, over half the letters now stand in spatial relationships — 30 out of 48, leaving 18, in fact an extreme-ratio division ($30:18 \rightarrow 48$, or $5:3 \rightarrow 8$). Suppose we link them graphically, drawing little frames around those involved: And now, turning the page to put the right margin at the bottom and half-closing the eyes,

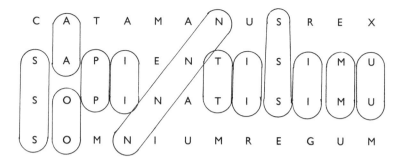

one may discern a kind of Lego-man outline; of a person with a clustering of SSS OO AA at the top or 'head', and then NNNN as a diagonal that could be an outstretched arm — and, as horrid realisation dawns, a bar of S S S that might very well represent an erect male organ. What can be happening? Is it thinkable that on this fine Cross-headed grandiloquent memorial, for a Christian monarch re-interred in his royal grandson's church or *memoria*, the wording is a cryptic joke, a spoof? Was Cadfan not, like king Solomon in 1 Kings, 4.31, *sapientior cunctis hominibus* 'wiser than all other men'? Or can there be a sly allusion to another Salomonic aspect, the King who (11.1) *amavit mulieres alienigenas multas* 'loved many foreign women'? Has an author dared to generate in one step a devised profile portraying the long-dead Cadfan as sexually aroused?

As a lone instance one might dismiss the whole idea, though the grid shows no acrostics nor relevant LaN or LNu totals. However we have this extravagant wording which might be intended ironically and, with its side-allusion to Maelgwn and his shortcomings, unkindly. We shall also discover in *Fig. 70* a pointed little display-profile image and then two wholly-relevant anagrams. Last, the 'Lego-man' picture is more than implied by drawing around linked letters in the 12-by-4 grid. It is *labelled*. At Llangadwaladr we are in the north-west of Wales, in Gwynedd, and there are earlier instances of low-key corporeal or 'body-part' labelling from the same region.

In Viola's display profile of Carausius entombed, seated, in his *congeries* (*Fig. 58*) it appeared that the letters CAU, CO and PD would correspond to, would suitably label, Carausius's *caput, corpus* and *pedes*; his head, body and feet. Something very similar occurs in another early sixth-century Gwynedd inscription, 420 *Porius* from Trawsfynydd (= *ECMW* no.289, correct reading) shown in *Fig.69*. Its 8-word, 36-letter (*LM*) text has a limited computus, but the interest is that this granite slab may unusually have been meant to stand, to be planted upright in, a grave-mound on its longer E-W axis (and thus to be read or viewed standing on the N side of the grave). As the illustration shows, P(oriu)S points left (E) to his *pedes*, feet, where the two H's each with *five* components depict his toes; we can find all of CAPUT 'head' within *Porius/iacit*, and most of CORPUS 'body' in the bottom line. This is by no means as accomplished a production as Viola's for her departed sweetheart, but it may be of much the same date (and the two stones, 393 and 420, are only some 10 miles apart) and represent the first stage of the display-profile innovation that involves human figures.

Now, moving on in time at least a century and a half, we can re-examine the *Catamanus* grid column by column starting on the left. We are expected to guess the relevant Latin

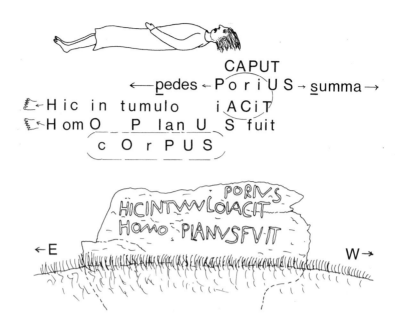

Fig.69 420 Porius *(redrawn from Macalister), seen from N on the assumption that this granite slab stood on the E-W axis of his grave. P(oriu)S points to his* pedes *'feet' and* summa *'top(of head)',* PoriUsiACiT *is an anagram of* caput *'head',* OPlanUS *labels his* corpus *'body' and the two five-component H's represent the ten toes. This tentative interpretation might be called a preliminary (and partly labelled) display-profile image.*

nouns of which the grouped letters might be initials. The first two columns are the head area — C for *caput* (or *crines* 'hairs'?), S S S *summae* (*partes*) 'the top portions', A A *aures* 'ears' and O O (cut like two small eyes in the inscription) *oculi* (eyes). The throat-neck area, P P, could for want of more suitable letters stand for *palatum* 'palate' and I I, next along, *iugula* 'collar-bones'. As the diagonal arm, N N N N suggests *nexus* 'a grasping, entwining', as when a priapic king grasps a submissive woman, and the topmost N forms part of *maNu* 'in or by the hand' Next, T T would be *thorax* 'chest', a loanword from Greek and I I, obviously, *intestina* 'the guts, stomach' appropriately surmounted by the single U for *umbilicus* 'the navel'. The other I I, col. 10, with G below, could stand for *inguen* 'the groin'; then M M, with U below, must surely be *membra ulteriora* 'the nether limbs, the legs'. The final U U, matching the opening S S S (*summae*), is for *ultimae* (*partes*) 'the last or lowest portions = feet, toes'. That leaves col.9, the pillar of S S S, with E below; we are obliged to propose *sexuale* (*membrum*) 'the sexual organ' with the E to draw attention to its *erectum* condition. Any reader is of course free to think up a completely different suite of Latin words, but it would have to comply with this consistent head-to-toe ordering and relate to the preliminary depiction.

Because the letters in the grid, letters that must at the same time constitute the words

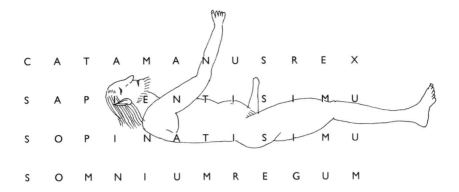

C A T A M A N U S R E X

S A P E N T I S I M U

S O P I N A T I S I M U

S O M N I U M R E G U M

of the memorial, are evenly spaced we cannot impose a complete, correctly-proportioned picture of dead Cadfan on them. But borrowing a recumbent male nude from, appropriately enough, Eric Gill's engravings, one probably can give an idea of what anyone who scratched out the grid, and (as I myself did) burst out laughing when the penny dropped, would generate as a purely mental image.

When the large 'A' spanning lines 3 and 4 is plucked out and tilted about 80 degrees left, pairing it with 'A' of sApientisimus, we have the ears of a face-on donkey (*Fig. 70*), enclosing the central letters of as)**INU**(S 'ass'. Was Cadfan also stupid and rich like the ass-eared king Midas? His epithet OPINATISIMUS offers one anagram, OPTIMUS ASINI 'the best(?) of an ass', a masc.noun like *ornatus* 'embellishment' being understood (no prizes are offered for guessing *which* feature is meant!) and SAPIENTISIMUS could be IPSE ASINUS T I M 'Himself, the ass — TIM' where T I M, 18.9.11 = 38, *triginta octo* provides the identity because the LaN total is the converse of CATAMANUS = 83, *octoginta tres*.

These convoluted insults from four different angles — a devised and labelled profile, minor display profiles, anagrams and literary allusions — imply a composer who knew descriptive Latin, the Vulgate, the DEB of Gildas and Ovid's *Metamorphoses,* xi (the Midas story). Why he chose to perpetrate this, why he judged that he could get away with it — and because this stone was never defaced we can assume that his joke remained undetected, at least by Cadfan's descendants — remain unanswerable questions. Another reasonable assumption would be that Cadfan's private life was remembered as open to censure in much the same way as his ancestor's from what Gildas writes about Maelgwn.[9] Who was the author? The set 4.9.13.22.35 tells us. Omitting CATAMANUS REX as inapposite to contain the reading, those numbers may be used, not as intervals, but as *indicators*:

sap **I** enti **S** imu **S** opinatis **I** mus omnium reg **U** (m = **I S S I U**
       4   9   13   22   35

Additionally, there is a split *rursus* anagram within the wording:

catamanus / **R** ex sapientisim **US** opinatisim **US** omnium **R** / egum = 48
         9   (13)   35   4

R US US R = RURSUS, and the 4 letters after, 9 before (=13), and span of 35 provide validation from *4.9.13.22.35.57…*, as expected. Reversing the text, precession-and-interval

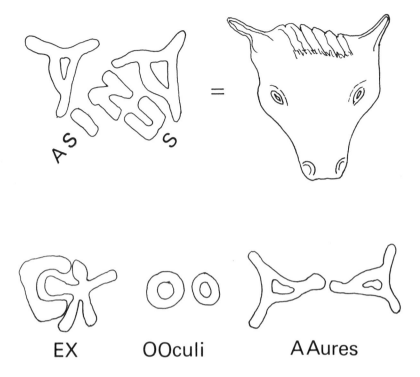

EX   OOculi   A Aures

Fig.70   970 Catamanus *; selected features from the inscription that can be classed as little display profiles. Above, how two large A's with (as)INU(s) between them suggest an ass's head and ears, face on. Below, suggestive 'EX' of REX, two little round eyes and two more ears.*

using an arbitrary *seven* — probably signalled,[10] but we can leave that — gives:

mugermu **I** nmosumi **S** itanipo **S** umisitne **I** pasxers **U** namatac = **ISSIU**

    7   7   7   8   7   7

Because 48 letters, minus 5 (ISSIU), is *43*, not 42, one interval is irregularly 8, not 7; as however the same name is delivered it could be accepted.

Old Welsh *Issiu* occurs as the patronal name of the little Merthir Issiu church (twelfth century; now 'Partrishow(e), Patrishow') in south-east Brecon.[11] The bearer of the same name in seventh-century Anglesey has left us a quite extraordinary composition; no record of him otherwise survives. In proposing the interpretation above I have left out some minor items — for instance, in a square of the last 36 letters, col.4 with I I I I, rooted in letters N I E G U, for *ingue(n)* 'groin' again?, might be taken as a devised profile, but endways-on, image of the erect monarch. What we have already is difficult enough to accept; but the display details, labelling, grid, extreme-ratio set, *rursus* and other anagrams, and precession-and-interval readings should not exclude 970 *Catamanus* from the company of seventh-century memorials in full inscriptional style.

A missing mausoleum

Caldey, Ynyr Bŷr ('Piro's Isle') is a 500-acre isle lying off Tenby and easily reached by boat. It now has some woodland, a Cistercian community and, by the farm-buildings, a ruined medieval priory. By 500 the island may have been held by Irish-descended settlers, one being commemorated on a slab with ogam *MAGL[I] DUBAR…[MA]QI INB* (?defective), a stone that may mark an ancient burial-ground at the Priory. The same slab, called from its later use 427 *Catuoconi*, was reportedly dug up here. In the early sixth century Caldey held a small monastery, under abbot Piro, probably an offshoot of Illtud's superior foundation along the coast at Llanilltud.[12] On this stone (*Fig.71*) an eight-line inscription surmounted by a cross, whose foot touches letter 'N', reads (cross)/ET SINGNO CR/UCIS IN ILLAM / FINGSI ROGO / OMNIBUS AM/MULANTIBUS / IBI EXORENT / PRO ANIMAE / CATUOCONI. Despite ligatured AE, ANIMA and E are separate. This means 'And by '(or with)' the sign of the Cross I have devised on that (?), I ask to all those walking-about there, that they pray for the soul out-of-Catuoconus (or from-within of-Catuoconus)'. The words *illam* 'that' (fem.) and *ibi* 'there' make it clear the message refers to another cross, carved or shaped, at or on(?) some *cella*, *memoria*, even *ecclesia* (all fem.); at a guess, a private burial-place or mausoleum. Prayers are asked, in advance, for the souls of those to be buried there, starting with CATUOCONI (IOC: CATUUOCONUS, nom.?), whom we might identify as the king of Dyfed, from genealogies a man born in the late seventh century, the date here being early eighth — *Catuocaun, Catgocaun/kad.wəgo:n/, which survives as 'Cadogan'. A likely royal Demetian seat lay close by, under the Norman remains on Tenby's Castle Head.[13] The main interest of the text lies in its use of acrostics, and the revelation of its authorship. Here is the inscription, analysed:

		W	S	LD	LM
1	E T S I N G N O C R	5	8	9	10
2	U C I S I N I L L A M			11	11
3	F I N G S I R O G O	2	4	10	10
4	O M N I B U S A M	2	4	9	9
5	M U L A N T I B U S		4	10	10
6	I B I E X O R E N T	2	5	9	10
7	P R O A N I M A E	3	5	8	9
8	C A T U O C O N I	1	5	9	9
		15	35	75	78

In line 7, despite Æ ligatured, we are to read: *pro anima* (abl.) *e Catuoconi* (gen.) 'for-the-sake-of/the soul/out-of/Catuoconi', i.e. after his eventual death; and the name has five syllables, the *-u-* being the retained (IOC) compositional vowel in *catu-*. David Howlett first observed that the whole text is a specimen of adonic verse,[14] with *seven* pairs of feet that can be written out thus:

Fig.71 427 Catuoconi, *Caldey Is., Pembroke; early 8th century, not a memorial and apparently referring to another monument nearby. Macalister's drawing, modified from (1995) photographs; omitting the traces of ogam (shown in CIIC) and two small crosses on the edges. Right, three ligatures; Æ is remarkable because computus and scansion require separation as* ANIMA / E

E ET

& EX

Œ AE

E	t singno cruci S
I	n illam fings I
R	ogo omnibu S
A	mmulantibu S
I	bi exoren T
P	ro anima E
C	atuocon I

each having *five* syllables (total, 35). Note, first, that lines 5 to 7, as verse, correspond to lines 6 to 8, as cut and displayed; and, second, that the initials E I R A I P C add to 57, and the final letters S I S S T E I to 92 (total, 149). This is not only in extreme ratio, but apparently a computus clue; see in a moment.

Clearly the prime key number is *five*; *W, S* and *LD* are all five-divisible and their total (125) is the cube of *five*. The second key number is *seven*. Their total (12) is apparent in

LM, since 78 is triangular from *twelve*. In fact this must be the convention *5.7.12.19.31.50.80...*, and the other non-Fibonacci conventional set (p. 168), as *4.9.13.22.35.57.92.149...* appears in the initials and last letters of the adonic verse-form.

Continuing with the computus, we have two triangulars; *LM* at 78, which is Δ12, and also the final five words (IBI to the end), with 28 letters, Δ7. Triangularisations were often intended to convey two symbolic numbers, 144 as the Heavenly City and 33 as a marker of Christian death. The likelihood is that these, so commonly found together in earlier inscriptions, were meant to refer not to the name *Catuocon* but to all those who would be buried in whatever monument the inscription adjoined. The first pyramid (Δ7) goes:

9	I	9
2	B I	9
5	E X O	13
16	R E N T	18
14	P R O A N	12
9	I M A E C A	1
18	T U O C O N I	9
	(87)	
73		**71**

The full triangle of all 78 letters produces this:

5	E	5
18	T S	17
9	I N G	7
12	N O C R	16
19	U C I S I	9
12	N I L L A M	11
6	F I N G S I R	16
13	O G O O M N I B	2
19	U S A M M U L A N	12
18	T I B U S I B I E X	20
13	O R E N T P R O A N I	9
11	M A E C A T U O C O N I	9
	(108)	
155		**133**

In the smaller pyramid, the sides add to *144*; this, plus the bottom line (87), gives 231, or (key number) *seven* times *33*. In the larger, the sides add to 288, or twice *144*; this, plus the bottom 108, makes 396, which is *twelve* times *33*.

Now we continue to explore 427 *Catuoconi* along two further lines. The second will be application of appropriate intervals, derived from a number-set (probably 5.7.12.19.31…), to the 78 letters to reveal hidden words. The first harks all the way back to the fourth century, Lullingstone, *Avitus* and the multiple games with letter grids to show acrostics. Since 78 is 13 by 6, and 6 by 13, and also 12 by 6½ with further possible staggered or irregular grids, we need to look for acrostics that not only say something in acceptably correct Latin but are relevant to the themes of the text — the Divinity, in particular. Beginning with 13 across and 6 down, we find

```
       e  t  s  i  n  g  N  O  c  r  U  c  i
       s  i  n  i  l  l  A  M  f  i  N  g  s
       i  r  o  g  o  o  M  N  i  b  U  s  a
  6    m  m  u  l  a  n  t  I  b  u  S  i  b
       i  e  x  o  r  e  n  T  p  r  o  a  n
       i  m  a  e  c  a  t  U  o  c  o  n  i
                      13
```

The Latin language may appear to have too many polysyllabic aspects (*sapientissimus; superabundaverunt*) but is actually rich in words that are closed (*tum, hac*) or open (*tu, de*) monosyllables. By accident, or design, or more likely their combination, letter grids from these texts usually contain short words and as at Lullingstone they can produce relevant phrases and comments. The 6 by 13 grid is tied to the key numbers; col.1 adds (LaN) to 60, *5* times *12*, col.13 to 50, twice *five* squared, and the reading starts with the *seventh* letter. We can see NAM . OMNITU . UNUS, perhaps *nam omni, Tu, Unus* 'For all [Creation], Thou [art] the One [Creator]'. Or using *twelve* again, a grid which is 12 across and 7 down, its bottom line having only 6 letters, shows:

```
       e  t  s  i  n  g  n  O  c  r  u  c
       i  s  i  n  i  l  l  A  m  f  i  n
       g  s  i  r  o  g  o  O  m  n  i  b
  7    u  s  a  m  m  u  l  A  n  t  i  b
       u  s  i  b  i  e  x  O  r  e  n  t
       p  r  o  a  n  i  m  A  e  c  a  t
       .  .  .  .  .  .  u  O  c  o  n  i
                      12
```

Though this throws up vertical sets reminiscent of *Catamanus* — SSSS in col.2 and III in col.11 (but no actual words like *nam omni*) — there can be litle doubt that the desired display is the O A O A O A O of col.8 which is a further allusion to the Almighty. It comes from Apocalypsis, at several points; 'I am the Beginning and the End…', and the alternating *omega-alpha* string is there because of the word-order and, more significantly, because the text has *singno* and not *signo*; *fingsi* and not *finxi*. In other words, this had all been worked out on a writing-surface.

Clever games and tricks of this sort, starting with the fourth-century Avitus compositions and from the Welsh evidence alone part of a taught compositional technique throughout subsequent centuries, go some way (along with triangularisation) to explain what have wrongly been described as aberrant or ignorant or rustic 'mis-spellings' of Latin words. *Singno* is as essential here as was *opinatisimus*, not *opinatissimus*, in the Cadfan lampoon. On top of everything else there was the final goal for which such precise arrangement was essential; inclusion of words and especially auctorial names by precession-and-interval. Letters R and S occur quite frequently in this text (R,4; S,5) and suggest a search for split anagrams that might direct us to backward readings. Here they are:

etsingnocrucisinillamfingsi		27
R ogoomnib **US** amm **U** lantibu **S** ibiexo **R**	30	
entproanimaecatuoconi		21
— giving **R US U S R** = *rursus*, and:	**30**	**48**
etsingnoc	9	
RU ci **S** inilla **M** fingsi **RO**		20
goomnibusammulan **T** ibusibi **E** xo **R**		28
entproanimaecatuoconi	21	
— giving **RU S M RO T E R** — *retrorsum*.	**30**	**48**

Both are similarly validated, by 30:48 → 78 (x 6, 1.2.3.*5*.*8*.*13*.21....). Readers will naturally be impatient to know the composer's name. A backward precession-and-interval reading using 4.9.13.22.(35) does not suit because it yields a meaningless OASI and last-interval 26. With the commoner 5.7.12.19.31.50… set we get the answer.

> inoco **U** taceami **N** aorptneroxei **B** isubitnalummasubinm **O** ogor…iste/
>   5   7   12   19   31

This fits precisely; UNBO is four letters, and 5 + 7 + 12 +19 +32 is 74, in the complete text of 78 letters. We can accept this as the author's name. Like Elri, *Unbo* as a masc. Archaic OW proper name may be unattested but both its elements are well-known.[15]

The text of *Catuoconi* is, relatively, a long one and other readings by precession-and-interval or gridding can be expected. Looking at the reversed version of the inscription above and bearing 5.7.12 particularly in mind (for modern readers, *Fig.8* earlier here as well) sharp eyes might readily spot that (backwards) the *second* 'I' is followed by *seven* letters to reach an 'E', and then by another *seven* to reach an 'S' (thus: **I** naorptn **E** roxeibi **S**), with a possibility of IESUS in the offing. But, with *equal* intervals, a grid is more likely than a precession-and-interval scheme. It turns out to be:

i n o c o		
5	u t a c e a m	**I**
	n a o r p t n	**E**
	r o x e i b i	**S**
	u b i t n a l	**U**
	7	

— containing, significantly, **5** + (4 x 7) = **33** letters as well as IESU. If we go on, we then find:

m	m	a	s	u	b	i	**N**
•	•	•	m	o	o	g	**O**
r	i	s	g	n	i	f	**M**
a	l	l	i	n	i	s	**I**
c	u	r	c	o	n	g	**N**
•	•	•	•	i	s	t	**E** = (IESU) **N O M I N E**

Because the final interval to give the 'E' *can* only be 3, one of the sevens is split 4/3 as shown. *Iesu nomine* assures the readers that this text, with its computus, is composed wholly 'in Jesu's name'. Who exactly, then, was Unbo? This too we learn, in another staggered grid that uses key number *five*:

•	•	•	•	i	n	o	c	o	u	t	a	c	e	**A**
m	i	n	a	o	r	p	t	n	e	r	o	x	e	i	**B**
i	s	u	b	i	t	n	a	l	u	m	m	a	s	u	**B**
i	n	mo	o	g	o	r	i	s	g	n	i	f	m	**A**
(•	•	•	•	•)(•	•	•	•	•)	l	l	i	n	i	**S** = **A B B A S**

This is based on a grid of *five*-times-three by *five*. It gives a *five*-letter telestich; the interval letters total 60, *five* times *twelve*; and the whole reading occupies 65, *five*-sixths, of the total of 78 letters(note how the 'corner' letters, initals and last of lines 1 and 5, i e l i, 9.5.10.9, make 33.) Unbo, in the name of *Iesu*, was the abbot (*abbas*) of the monastery on Caldey. If it can be accepted that CATUOCONI names a contemporary king of Dyfed, it would be natural for Unbo to have provided a suitable inscription to accompany any creation of a burial-monument linked to the monastery.

We find here in the eighth century a composition containing most of the known devices. It is metrical (though not additionally chiastic), immediately offers key numbers — notably *five*, from *W* 15, *S* 35, *LD* 75, and *seven* from the adonic verse — with reference to the 5.7.12.19.31.50 convention. Regular and staggered grids, validated by 5 and 7, provide Christian sentiments; in reverse, precession-and-interval yields the name *Unbo*, while some more grids disclose *Iesu nomine*, *abbas* as telestichs. The appropriate numbers 144 and 33 arise from triangulars, 33 being found elsewhere. The LaN base is still of 20 letters.[16] Lastly, and this must be important for any future archaeological investigation, the best sense of the text is that the royal donor was still alive, and that whatever he caused to be founded on Caldey adjoined this dedicatory slab. It is at least possible that the words *signo crucis* denote a separate stone cross, larger and free-standing, that may yet be found.

Towards some typological conclusions

This study has concentrated upon demonstrations of the more interesting stones, image-generating or not. There are others, not all in Wales, of less interest but with, at the very least, hints of a computus or minimal Biblical-style construction. I do not think it would be helpful yet to produce lengthy analytical summaries, listing by inscription every possible device and feature as these appear (irregularly) from the fourth to the eleventh century. The previous chapters should have shown how, from what will now seem comparatively simple beginnings before 400, a plateau of complexity is reached after 600

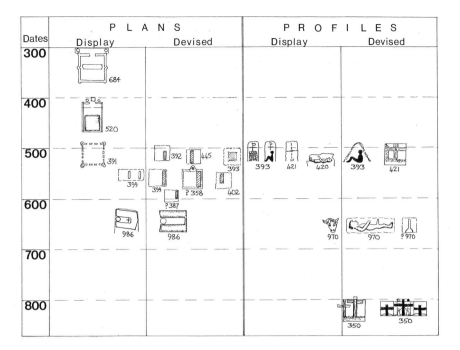

Fig. 72 Diagram; mental images generated by inscriptions, divided as in Fig. 50. The instances are arranged by cautious estimates of relative dates as discussed in the text, identified by CIIC numbers. Except for the first two display plans (RIB 684: 520) all are from Wales; the 6th-century devised plans are of small grave-plots.

because so many Insular innovations are added. To select one obvious occurrence, unless quite unexpected (and exact) parallels are found in Gaulish or Spanish memorials the combination of *rursus-retrorsum* pointers, reversed reading, indicated number sets and the discovery of auctorial names by precession-and-interval readings has to be regarded as something invented in seventh-century Wales. The geographical spread could tell us that the invention was shared among centres of learning, a part of taught composition; and in fact we could probably infer as much, because this encoding trick would have been a dead-end unless a composer's intellectual peers were expected to know the rules.

Specifically British was the invention of *profile* images. It is no accident that some of them involve human figures, though the climax of 350 *Idnert* (*Fig. 73*) goes outside the sequence because the images lead to an existing picture, Iago's starting-point and also goal. But we should be prepared to see the inscription images that depict humans, from Christ downwards, as a wider artistic trait documented in incised and relief sculpture, decorated manuscripts and other media in Britain and Ireland by the eighth century. *Fig. 72* is a first summary of the images. If this were a typological diagram in a venerable archaeological way, presenting all known specimens of a dual-format artefact (a bronze socketed axe with/without basal loops, say) in time and space, it would be taken to offer provisional conclusions. But it *is* a typological diagram, albeit for an extremely complex artefact. And

The grid letters read:
- Row 1: H I C | I A C | B I | O P T E R
- Row 2: A C E T | QUI | P R E D
- Row 3: I D N E R | O C C I S | A M S A
- Row 4: T F I L | U S | F U N C T I
- Row 5: I U S | I | I T | P R | D A V I D

Fig. 73   *350* Idnert; *the final Calvary scene using the three 25-letter squares in Fig.9. Technically a devised profile, 75 letters and blanks are superimposed on a Gospel scene, of the type shown here from the Rabbula Gospels of 586 (at Biblioteca Medicea-Laurenziana, Florence, Plut.I.56, on f.13a, sup.). Two thieves, named in the apocryphal NT, are Dismas, left, letters* **DI***sm***A***s, and Gestas, right, g***ESTA***s. But 'Dismas' is really* IDNER(t), *crucified beside his Lord when (Matthew, 27.45) there was darkness from the sixth to ninth hour; on the cross-arm* **T** *= tenebrae,* **F** *(6) and* **I** *(9) the hours in question. Centre, the 'O' of* ACOBI *becomes the Nimbus; 'C' is the crescent moon, dust-storm reddened, and 'O' four places right, the sun. Lower left below Christ, 'Stephaton' proffers the sponge full of wine-vinegar; 27.48, spongiam implevit aceto – we see around him letters* **S***(pongiam)* **I***(mplevi)***T***, and* ACET*(o) top left. Below the crucified Idnert, acrostic* IUS.IIT *tells us that 'righteousness hath departed'. Christ's Head is central in* ACOBI, *LaN total perfect-28. There are many more allusive LaN totals and part-labellings but the above is enough to show the richness of Iago's composition in AD 806.*

it does offer at least one conclusion; that profile image-generation was invented in Wales, perhaps around 500. We can also see this from a map (*Fig.74*) showing inscriptions in Biblical style and distinguishing those that generate images, plans or profiles. The emphasis on the north and north-west of Wales (with 11 examples) is obvious. To highlight the concept of an intellectual bastion the line of the late eighth-century linear earthwork system, Offa's Dyke, is shown[17] — of partial relevance even if built to *in*clude Britons in their own land, and built by Mercian English; not by Britons to *ex*clude those unequipped to participate in their own Britishness.

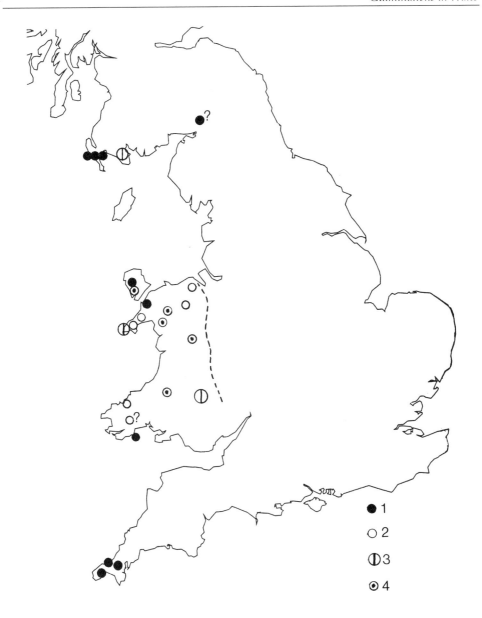

Fig.74 Distribution, to early 1998, of inscriptions identified as being in Biblical style. Symbols:
1, not generating any images. 2, simple 'grave-plot' plans only. 3, elaborate labelled plans
(520, 391, 986). 4, profiles of any kind. Dotted line = the course of Offa's Dyke, a
cultural frontier.

Inscriptional authors as native bards?

There have been suggestions in these pages, and others have voiced them elsewhere, that the composers of inscriptions on stone and of longer Latin works surviving as MSS were, if British, likely to have been intellectually bilingual; educated through the medium of Latin, familiar with Latin as a written and spoken language, but also users of what had formerly been British as a vernacular (and in some cases sufficiently versed in British to produce IOC spellings). The suggestion is that any such creative literary caste, however small within post-Roman Insular society, was responsible both for Latin composition and our surviving scraps of written Old Welsh, *and* for a much larger body of oral composition that we assume existed. Can we perhaps recognise in the Latin inscriptional texts any features that stand outside what has been defined as Biblical style? Was there any measure of overlap between Latin and British?

Classical Latin has always been taught analytically; it has to be. *Titulum posuerunt* 'they have set up an inscription', the syllables in the verb are *po.su.e.runt* and they carry information — *u* marks the perfect tense, 'have (done something)' and the *-unt* the 3rd person plur., 'they'. Our composers mastered Latin with grammatically correct syllable-division, because precise syllable counts were essential in a computus and in any kind of metrical scansion. But there is something more, and this is apposite to the public use of any language at the period in question. It is a form of audience participation and it is bipartite. For those who knew some Latin but could not read the letters, the reading or reciting of a text aloud was directed to the *ear*; an occasion for the measured voice, strong spoken stress, even chanting. It is commonplace to suppose that early poets spoke aloud their stirring and heroic verse-compositions in this manner. But — and this is obviously relevant to inscriptions on stone, when new and clearly-cut, because the lettering is much larger than it would ever be in MSS and can be further emphasised by line-arrangement — the other direction is to the *eye*; to readers who may see patterns of letters and syllables repeated, even more so to readers who (as in this book) examine texts transferred from stone to a writing-medium.

If we accept this as applicable to inscriptions, we can discover presentations of texts differing considerably from structural analyses. In what follows, selected texts are syllabically divided as a Latin grammarian might do so (there were standard rules for this), but we take into consideration that the divisions would be almost entirely lost in reading aloud (for the ear) and in continuous writing (for the eye). On the *left* are repetitive elements, mostly vowel-consonant(s), noticeable in a measured recitation. On the *right* are other features that could also be discerned in speech but which, either within *scriptio continua* or a written re-arrangement, any reader of Latin would be more likely to notice as visible repetitions. 'Correspondences' is a better label than consonances or alliterations. With these, the mark 1/2 means 'Features in line 1 that are visually matched in line 2' (and 2/1 means the reverse; the 1/4, 4/1 pairings are the most interesting).

We open by taking Elri's 986 *Ioruert*, with its two non-Latin names, and followed him by writing it out quartered, in four lines thus:

		IN IND MU	1/4
in si/in on ti	(1) IN SIN DO NE MU TI		
		ON E	1/2
		AUN E	2/1
ru al (l) ul ri	(2) IOR UERT RU A LLAUN QUE SE PUL CRIS		
		AUN SEP	2/3
		EN SPE	3/2
iud ad ent ant	(3) IU DIC I I AD VEN TUM SPEC TANT		
		EN PEC AN	3/4
		IN PAC EN	4/3
in em en um	(4) IN PA CE TRE MEN DUM		
		IN END UM	4/1

Set out in this manner, on paper it gives four lines; syllables superficially 6.9.9.6 (total *30*, not the same as when properly scanned as Latin verse[18] because it is then a couplet of dactylic hexameters with syllables 14.14 (=*28*) because two are lost through synizesis, in Ruallaun and iudicii). The rhymes, *left*, could be abab. abba.aabb.abab. Because in spoken Vulgar Latin some of the vowel distinctions as well as lengths (short or long) had become blurred, in line (4) the *en* and *in* (trem*en*dum, *in*) probably sounded the same. Notice specially in the correspondences, right, the visible match between the opening and closing lines where IN IND MU, from **INSINDONEMUTI**, is repeated with near-entirety by IN END UM, from **INPACETREMENDUM**; and again with MU UM, and from (2) and (3) SEP and SPE, this is bound to be reminiscent of the partly or completely inverted letters common to terms in inscriptional chiasmus (e.g., p. 158). It might even be suggested that this is related to inscriptional chiasmus and that the latter, in this respect, was prompted by a recognition of 'pairs' like MU.UM, ANT-IB.IB-END in a context other than inscriptions.

Whatever this is, whatever verse-tradition (if it can be called that) the alternative construction represents, it is certainly not Classical Latin versification with all its grammarians' rules. For a good indication of departure from the (Classical) norm, around 500, we can take a second look at 393 *Carausius*. Viola did not include any backward readings in her 7-word text. We cannot find any signposting split anagram, because a hypothetical one like ca / **R** a **US** i **US** hiciacitinhocconge **R** / ieslapidum (= R US US R) divided 2/26/10, the *rursus* span as 6/20, is just not validated. However, as David Howlett found in 1997[19], Viola did manage a most extraordinary dactylic hexameter by reversing, not all the text, but some of the constituent syllables. What this produced was

$$\text{ūm lăpĭd / ēs gĕrĭ / cōn hōc / ĭn iăcĭt / hīc ĭŭs / aūs Cār}$$

and when this hexameter is projected back into the text retaining its scansion it would have meant that Viola, presumably recipient of a full classical education in the Roman mould, thereby committed her text to (Latin) vowel-quantities throughout. But this does not preclude its presentation in the alternative mode. Since her text has 16 (spoken and written) syllables we can again quarter it.

							A	I	US	1/4
aus	*ŭs*	(1)	CĀ	RĀU	SĬ	ŪS				
							C	A	I	1/2
							C	A	I	2/1
ĭc	*ăc*	(2)	HĪC	IĂ	CĬT	ĪN				
							I	C	IN	2/3
							O	C	ON	3/2
ō(c)	*(c)ō*	(3)	HŌC	CŌN	GĔ	RĬ	E	I		3/4
							E	I		4/3
ă(p)	*ĭ(d)*	(4)	ĒS	LĂ	PĬ	DŪM				
							A	I	UM	1/4

The quantity-markings (left and centre) are the correct (Classical) metrics; by *c*.500 these were not necessarily followed in spoken British (Vulgar) Latin. The text, forward as above (not backward), again has these quasi-chiastic correspondences and again lines 1 and 4 can be paired. We can turn to a third and considerably later (AD 806) text which is also complete — model and display are the same — and which can also be scanned (in writing) as five Latin dimetric lines (they run dactyl - ⌣⌣ spondee - - ; dactyl.spondee; spondee.dactyl; spondee.spondee; spondee.spondee). The textual, analytical, syllable count of 25 is reduced to a metric 23 with one synizesis and one elision.[20] This is of course 350 *Idnert*, an inscription whose display was cut in three lines, the 12 words as 5.5.3 (key numbers being 5 and 7). Can this, too, be re-presented? We might try it in *five* parts.

								AC T	ID		1/5
ī̆c ăc ĕt ērt	(1)	HIC	IA		CET	ID	NERT				
								I	IAC I		1/2
								I	IAC I		2/1
iŭs iăc	(2)	FI	LI	US	IA	CO	BI				
								F	IU O		2/3
								O	FU I		3/2
i i	(3)	QUI	OC	CI	SUS	FU	IT				
								OC	T		3/4
								O P	T		4/3
pr pr	(4)	PROP	TER	PRE	DAM						
								DAM			4/5
								DA			5/4
ā ī ā ī	(5)	SANC	TI	DA	VID						
								A	CT ID		5/1

As a just post-800 example, this fits the pattern less readily. A face value count of 25 syllables is intended by its computus (for key number *5* squared, the 3 x *25* letter squares in Fig. *9*, etc.) but its author Iago would himself have chanted this, as Latin verse, with 23 syllables only. In (2), FILIUS is not fil-I-us but /fil-yus/, in (3) we would hear qu.occisus, not quI occisus (four syllables). Returning to the seventh century, however, there is the long *Catuoconi* text, now shown by Dr Howlett to be structured as seven lines of adonic verse,[21] but syllabic, not metric (adonic metre, dactyl-spondee, reads long-short-short/long-long). We can follow by organising its 35 syllables as 5.5.5.5.5.5.5, which produces this:

							ET O UC I	1/7
si in no is	(1) ET SING NO CRU CIS								
							SING N IS	1/2
							IN ING SI	2/1
in i in i	(2) IN IL LAM FING SI								
							AM I	2/3
							OM I	3/2
o o	(3) RO GO OM NI BUS								
							OM IBUS	3/4
							AM IBUS	4/3
am u an u	(4) AM MU LAN TI BUS								
							ANT IB	4/5
							IB ENT	5/4
i i e e	(5) I BI EX OR ENT								
							I EN	5/6
							AN I	6/5
a a	(6) PRO A NI MA E								
							O NI	6/7
							O NI	7/6
c o c o	(7) CA TU O CO NI								
							AT U OC I	7/1

Notable here must be the 'framing', the close linking of (1) and (7) with ET O UC I = AT U OC I and, in the correspondences, right, the similarity in, e.g., ANT IB / IB ENT to inscriptional chiasmus. If this was strict metrical adonics, the rhymes (left) would over-ride the vowel lengths; e.g., in (5), ī ĭ ĕ ē ought to be recited, and heard, as ĭ ĭ ĕ ĕ ; in (6) ă ā as ă ă .

If we put forward the idea — without prejudice as to exactly where, when, how and whence these apparently non-Latin versions of the texts as metrical compositions originated — that the phenomenon, most marked in Wales, is in some fashion *British*, two other conditions must come to mind. The first is that any of the few early inscriptional texts provisionally attributed to incoming *Gaulish* clerics ought not to exhibit the same features. Certainly for 391 *Senacus*, this is so; it is unclear how its 7 words and 17 syllables could ever be so divided and the alliteration noticeable in, say, cUM MUltitudinEM fratrUM is a near-universal Latin feature. The same goes for 516 *Viventius* and, as far as can be made out, for a third probable exotic, 479 *Cunaide* in fifth-century west Cornwall. The second condition is that we should be able to find a memorial of suitable length, in Latin, in Wales, that does *not* contain any Biblical style computus nor image-generating capacity, yet is British from context and *does* exhibit the alternative verse-scheme.

One such exists. It is 360 *Paulinus* from Maes Llanwrthwl in the depths of Carmarthenshire, an inscribed slab that I believe was the (head-end) grave cover — somewhat in the Gaulish manner — for a pious aristocrat buried on his own estate in the sixth century. There are five lines of capitals with numerous ligatures. The text scans as two correct hexameters and, with David Howlett's translation, reads *servatur fidaei patrieque semper amator hic Paulinus iacit cultor pientisimus aequi.* 'A lover, always, of Faith and Fatherland is saved. Here Paulinus lies, most pious cultivator of the just'.[22] Five lines, 11 words, 73 letters (*LM*) reduced by ligatures to 67; but repeated scrutinies completely fail to find any computus in it.

			TUR I AE	1/4
er ur i i	(1) SER VA TUR FI DAE I			
			ER ATUR	1/2
			ER ATOR	2/1
atr e e a t r	(2) PA TRI E QUE SEM PER A MA TOR			
			PA AT	2/3
			PAU IT	3/2
ic i aci	(3) HIC PAU LI NUS IA CIT			
			C PAUL IN	3/4
			CUL PI EN	4/3
i is us i	(4) CUL TOR PI EN TI SI MUS AE QUI			
			TOR I AE I	4/1

With no difficulty, *Paulinus* as a hexametric Latin couplet is now presented as a four-part 'verse', 6.9.6.9 (ignoring any of the Latin elisions), rhymes as aabb.abba.abab.abba, and a clear run of visible consonances, notably the TUR I AEI — TOR I AE I, linking start to finish. For the ear, it could be pointed out that in the speech of uncultivated persons reciting (British) Latin in a way that would have made a Roman litterateur shudder, SERVATUR and AMATOR as more like 'Sher-WAH-der, A-VAH-der' emphasise the rhymes.

The foregoing instances are presented as no more than something observable in respect of selected Latin inscriptions. What they share is a pattern of syllabic lines, audible rhymes per line and detectable correspondences of letters as between adjacent lines (and first and last lines, particularly) that not only diverge from a maintained tradition of, generally correct, Latin metrical verse but demonstrably slight the stated Latin vowel-quantities and the necessary Latin synizesis and elision. So far, it can be stated that our re-arrangements are applicable to texts in Wales that are otherwise Latin metrical compositions of identifiable type, but do not have to be in detectable Biblical style; and that those early texts provisionally seen as Gaulish are unaffected. The use of the word 'British' seems justifiable. The known authors (Elri, Viola, Iago, Unbo) can hardly be regarded as other than natives.

Is it conceivable that we have here an indication of a verse-form extracted from one language (Latin) which betrays an influence, deliberate rather than sub-conscious, of a verse-form proper to another language? Are the authors in question representative of a learned, Latin-schooled, clerical and aristocratic minority accustomed to compose, formally and metrically, in vernacular British? Are patterns of short lines, like 4.4.4.4, 6.9.6.9, and audible internal rhymes and alliterations, and (on stone) visible correspondences that are also to some extent rhymes or consonances, together in any way characteristic of what is now believed about the missing British (neo-Brittonic) verse; short poems or long heroic sagas? Could a resemblance have been heightened because, in sixth-century Wales, in *spoken* Latin the correct vowel quantities and certain vowel distinctions (like *e - i*) had become ignored?

This is offered as a suggestion, an idea; no more. The main obstacle is that there is virtually no *direct* evidence for *written* neo-Brittonic, Archaic Old Welsh, poetry, however structured. Its nature has to be inferred from linguistic reconstruction and from the intricacies of the later *cerdd dafod*, the numerous compositional rules of Middle Welsh verse. But any such comment raises a further suggestion, and it is not dependent on negative evidence (for instance, that no early writings in British have survived because most of them were on imported and rapidly-perishable papyrus). It is that, along with what must be inferred about the continuity of Latin education, penning of models underlying stone-cut texts, necessity of resolving final computus details in writing and the obvious circulation of multiple-copied Christian and secular Latin literature, we have to postulate not simply the existence of *written* British, to whatever end, but of writing itself as a widespread social activity. After 500 or so (or before then?), there may have been writing in both languages as an everyday occurrence. If there was an interaction between conventional Latin metrics and a lost system of British metrics, it probably left unaffected the highest register, the most mandarin, of Insular Latin writings (Gildas, with *DEB*). Short inscriptions publicly aimed at the faithful and semi-literate as well as at cognoscenti may be thought rather more demotic in character. But the provisional evidence collected here does not suggest that an interaction only took place at the spoken level, or that it was necessarily one-sided. These are deep questions and they must await proper exploration. For now, it may be possible to picture (in Wales, 500 to 700) a currency of *written* poetry; in both languages, and by the same group of authors.

Notes to Chapter 7

1   Surviving from Roman practice, this is found a century earlier in the same district; 360 *Paulinus*, with PATRIEQ(ue) SEMPER.
2   Bartrum, *EWGT*, 45, Jesus College 2, no.8. I do not discuss Nash-William's views on an epigraphic date, nor Jackson's on the spellings of names, because they are not really relevant if the historical setting is preferred.
3   *Cf.*, in *Land*, Elcu, Elhaern, Eliud, etc., and of course 'Illtud' as Eltutus; and the many names like (IOC) CLUTORIGI > OW *Clotri*.
4   A reconstruction (on paper) of this monument, other pieces of which may lie around Llanllywenfel churchyard, is planned to appear in a separate and longer publication discussing it; it belongs to a small class of 'royal' or 'special' tombs.

5   Bartrum, *EWGT*, 9, Harl.3859, Gwynedd, *Catman*; *ibid.*,50, *Catuan*; more fully in R.Bromwich, *Trioedd Ynys Prydein* (Cardiff 1971), 290.

6   The church may be the latest of successive re-builds on the first 7th-century site; see RCAMW *Anglesey Inventory* (1937), 85-7.

7   Bromwich, *Trioedd Ynys Prydein*, 293-6; he fell in battle in 634. The rulers of Gwynedd are relatively well documented in both Welsh and English sources.

8   Greek corporeal nouns were borrowed into Latin (e.g. *thorax*, used by Pliny and Celsius); *pharynx/*pharinx* 'throat, gullet' would have fitted well but I cannot find that it was any such early loanword.

9   Maelgwn allegedly (*DEB* 33-35) married after taking monastic vows, then lusted after his own nephew's wife, whom he wed publicly after arranging for the deaths of both his nephew and his queen. There is a reference to him being 'like a man drunk on wine pressed from the vine of the Sodomites'.

11   What may be a cognate Irish name, *Essiu*, belonged to one of Patrick's three (Irish) artisans; K.Mulchrone, *Bethu Phátraic, The Tripartite Life of Patrick, I* (Dublin 1939), 155.

10   There are actually many 'seven' clues; first and last letters overall, C M, 3.11 = *seven* twice, and by LNu the text contains I I I I I I I = 7, and also X V V V V V = *seven* times 5.

12   Accepting the identification with Caldey (as I am convinced we must), from *Vita Prima Sancti Samsonis*, caps.20, 33-37. A text of this Life may well have existed at Caldey; if so, note in cap. 35 where Samson makes the sign of the cross on some honey-jars — *lanternis signum crucis imposuit*.

13   See Sir Ifor Williams's annotated edn.transl. of the archaic poem *Etmic Dinbych* 'The Praise of Tenby', in his *The Beginnings of Welsh Poetry* (ed. Rachel Bromwich, Cardiff 1972), for this citadel.

14   Now in his *Cambro-Latin Compositions*; I owe much of the analysis here to our long discussions about this fascinating inscription.

15   *Un* 'one, single', *-bo* probably from **bog* — 'battle, hitting'. In *Land*, we find *U*ngust, *U*nhu, and the quite common name Con*boe*, Con*uoe* (where u =/v/). *Cf.* Old Breton Dosar*boe*, Riski*boe* (9th cent.).

16   As we would expect for the 8th century; until there is rather more evidence, I postpone discussing further the timing (and reasons?) for a, probably 9th century, shift from the 20-letter convention to a 23-letter one that was used from Roman times for literary purposes (*cf.*, in *H.E.*iv.20, Bede's poem on abbess Aedilthryda, 27 couplets, A to Z (23) plus A M E N).

17   The Dyke runs down most, but not all, of the 'frontier'; (Sir) Cyril Fox, *Offa's Dyke; a field survey* (Brit.Academy, London 1955).

18   In his *Cambro-Latin Compositions* (1998); see also in *Peritia*, 11 (1997), 80.

19   *Peritia*, 11 (1997), 78 ('An inscription that might at first sight suggest ignorance of rules really illustrates a knowledge of rules deep enough to play with them').

20   *Peritia*, 10 (1996), 142, n.24.

21   *Cambro-Latin Compositions* (1998).

22 *Peritia*, 1 (1997), 79-80; this corrects the (*ECMW*) reading of *servatur* 'is saved, preserved' as *servator* 'Preserver (of the Faith)', a mistranslation frequently repeated; e.g., the CBA's *British Archaeology*, 32 (March 1998), 9,with photograph. For Paulinus himself, see *Mute Stones*, 104 and refs.

8 Pre-Norman Cornwall

Though neither the title nor the proclaimed scope of this book use the word 'early', discussion of the various inscriptions and their background could be said to have peaked within the seventh and eighth centuries, and so far to have reached no later than AD 806, the supposed date of 350 *Idnert*. How long did this special compositional mode persist? Did it at any later and secondary stage affect memorials in Latin, or any other language, in Ireland or any part of Britain outside Wales? The short answer is that at the moment nobody knows, and that no appropriate search has taken place. What V.E.Nash-Williams called his (Welsh) Group III stones, many of them tall free-standing crosses with dedicatory inscriptions (alas, usually damaged or defective), have texts long enough to be interesting, but it requires a lot of time to investigate them. David Howlett has shown that the Pillar of Eliseg (*CIIC* 1000 = *ECMW* 182; ninth century) is a largely-restorable text of complex structure, and in many ways unique.[1] It would be a guess only, but a guess that might understandably be entertained, that the particular inscriptional style described here continued to surface for some centuries after AD 806. The closer we come to the ecclesiastical Great Re-build, the wave of construction of new churches on ancient sites linked to the Norman conquest, the more intense was the recycling of usefully-large but (to the Normans) meaningless lettered crosses and other memorials. We should therefore concentrate on likely marginal survivals.

One of these, happily, survives in west Cornwall, last visited for the fifth-century 479 *Cunaide* stone, p. 151. It is the tall granite cross, 1051 Penzance (Market Cross), which has just — Autumn 1997 — been moved for the fifth (and one hopes the last) time to the new west-front terrace of Penlee House Art Gallery and Museum (*Fig.75*).[2]

Still called Penzance *Market* Cross (because it stood for many years in the town's Greenmarket), a single pillar originally at least 8ft high and ornamented on all four faces, its most likely provenance would have been at some late pre-Norman burial ground and chapel just west of Penzance; in the district called Alverton, Domesday *Alwaretone*, by then an English fief held by one Alward. Macalister's 1920s drawing (*Fig.75*: *CIIC* ii, p1.LXI) shows all the essential features. The ornamentation (not discussed here), shape and form, combine to suggest a late tenth or eleventh century date. There are two basal-panel inscriptions of vertically-set lettering in tenth-twelfth-century bookhand. The shorter (two lines) is almost illegible — Macalister thought it read REGIS RI/CATI CRUX 'Cross of king Ricatus' (grossly improbable), but it may have been ...I / C R U X 'The Cross of...' (male name, gen., of the donor; see now p. 192).

The longer inscription is in three lines, the endings of which run across a groove into the last panel (*Fig.75*). The first letters were seen and recorded in the last century before damage took place, and the last few in each line (also scarred away, in the modern base) have to be restored. This is both possible and permissible because, late as it may be, the inscription is in Biblical style. By far and away the most likely version is this: restorations, italics.

1	*p*	)	c	u	m	b	u	i	n	/	f	o	(	*r*	*i*	*s*
2	*q*	)	u	i	c	u	m	q	:	/	p	(	*a*	*c*	*e*	
3	*u*	)	e	n	i	t	h	i		/	c	(	*o*	*r*	*e*	*t*

which, expanded, gives PROCUM*BUNT* IN FORIS / QUICUMQUE PACE / VENIT HI*NC* ORET — 'They lie here in the open. Whosoever in peace comes here, let him pray (for their souls)'. At this late date, similar exhortatory public messages were being used in Ireland and Wales[3], of the 'Whosoever…let him pray (read)' kind; on 427 *Catuoconi*, p. 169, EXORENT PRO ANIMA 'let them pray for the soul' foreshadows this tradition.

The fascination of this very short text is the sheer amount crammed into it; here is the usual analysis, by semantic parts.

		W	*S*	*LD*	*LM*
(a) Line 1	P (r o) C U M B U (n t) I N F O R I S	3	6	13	17
(b) Line 2-3	Q U I C U M Q (u e) P A C E				
	V E N I T H I (n) C O R E T	5	10	23	26
		8	16	36	43

The totals show extreme ratio; *W*, 3:5 → 8, *S*, 6:10 → 16 (the same), and *LM*, 17:26 → 43 (from 1.8.9.*17*.26.43.69…). Note that, by this date and apparently following a general change-over during the ninth century, the LaN base is twenty-three letters (with K, Y and Z);

A	B	C	D	E	F	G	H	I	K	L	M	N	O	P	Q	R	S	T	U/V	X	Y	Z
1	2	3	4	5	6	7	8	9	10	11	12	13	14	15	16	17	18	19	20	21	22	23

Overwhelmingly, a key number is *seventeen*. There are *17* letters in (a). Dividing 8 words as 4:4, *pace venit hinc oret* = *17* letters. Three line-initials P Q V, 15.16.20 = 51, *17* x 3. Initials and last of (a), P S, and of (b), Q T = 68, *17* x 4. Initials of all eight words (=103) and their last letters (=101) make 204 =*17* x 12. In part (a), the 23-letter LaN of all 17 letters gives 221 = 17 x 13.

The text is chiastic; here are the terms:

a	Procumbunt	Verb, plur., letters **R O T**
b	in foris	Adverbial, plur., **I N**
c	quicumque	9 letters, subj. single, **U I C E**
c'	pace uenit	9 letters, verb single, **C E U I**
b'	hinc	Adverbial, single, **I N**
a'	oret	Verb, single, letters **O R T**

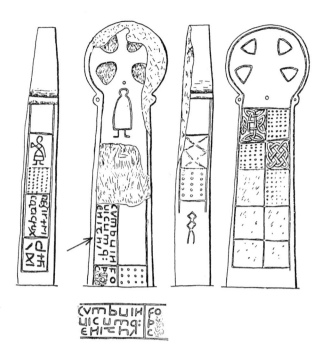

*Fig. 75 The Penzance
Market cross,
now at Penlee
House Art
Gallery and
Museum;
Macalister's
drawing (CIIC,
1051, by courtesy
of the controller,
Stationery Office,
Dublin). The
main inscription
is arrowed and
shown below.*

and it also holds *chronograms*, devices to indicate the date AD. No less than three exist:

(a) p r o c u   5 letters

$\mathbf{M}$ b $\mathbf{V}$ n t $\mathbf{I}$ n f o r $\mathbf{I}$ = MVII = 1007   11

s $-$ $\underline{1}$

                                                                  11   6   (5:6 →11)

(b) q u i c u   5

$\mathbf{M}$ q $\mathbf{V}$ e p a c e v e n $\mathbf{I}$ t h $\mathbf{I}$ = MVII   15

n c o r e t $-$ $\underline{6}$

                                                                  15   11

Add the *spans* in (a) and (b), 11 + 15 = *26*, and unused, 6 + 11 = *17*, and we are back to *LM*'s extreme ratio as 17:26 → 43.

Part (b) holds the third; validated by *mean*, not extreme, ratio:

q u i c u   5

$\mathbf{M}$ q u e p a c e $\mathbf{V}$ 9

e n   2

$\mathbf{I}$ t h $\mathbf{I}$ 4

n c o r e t $\underline{6}$ $-$

                                                                  13:   13

This date of AD 1007 accords with what have been, necessarily loose, art-historical and typological estimates of this cross's age.

If it is supposed, as for this period in Cornish history it might well be, that the text represents an Old English (Anglo-Saxon) Latin composition rather than a purely Cornish one, we then have the possibility that the oddly-chosen word *procumbunt* 'they lie down

Fig. 76   1051 Penzance; the main inscription. Three initial letters, now chipped off, are recorded, the main part has been drawn in situ and from photographs and the closing letters in each line may seem conjectural but are supported by analysis and computus.

forwards, prone, on their faces' conceals a shorter word through precession-and-interval, perhaps from the 1.2.3.5.8.13… set. Is this p_1 **R** o_2 c **U** m b_3 u **N** (t? It yields RUN, rūn, Old English for the notion of 'mystery; a secret writing'. And noticing that the *display* letter-total is 36 words, or the *square* of 6, as:

P	C	U M	B		**U**
I	N	F O	R		**I**
S	Q	U I	C		**U**
M	Q	P A	C		**E**
V	E	N I	T		**H**
I	C	O R	E		**T**

— its telestich, or last-letters downward-acrostic, is UIUEHT. The (23-letter) alphabet, a vehicle whose primary load was Latin, was not entirely suited to conveying Old English names[4]; but one can suggest that the above provides us with an (unattested) **Wi(g)weht* as the composer.

What is the *seventeen*, which is further signalled by other computus devices and LaN totals omitted here? The text is a part-memorial to a crowd, not an individual; all those who lie, open-air, in the adjacent cemetery. It is the triangular, Δ17 giving 153, that is meant; bodies on this earth, whose souls are gathered into God's net, as the 153 fishes in the lake (John, 21.11) fell into the Disciples' net in the presence of the Risen Christ. Singularly apt for the Penzance-Newlyn district, the home of Cornwall's oldest fishery, the allusion would not have been missed.

The fascination of this eleventh-century text, the latest to be included here, is its general echo of compositions stretching back to the fourth century. The 36-letter square giving the telestich UIUEHT, if (like 393 *Carausius* with VIOLA) that represents the author's name, is of course triangular, with 36 as Δ8. Triangularised, a pyramid shows lateral totals of (left) 85, *seventeen* times 5; and (right) 99, surely for the sheep that cannot now go astray, being in God's Net.

There is a remarkable finale, too. 'Wiweht', if we may call him that, seems to have read his Vulgate, John 21, with greater attention than I did in first publishing an interpretation of 1051 Penzance. His focus narrowed to a single but vital point; certainly that Christ had arisen, because God's Word stated beyond any doubt that seven of the twelve Disciples were there when the Risen Lord appeared to them and arranged the miraculous draught of 153 fishes. How was this conveyed to readers? First, the *numbers* were re-stated. In the square of 36 letters, col.1 has a part-acrostic; in the display, we can surely pick out

P C um**bu** in for **I S**	**P C B U I I S**
Q U icumq: pace venit hic **O** re **T**	**Q U O T**

— asking Piscibus, quot? 'With the Fishes, how many?' (answer, 153). The hint, here, is to look more closely at the lines of text. Let us re-examine the relevant Vulgate passage. In John 21, 2, we are given the names of those (among the Disciples) who were present; in all, seven, and described in what can be taken as Jerome's exact wording (the manuscript tradition allows no variant reading here).

> Jerome chose to write: Simon Petrus
> et Thomas qui dicitur Didymus
> et Nathanahel qui erat a Cana Galilaeae
> et filii Zebedaei

This extract, which we can call *(i)*, identifies Simon Peter; Thomas; Nathaniel from Cana;[5] and the two sons of Zebedee (James and John). That makes five. Extract *(ii)*, *et alii ex discipulis eius duo* 'and two others from His disciples' (not named), brings the total to seven.

Now do what Wiweht obviously did in AD 1007. Count the number of *words* in Jerome's extract *(i)*; there are *seventeen*. Then count up all the *letters*; divide their sum (84) by the *seven*, for those who were present, to find the *twelve* Disciples. Lastly, set out the 17 initials of the words, and add them up as 20-letter LaN; in groups, S P E T = 54, Q D D E = 28, N Q E A = 33, C G E F Z (remembering that Z counts as S, 17, in Jerome's computus) = 38. Inevitably, the answer is 153.[6] We therefore return to the model text,

proc **V** mb **V** nt.**I** n. for **I** s

having in its *three* words a mark of the Triune God, and in its own LNu content (V V I I, 5.5.1.1 = 12) a reference to the Disciples. Select the first *twelve* letters (*procumbunt in*), and observe Wiweht's latter-day labelling; an echo of 986 *Ioruert Ruallaunque* (p. 157).

P R ocumb **U**	(Simon)	**P** et **RU** s
N		**N** athanahel
T		**T** homas
I N		**I** oha **N** nes (f. Zebedaei)

Dividing the eight words of the text by mean ratio, 4.4, we see this again in the second half (its first *twelve* letters, naturally):

P ac **E V** e	**P E** tr **U** s
N i	**N** athanahel
T H	**T H** omas
I N	**I** oha **N** nes

To get the double set of names, *twenty-four* selected letters had to be used; twice the total of the Disciples. Suitably, if we go back to extract *(ii)*, *et alii ex discipulis eius duo* —

containing as it does the word *duo* 'two' — we see that Jerome arranged for the six initials, E A E D E D, 5.1.5.4.5.4, to add up to — *twenty-four*...And (above), the common letters in the first part, P R U N T I N, using Jerome's 20-letter LaN and *not* Wiweht's 23-letter, make 100 (symbol of the Lost Sheep Saved, as were all the souls in the 153-Net); it would be interesting if those in common in the second part, P E U N T H I N, came to the linked figure 99 (= the sheep that were not lost) but in fact they make 97. We are however taken back to the starting-point, the *seven* disciples out of *twelve*, by LNu. Take the second *twelve* letters to find

pace **V** en **I** th **I** n = V I I = *seven*

and then the first *seventeen* to find, a second time,

proc **V** mb **V** nt **I** n for **I** s = V V I I = *twelve*

and then perhaps pause to admire the skill of a man who could arrange these obvious and wholly convincing readings in double-harness with his use of M, V and I for a triple chronogram.[7]

We know nothing about this author save what is probably his name, his mastery of inscriptional Biblical style and the fact that he had subjected Jerome's translation of John, 21, to intimate scrutiny; but this is the only case known to me where any composer switches, logically and consistently, from the 23-letter LaN of his own day and his own computus to the 20-letter LaN that he knew was used by St Jerome. His little message addressed to the percipient far and wide, affirming the resurrection and salvation of all who lay around this tall granite cross, may today appear damaged, defective and even illegible. It has survived, triumphantly, the passage of almost ten centuries. It has done so because — and *only* because — its compositional mode was designed to lead, one day, to full recovery. Nine hundred and ninety-one years on, we might view this as little short of miraculous.[8]

Notes to Chapter 8

1 In his *Cambro-Latin Compositions* (Four Courts, Dublin 1998) at 27-32.

2 Its alarming tale of previous treatment is recorded by E. Okasha, *Corpus of Early Christian Inscribed Stones of South-west Britain* (Leicester UP, London 1993), 195 99, fully referenced.

3 Wales; see in *ECMW*, 40-41. Ireland; I.Henderson & E.Okasha, 'The Early Christian Inscribed and Carved Stones of Tullylease, Co. Cork', *Cambridge Med. Celtic Stud.*, 24 (1992), 1-36 — e.g., 9th cent., QUICUMQUAE HUNC TITULUM LEGERIT ORAT PRO BERECHTUINE.

4 *CIIC* 1045, Treslothan, inscribed altar, 11th century, appears to read æ g u r e d (=E(c) gfrith ?).

5 Nathanael from Cana (John 1, 43-51) does not figure by that name in the Matthew 10 list used in 986 *Ioruert* (p. 157); but from the 9th century he has been identified with 'Bartholomeus'.

6 Jerome, in his turn, must have closely examined John's Greek text of the 1st century. There the words corresponding to Jerome's passage *(i)* total 18, not 17, but they also

have 84 letters; the whole passage corresponding to Latin *manifestavit autem...ex discipulis eius duo* has *twelve* time 10 letters; and the Greek for 'with 153 great fishes', *ichthuon megalon (h)ekaton pentakonta trion*, has 34, *seventeen* times 2, letters.

7   It is not impossible that five centuries earlier a similar allusion to the John, 21 list of disciples named as witnesses was built into 391 *Senacus* (p. 92), a text that certainly uses 17 as a key number and that may refer to the (Luke,5) Draught of Fishes story through using MULTITUDINEM. Pairing the inscription with the names gives us: SENACUS PRSB/**Simo**n **Petrus** — HIC IACIT CUM **Thoma**s Didymus — MULTITUDINEM/**Na**thane**hel**. That involves 34 letters of the display. In the right order, 17 (50 percent) are contained in the proper names. FRATRUM would refer to the brothers John and James, sons of Zebedee. Of course 391 *Senacus* and 1051 (Penzance) are unconnected, as must be 986 *Ioruert* (intermediate in time and space) with its full, Matthew 10, roll of disciples. Allusion(s) to those who are recorded as meeting the Risen Lord must suggest a special weight attached to John, 21, as proof of the Resurrection.

8   For a recent powerful re-statement of what the use of Biblical style really signifies and why all these modern recoveries can be made (as intended), see David Howlett's remarks in *Peritia*, 11 (1997), at 119.

A further note on 1051 Penzance

Since the above was written, the author and Carl Thorpe have managed to read (June 1998) the large, straggling, peculiar and eroded letters of the smaller basal-panel inscription. Left (upper), 2 lines, is R . G I S I over the expected CRUX; 'Cross of (name)'. The second graph is either E C or A E internalised, for (Old English?) *Recgisi* or *Raegisi*, presumably the benefactor or donor of both cross and burial-ground. Right (lower) reads D + T I (conjoined) over another peculiar X; ? *Crux D(omini) Xti* (= *Christi*) 'the Cross of the Lord Christ'. Though now transcribed as capitals the letters are all bookhand; certainty is impossible but these readings go with the general tenor of the main inscriptions and its interpretation here.

Envoi

It is interesting to find that many of the devices in Biblical-style *arithmetica*, as well as resting on the Greek mathematicians' quite advanced work on properties of numbers, were still being recommended in cryptographic treatises of the Renaissance. During the present century the Baconians, those who believe that Francis Bacon wrote both the works attributed to him *and* all or most of those supposedly by William Shakespeare, made endless forays into this field. Within anything by 'Shakespeare', codes and ciphers of every imaginable nature yield readings like FRA.BACON, F.BACON, and his associated titles. They have to. In the pages of *Baconiana* we can even read about a 24-letter LaN system in which B A C O N, 2.1.3.14.13, makes 33, though we are not told why this should be significant![1]

Over the last few years the practical experience of seminars and public lectures has assured me that any audience, provided with pens and ruled paper and invited to undertake nothing more challenging than elementary addition and multiplication, can rapidly grasp the fundamentals of inscriptional style. It is the expected outcome of proper explanations in plain language. A second, sadder, experience has been that those whose instant reactions are that 'they have no head for figures' or 'mistrust anything with numbers in it' almost invariably have not bothered to read analyses and interpretations. For the main, there continues to be an abiding and well-informed national desire to know more about our protohistoric past in the first millennium AD. It deserves to be met with something better than tired old icons like 'King' Arthur, and any new discoveries help to relegate the ridiculous label of *The Dark Ages* to obsolescence.

Memorials in Latin are still occasionally set up; so, far more often in rural Wales, are tombstones wholly in British (=Welsh). In fact a good many of the simpler Biblical-style devices and adjuncts appear in print daily. Take the example in *Fig. 77* — a promotional 14-by-14 square in a local paper, December 1997. The answers (*left*) can be seen at once; four of them reading across, six acrostically downwards. Whoever composed this can never have intended that at least twenty short words are also detectable (*right*) reading across, down and diagonally. We could juggle them into a kind of nonsense-tale; 'Ammon — load dab, trout. Opt one oak urn; tie tent. Pop! Ell! Cut cost; rat cat, hoe, cab; Cad!' and we even have the name for something in Latin (col.12, centre) MALA ('cheek, jawbone'). The fruit-and-veg. names are *relevant*, to a pre-Christmas greengrocery promotion. Nothing else is. A subversive composer could easily have worked into this SUPERMARKETS RUIN TRADE or DEATH TO EUROPEAN UNION, which would have made it considerably more interesting.

HERE'S the first of three chances to win £20 worth of vouchers for healthy organic produce from the St Austell branch of Tesco.

The names of five fruits and five vegetables are hidden in the wordsearch.

Fig. 77   A contemporary letter square, left, with its intended acrostics (to win £20…) but right, a mass of unintentional and often diagonal acrostics. Only relevance, in this case to a theme of greengroceries, tells us which set must be an intentional one.

With the various acrostics, telestichs and horizontal readings in all the squares and grids discussed earlier, and they ranged from the 380s to 1007 (a very long run), the inducements to accept them as historically genuine and intended are, first, that the readings are also *relevant* to the short inscriptions as displayed, and second, that in common with most other devices they are not isolated curiosities. They occur far too often to be written out as fanciful impositions by modern interpreters on ancient texts. The same goes for many of the symbolic numbers (33, 99, 100, 144 and 153 in particular) that, given by LaN totals from columnar addition or triangularisation, occur again and again. The Vulgate still tells us, as it told countless Christian Celts in post-Roman times, what these numbers imply. In any memorial to a dead Christian, reference to Christ's archetypal 'death' on the Cross, to the Lost Sheep Saved, to the Heavenly City, is entirely relevant to the restricted theme of the display.

Looking back over the previous chapters, a reader might get the impression that intellectual life in protohistoric Western Britain was dominated by the Word of God, in Latin, allied to an obsession with numbers in a manner reminiscent of certain psychiatric disorders that (it has been pointed out)[2] accompany religious extremism. A sense of proportion, indeed plain commonsense, will correct this. The inscriptions represent a surviving fraction of a minority activity, probably not even an annual activity, by a priestly or scholastic minority within the upper reaches of society. They have assumed a disproportionate and unexpected importance because, being on stone, they have neither perished nor been detectably altered since first cut and because, being almost wholly in Latin and composed in their own arithmetically-dominated Biblical style, they provide a corpus of hard evidence for features we either know from different material — the longer MSS analysed by David Howlett, to a certain extent the use of *geometrica* in manuscript illuminations explored by Robert Stevick; or have begun to suspect were present for other reasons — the likely outline of post-Roman education, for example, discussed in Chap. 3

Fig.78   *358* Voteporigis, *drawn from photographs of the stone, now in Carmarthen Museum. Note how the slightly lowered -MO- may accommodate the ringed cross (carved first ?). The ogam has an imagined stem-line up the irregularly rounded surface.*

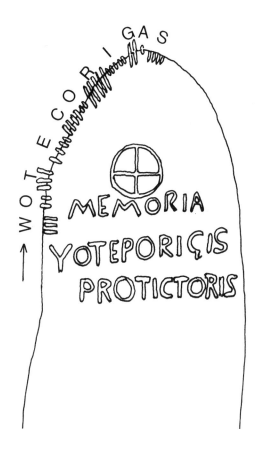

An aspect of scientific enquiry, the raising-up of a first hypothesis arising from observations open to all to the status of an embracing theory that may eventually be acceptable as fact, is prediction and verification. It could be predicted, from what has allegedly and hypothetically been discovered, that newly-found inscriptions should include those exhibiting the same features; strictly, not more than a tenth of them since only some ten per cent of the known texts have Biblical-style contents, or generate images. If so, it would help to verify the claims made in this book. However, most if not all of the post-Macalister discoveries in Wales and Cornwall are either too short or too defective[3] to offer any help, or seem to belong to the non-qualifying ninety per cent. There is a further interesting possibility, and it is neither a remote chance nor impermissible; that there could exist an inscription in full Biblical style, computus and all, yet by accident or design slightly altered between composition and cutting so that the display has lost any inner meaning — but would regain it, if the alteration was identified and reversed.

The boulder-slab memorial 358 *Voteporigis*, *ECMW* no.138, was found near Narberth, Pembrokeshire (actually just in Carmarthenshire) and is now is Carmarthen Museum, *Fig. 78*. It marks the grave or burial-plot, *memoria*, of a *Voteporix who can be accepted as the king of Demetia addressed about 540 (when he was no longer young) by Gildas, who called him *Vortipori* (voc.), *Demetarum tyranne* 'usurper-king of the Demetians'.[4] His name in sixth-century neo-Brittonic might have been written *Uotepir* /wodebir/. In IOC, we suppose its nominative would have been VOTEPORIX, the final element being British *rix* 'king'. The stone is demonstrably Christian, the 'hot-cross-bun' motif simplified from the encircled chi-rho seen in *Fig.40*. The text is MEMORIA / VOTEPORIGIS / PROTICTORIS 'the memorial of V., Protector' — we need not bother about this use of a revived Roman title — and because the dynasty may still have been conscious of its immigrant Irish origin the name is repeated in ogam (*Fig. 78*) as a translated Primitive Irish genitive *WOTECORIGAS*.[5]

What we should expect is that, short as it may be, this royal and Christian epitaph is in Biblical style. Putting the name as (a) and the other two words as (b), analysis produces:

		W	S	L
(a)	V O T E P O R I G I S	1	5	11
(b)	M E M O R I A … P R O T I C T O R I S	2	8	18
		3	**13**	**29**

The totals show extreme ratio; *W*, 1:2 → 3 and *S*, 5:8 →13 from *1.2.3.5.8.13.21.34…*, and *L*, 11:18 →29 from *1.3.4.7.11.18.29.47…*, but that is about all. First and last letters of the *display*, M and S, 11.17, make 28, which is Δ7, and therefore might look like a hint to triangularise the text. But we cannot triangularise from a letter total of twenty-*nine*. The *hypothesis* is that, from context and analogy, this memorial was originally designed with a computus going beyond mere totals in ER (and that it was somehow altered before the extant display was cut). The *prediction* is that, if an alteration can be found and reversed, the text will exhibit a structure with relevant details. *Verification* proceeds from a suspicion that VOTEPORIGIS may look like an IOC form, but appears not to be correct IOC. The reconstructed British name would be *Uo-tepo-rix* (the meaning is a matter of debate)[6], of which the proper genitive is *Uoteporigos* — the ogam *WOTECORIGAS* (where *-as* had developed from *-os*) is the correct (Irish) IOC shape. Now in other Welsh names given in IOC, compounded with *-rix*, we find, e.g., 455 *Camulorigi*, 318 *Ettorigi*, 413 *Monedorigi*; not *-rigos*, but *-rigi*, mock Latin genitives using the 'epitaphic-I' ending (see Glossary), and these quite soon became treated like nominatives (as on 435 *Clutorigi*). There have been various explanations for the unique VOTEPORIGIS spelling; it imitates the Latin (*rex*) *regis*, gen., it is to match and to rhyme with PROTICTORIS, it was chosen to echo the final -S of *WOTECORIGAS*.

What happens if we restore the name to read VOTEPORIGI? Look what follows, starting with the analysis:

		W	S	L
(a)	V O T E P O R I G I	1	5	10
(b)	M E M O R I A … P R O T I C T O R I S	2	8	18
		3	**13**	**28**

The totals are still in ER; the letters, dividing by two, show (10:18 → 28) 5:9 → 14, from *1.4.5.9.14.23.37…*. We now have 28, or Δ7, from *L* and also from initial and last letters of the name, V I, 19.9=28. Triangularisation gives this pyramid:

```
11              M            11
 5             E M           11
13            O R  I          9
 1           A V O T         18
 5          E P O R I         9
 7        G I P R O T        18
 9      I C T O R I S        17
51                           93
```

To obtain these totals we must have PROTICTORIS, not PROTECTORIS (and this might explain the choice of spelling); 51 plus 93 takes us to the familiar 144 of Apocalypsis 7.4 and 21.17, for the Heavenly City. As the combined totals *W*, *S* and *L* now make 44, and the display's three line initials M V P, 11.19.14 give the same, with 28 and 144 also being *four*-divisible, we can try a *four*-line grid:

```
11     M E M O R I A      1
19     V O T E P O R     16
 9     I G I P R O T     18
 9     I C T O R I S     17
48        = 100 =        52
```

Here, too, is a meaningful total. Moreover with this simple grid, only one step (device) from the letter total of the display, we may have another of these elementary Welsh devised plan images (*cf. Fig. 53* earlier). It could suggest a rectilinear grave-plot where the ringed cross, correctly placed, represents the whole cross-marked and inscribed boulder (as with 393 *Carausius*, *Fig. 57*). If so (*Fig. 79*), the plot is aligned N-S-E-W, with *A*(*quilo*), *M*(*eridies*), *O*(*riens*) and *O*(*ccidens*). Within the plot, the grave would be the column I O O I, which adds to 44 again, and the head would be at the west, *Occidens*, cross-marked end. From the symbolism of the numbers, it is the grave of a Lost Sheep Saved (one hundred) whose soul, revealed by perfect 28 triangularised, is now in the Heavenly City (one hundred and forty-four). With the spelling VOTEPORIGIS, this would be impossible.

What happened? We can make a guess, for historical reasons. The deceased ruler may have been a nominal Christian. Gildas tells us that he had become a *bad* son of a *good* king (probably of his royal predecessor *Aircol* (/airgol/; in IOC, this would be AGRICOLA)[7] who was elsewhere remembered as a church benefactor. Voteporix was prey to surges of violent sin; guilty of murder and adulteries; worse, of the rape of a shameless daughter after his wife's death. Was this too much for someone to accept? Is this another *Catamanus* episode? Before the epitaph was cut, an unknown hand inserted that innocent-seeming final -S, and the textual meaning was rendered null. Insofar as that previous prediction could ever be verified, a restored 358 *Voteporigis* text would exemplify a familiar pattern of Biblical style, and there may well have been good reason to tamper with it.

The past is indeed a foreign country, as Professor David Lowenthal wrote in 1985. The creation of a heritage industry can render its uncritical exploration an often lucrative activity. But which past? Longer ago, Stuart Piggott sketched a distinction between the Past-as-it-Really-Was, by its nature irrecoverable, and a parallel Past-as-Wished-For. The

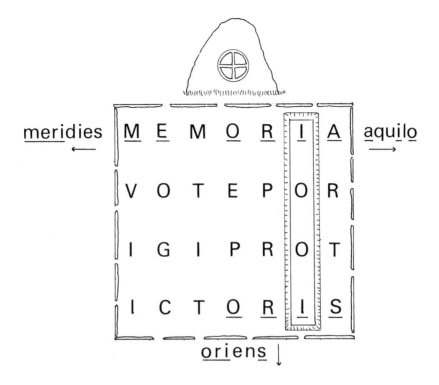

meridies M E M O R I A *aquilo*

V O T E P O R

I G I P R O T

I C T O R I S

oriens

Fig.79   *An image – a devised plan (of burial plot with E-W grave and cross-marked headstone at W end) – that would be generated by 358 with the spelling* VOTEPORIGI. *For the 'labelling' of three compass points by the text, cf. 391 Senacus in Fig. 32.*

latter manifests itself within most national groupings at (predictable) intervals: the signs are not hard to find. In Victorian England the upper social reaches became peopled with names like Alfred, Edgar, Harold, Oswald, even the odd Athelstan(e) — those of pre-Norman English kings — under discreet leads from Lord Tennyson, J.R. Green and now-forgotten publicists. In post-400 Celtic Britain, could we ever hope to define the impulses behind the continued use of Roman (even Imperial) non-Biblical names and the occasional record of older, probably legendary, British ones like 499 *Carataci*?

Our pre-Norman and, broadly, Celtic Christian past is a very remote country now. The materials for anything better than a series of partial reconstructions have vanished. In that distant landscape the historian's business, as an occasional explorer, must be to recall whatever details may be briefly lit by flashes of sudden discovery, realisation, intuition, and (as longer illumination) the re-working of established sources; from that, to offer reports in the shape of structured narratives; and lastly, back home again, to suggest explanations. In this book, the chapters have represented my first reports from a Vanished Land that none can know fully, but which after a half-century of visits I may know a little better than I did, and the explanations have been mainly confined to technicalities.

My closing explanation — at least, the one that I feel most confident in proposing — is that all these post-Roman inscriptions on stone, still our largest single body of evidence for the period and area, can be interpreted as a manifestation of something called *Britishness*. It could be further defined as the planned exploitation, during a time of instability and external menace, of an exclusive intellectual heritage. We have observed its components; *romanitas*, hierarchical Christianity, an international literary language, artificial prolongation of the remote heroic past, the purely internal fostering of a compositional style to the stage where it fragments into cryptography and image-generation, in short, all the signs of communal intent to be (and to remain) different. Wales, Cymru, the largest homeland of the *Combrogi*, the dwellers within the same frontier, became and long remained the centre of Britishness. There was a repeat performance, certainly at a high social and intellectual level, of this raising of the cultural defences in the late eleventh and the twelfth centuries. There arose an urgent need to re-state the British past, its far-off Roman inheritance, its half-remembered kings and saints, against certain preposterous claims and assumptions from the Anglo-Norman conquerors.

Who undertook this considerable task? If, for a moment, we can equate at least a part of this Britishness with a (necessarily, by then uncritical) image of the British historical past — in other words, as a British historical *mythology* — a clear answer has been provided in the following words:

> In Ireland, Wales and Gaelic Scotland the preservers and presenters of historical mythology were pre-eminently a mandarin and often hereditary literate caste, whose expertise ranged across poetry, mythology, story-telling and genealogy and who drew distinctions between these various categories. They were the conservative keepers and remembrancers of highly conservative and past-oriented societies, drawing upon a vast corpus of triads, genealogies, foundation-legends and a mass of literary, toponymic and onomastic lore...It is arguable that it is only societies uncertain of their present status and even more unsure of their future prospects which need the self-assurance of nostalgia and historic mythology.

Here, Professor R.R.Davies is writing[8] about non-English societies in Britain and Ireland during the twelfth to fourteenth centuries; for that age, we possess very much more literature in all the categories he names than we do, or ever will, for the fifth to seventh centuries. Nevertheless, stretching the definition of his 'mandarin and literate caste' to cover the Christian priesthood, it becomes as apposite to the earlier period as to Norman time. In respect of the repertoire of traditional knowledge (embraced by several languages) the short inscriptions are one rather special tip of the inferred iceberg. And in terms of both past-orientation and historical mythology we must also remember that, imperfectly transmitted as many details certainly were, until we reach the early sixth century the outside limits of orally-transmitted knowledge (about a century, or three generations) would still have stretched back to the last days of Roman Britain.[9]

Does Britishness, in opposition to 'Englishness', exist today in a supposedly multicultural Britain that has in fact been thoroughly multicultural (and multilingual) since the Iron Age? Possibly. Before me is an August 1997 issue of *Y Cymro*, a lively all-Welsh newspaper published at Yr Wyddgrug (=Mold, Flints.), mainly about *y tymor rygbi*

Fig. 80   Fresh delights and unexpected implications; the vicarage garden, St Clement, Cornwall, probably 1928. R.A.S. Macalister (left) explains details of 473 Vitali, including a non-existent ogam, to Rev. Frederick A. O'Flynn, incumbent 1922-1932, whose little daughter (now aged 79) recalls the incident; because all Macalister's archive was inadvertently destroyed on his death (1950), views of the Master in the field are rare discoveries.

newydd ('the new Rugby season'). The Welsh for 'at' somewhere is *yn*, like Latin with *in* meaning both 'in' and 'at'. To explain fully why 'at Twickenham' must be written *yn Nhwickenham* would need several pages or, lecturing, quarter of an hour with a blackboard. The Us-and-Them assertion lurking behind *Nhwickenham* would have been found in AD

700; showing a learned Anglo-Saxon visitor a tombstone with CVNOMAGLI, letting him read it, telling him the deceased was called / ˈconˌṽail/ and watching him write it down as c o i n m a i l.[10] The sub-title to David Lowenthal's *The Past is a Foreign County* is: *They do things differently there*. Do they? Britain's past caught us up years ago.

Writers of supposedly non-fictional works (myself included) stand, at the end, too close to the completed task to evaluate either the product or the likely reactions of reasonably-minded general readers and professional colleagues. I see this book as an exposition that begins with archaeological objects (old stones, standing in the landscape, humanly-adorned with ancient letters and occasional ornaments), made to take part in a kind of Dance of the Seven Veils. As each veil is whisked aside, not only fresh delights, but little star-bursts of unexpected implications too are laid bare (*Fig. 80*). In no special order, the latter concern the legacy of *romanitas*, literacy in Latin and other languages, schooling in the byways of Latin and in Greek-originating mathematics, the growth of hierarchical Christianity, the lasting model of the Vulgate with its forgotten inner intricacies, inequalities in post-Roman society, intellectual bilingualism (and exclusiveness), an heroic scale of ingenuity, lost attitudes to how sight and sound relate to each other, composition as an end in itself transcending conventional divisions, and perhaps (as a common backdrop to much of this) a sense that our limited knowledge and over-many preconceptions about our own not-too-distant, and by no means unitary, national past can remain stultified; unless given the kind of sharp jolt that I became determined to administer. Any published work claiming to explore uncharted territory, break new ground, point to new horizons (etc.) must anticipate a reception ranging from uncritical praise to downright onslaught. That is fair play but it does not matter. Reading the book rapidly in one go, I believe that — with its many imperfections — it describes findings far beyond coincidence; things that existed; just for once, a peephole view into a British Past-as-it-Really-Was.

Since the first chapter of this book began with the fictional William Hanks, it would be appropriate to end it with the once-real Gildas. From his writings Gildas the Briton, priest and polemicist, does not come across as a comfortable person. He wrote during a lull in extremely uncomfortable times. His contemporaries and subsequent admirers were certain that Gildas had been pre-eminently a wise man; *sapiens, sapientissimus*. Attributed to him is a saying: *veritas sapienti nitet / cuiusque ore fuerit prolata*[11] and, regarding myself auctorially as no more than a mouthpiece for revelations that others must now work upon, I am more than happy to adopt these words. The emphatic noun is *veritas* 'truth, reality; what genuinely is'. It has seven letters. And of course we see there are *seven* words, divided 3:4 (as if from 1.3.4.7.11…), and thrice-*seven* syllables divided 9:12 (=3:4, thrice). The last word *prolata* also has *seven* letters; all *seven* word-initials add up, in 20-letter LaN, to *seven* times twelve. As Gildas was probably the brightest of all products from Illtud's famous school, we would rightly be disappointed unless Gildas's saying showed the same easy, throwaway, numerical trademark as any piece on similar lines by St Jerome or Rufinus the Syrian. Probably the purpose was to give special weight to the word *veritas*. Michael Winterbottom translates this as 'A wise man recognises the gleam of truth whoever utters it'. Content in this setting to be no more than *whoever*, I hope that readers who have borne with me to the end will, in their turn, accept the veracity of these Christian Celtic messages and images, our legacy of compositions in Insular inscriptional Biblical style and inheritance of unique cultural significance.

Notes to Envoi

1   Alfred Dodd, *The Personal Poems of Francis Bacon* (Our Shake-speare), 2nd edn. (Liverpool 1931), 18, has this and similar solutions.
2   See Robert Sapolsky's essay 'Circling the Blanket of God' (on the link between schizotypal disorders and religious extremism) in his *Junk food Monkeys* (Headline, 1997), at 246-7; I owe this reference to the kindness of David Miles, Oxford.
3   E.g. (numbers from my *Mute Stones*), Lundy, 1400 O/P/TIMI, 1402 (ring cross)/POTITI; Cornwall, 1202 EVOCA(T?)./CAT...; or Wales (Anglesey), ERCAGNI. No multiline inscriptions have been found for some decades now.
4   *De Excidio Britonum* (ed.transl.M.Winterbottom, Chichester 1978) cap.31 (with 'Your head is already whitening...the end of your life is gradually drawing near'). This, if written around 540, suggests a death within the next 10-20 years.
5   I do not believe any parallel name existed in Irish; this is a court scholar's learned 'translation' into a PrIr.genitive.
6   Most recently, Eric Hamp, 'Voteporigis Protictoris', *Studia Celtica*, 30 (1996), 293-4. Hamp reads the name as 'succouring king'or 'shelterer', for which Latin *protector* would be 'a sort of onomastic explicatory gloss'.
7   Bartum, *EWGT* 10 (Harl.3859), *Guortepir map Aircol*, and 45, *Aircol lawhir (lau, hir,* 'Long-Hand', i.e., The Generous). The original borrowing from the (Imperial) name Agricola may have been in Ireland.
8   See Further Reading: this is from his pt.iv (*Trans.R.Hist.Soc.*, 6th ser.7 (1997), at p.18.).
9   But the mixture of historical fact and historical mythology (or compression, confusion and re-writing) in *DEB* shows how Gildas, b.(?)496, was almost beyond such outside limits.
10 *Anglo-Saxon Chronicle*, A text, under year 577 — deaths of three British Kings, entered as *Coinmail, Condidan. Farinmail* (and see *LHEB*, 464, for comment).
11 *DEB* (ed.transl.Winterbottom), 88, fragment 8.

Further Reading

Chapter 1

There is no single work devoted to all the post-Roman British inscriptions. I have tried to provide an archaeological background in my *And Shall These Mute Stones Speak? Post-Roman Inscriptions in Western Britain* (Cardiff 1994), which updates in detail those of the south-west, mainly Cornwall and part of Devon; E. Okasha's *Corpus of Early Christian Inscribed Stones of South-west Britain* (London 1993) while bibliographically exhaustive has too many incomplete readings to be of use here. Chap.V ('The Early Christian Inscriptions') of Kenneth Jackson's *Language and History in Early Britain* (Edinburgh 1953=*LHEB*) is eminently worth reading. The main, numbered, descriptive catalogue is R.A.S. Macalister, *Corpus Inscriptionum Insularum Celticarum* (2 vols., Dublin 1945,1949=*CIIC*), and for Wales alone V.E.Nash-Williams, *The Early Christian Monuments of Wales* (Cardiff 1950=*ECMW*). The few Lowland Scottish stones are most recently covered by my paper 'The Early Christian Inscriptions of Southern Scotland', *Glasgow Archaeological Journal, 17* (1991-2), 1-10. (All the foregoing were written before the discovery that any of the inscriptions were composed in Biblical style.) From the cutter's standpoint, which needs to be properly understood, two useful short works are Giancarlo Susini, *The Roman Stonecutter, An Introduction to Latin Epigraphy* (Oxford 1973), and the master-mason Harold Crossley's *Lettering in Stone* (Self Publ. Assoc., Upton-upon-Severn 1991). Those who are fascinated by the design and production of letters should read the classic handbook, Edward Johnston, *Writing & Illuminating, & Lettering* (Pitman, London 1906, with numerous reprintings; now in paperback, A. & C. Black, London 1994).

Chapter 2

Martin Henig's *Religion in Roman Britain* (London 1984) offers a full and thoughtful survey of the whole topic, in which Christianity is placed in context as one of the later exotic cults, eventually triumphing; its companion volume, my *Christianity in Roman Britain to AD 500* (London 1981; 2nd impr. 1985.) ought now to be re-written to take new ideas into account, but will serve as a general picture. The cult of Isis in the Roman period is fully examined by R.E. Witt, *Isis in the Ancient World* (Johns Hopkins Univ. Press, 1997). For Roman Britain generally, a standard work is Peter Salway, *Roman Britain* (Oxford 1981) supplemented by Barri Jones and David Mattingly, *An Atlas of Roman Britain* (Oxford 1990). The relationship between the principal languages, Latin and British, was explored in *LHEB* by Kenneth Jackson — his views have been inevitably modified since 1950 by others — and another side of it emerges from A.L.F. Rivet and Colin Smith, *The Place-*

names of Roman Britain (London 1979), containing the main record of how the Romans actually wrote and spelled so many names in British.

The preliminary description of Lullingstone was Col. G.W. Meates's very readable short book, *Lullingstone Roman Villa* (London 1955). The full report appeared (under his name) in the Kent Archaeological Society's two-volume monograph, *The Lullingstone Roman Villa* (1979). The Europa mosaic panel, in subdued colour, forms the frontispiece to the first volume. The background to the York inscriptions is the *RCHM England The City of York: Vol.1, Roman York — Eburacum* (HMSO, 1962), arranged in a near-unuseable manner (Corellia Optata is at p.96). All inscriptions from Roman Britain, on every surface and medium, are listed in *RIB* (see Abbreviations, p. 11), with annual Supplements in the journal *Britannia*.

Inevitably there has been a great deal about languages, ancient *and* modern, in a work discussing Latin inscriptions containing Celtic and Germanic names and employing analogies in English. For readers particularly interested, perhaps taking part in the revival of self-taught Latin and Greek spearheaded by Dr Peter Jones, the best (Classical Latin) dictionary is the *Oxford Latin Dictionary* (7 parts, Clarendon Press, Oxford 1968-80), and for standard post-Classical reference, Alexander Souter, *A Glossary of Later Latin to 600 A.D.* (Oxford 1949), with what is so far available — vol.I, A-L — of the great *Dictionary of Medieval Latin from British Sources* (O.U.P. for British Academy, 1997). The most comprehensive grammar of Latin in English, with a full discussion of verse and metrics ('Prosody') at the end, is still the old favourite; B.L. Gildersleeve & Gonzalez Lodge, *Latin Grammar* (rev. edn. 1895; constantly re-issued, and now (1997) by Bristol Classical Press/Duckworth, London, paperback). There is no point in looking for some of the words here and their many meanings in a pocket dictionary.

Welsh frightens many English-speakers because of its supposed traps, like -LL- and the different sounds of its W and Y, but colloquial Welsh is no harder to learn than French and easier than correct German. Now fortunately available is Paul Russell, *An Introduction to the Celtic Languages* (Longman, London & N.Y. 1995), a proper survey by a skilled linguist, to be read carefully, and warmly recommended. Need I point out that in the sister-isles during the period of the inscriptions early Irish and early Welsh were the *majority* languages?

Chapter 3

There is very little direct evidence about Insular post-Roman education and correspondingly little in print. Professor Michael Lapidge, 'Gildas's education and the Latin culture of sub-Roman Britain', pp.27-50 in: M. Lapidge & D.N. Dumville, eds., *Gildas: New Approaches* (Woodbridge 1984), puts forward certain conclusions that are now hard to reconcile with specific indicators from these Latin texts. A new collection of essays, *Literacy in Medieval Celtic Societies* (ed. Huw Pryce, Cambridge 1998), provides insights — mainly by inference — into a limited retention after 400 of structured Insular schooling, the three stages of primary, by a *grammaticus* and finally by a *rhetor*. For those who may be particularly interested in Roman education and the status of the grammarian (*grammaticus*), Robert A. Kaster's full study *Guardians of Language. The Grammarian and Society in Late Antiquity* (Univ. of California Press 1988) can be recommended. For a wider question of transmission of learning, how the whole Latin culture was promoted and how the early counterparts of libraries, reading facilities and publication were organised, two admirable guides are: Harry Y. Gamble, *Books and Readers in the Early Church* (Yale Univ. Press, New Haven & London 1995), and Jocelyn Penny Small, *Wax Tablets of the Mind. Cognitive studies of memory and literacy in Classical antiquity* (Routledge, London 1997). Chaps.10 & 11 of the latter form an illuminating and rare account of the material and mechanics of reading.

As to the minority commemorated by stone memorials — indeed, who in society were the early Christians — Rodney Stark's *The Rise of Christianity: a Sociologist Reconsiders History* (Princeton Univ. Press, Princeton 1996) is fresh, well documented, provocative, and must challenge a deal of loose thinking on this score. Professor Stark's findings strike me as entirely relevant to the Insular scene. Finally, each year now, more books about 'Celtic' Christianity (most of them historical rather than archaeological or analytical) spatter down like the gentle dew from Heaven. Evidence from inscriptions is seldom if ever included, and I can find none to recommend as enlightenment for the topics considered here.

Interlude

Many readers of this book will, like its author, be lost at an early stage in the world of mathematics; even that old standby, Lancelot Hogben's *Mathematics for the Million* (the 1968 rev. ed., still in print), proves impenetrable soon after its Introduction. The arithmetic here is actually quite simple and the focus is very much on the properties of numbers. In that respect, any reader would enjoy, and be informed by, Karl Menninger's *Number Words and Number Symbols. A Cultural History of Numbers* (originally, German, 1957-8; transl. Paul Broneer, now Dover Publications, New York 1992). There are explanatory sections about the arithmetical adjuncts of Biblical style in David Howlett's books (*Saint Patrick, Celtic Latin Tradition*, and *British Books*), much of it relevant to inscriptional computus.

The classic source for the discoveries and accomplishments of the Greek mathematicians (on which Roman *geometrica* and *arithmetica* rested) remains Sir Thomas Heath's 2-vol. *A History of Greek Mathematics* (Oxford 1921; available again as a reprint, Dover Publications, New York 1981). The Greek texts themselves, with some diagrams, are in Ivor Thomas (transl.), *Selections illustrating the history of Greek mathematics* (rev. ed., Harvard 'Loeb' ser., 335, 362, 1991, 1993). Here, it would have been inappropriate to go further into the hugely complex world of early symbolic numerology, where there are or were systems other than those mentioned in the book; enthusiastic seekers might try, for instance, Adela Yarbro Collins, 'Numerical Symbolism in Jewish and Early Christian Apocalyptic Literature', pp.1221-1286 in: W. Haase, ed., *Aufstieg und Niedergang der Römischen Welt*, II, 21.2 (Berlin 1984). A different approach to numerical and allusive composition, but with familiar aspects, is outlined in Professor John MacQueen's *Numerology* (Edinburgh Univ. Press, Edinburgh 1985).

It seems to me that the computistic and allusive system used, or developed, in post-Roman Britain for inscriptional ends to a large extent went its own way (though certainly owing much to the Vulgate). The older and mathematically very complex system of symbolic numbers known as *gematria* is however described by John Michell, in his *The Dimensions of Paradise. The Proportions and Symbolic Numbers of Ancient Cosmology* (Thames &

Hudson 1988). Lastly, note that what happened in the Celtic-speaking world by no means precluded the use, from time to time, of simpler approaches to cryptic writing. Revival of the 'Caesar' substitution-code in the eleventh century is described by Wilhelm Levison, *England and the Continent in the Eighth Century* (Oxford 1946), appendix viii, 'St. Boniface and Cryptography'.

Chapter 4

The evidence (such as it is) for bishops and other orders of priesthood in Roman Britain is summarised in my *Christianity in Roman Britain to AD 500* (Batsford, London 1981); there is a further summary, for Wales, in chaps.7 & 8 of Professor Wendy Davies, *An Early Welsh Microcosm. Studies in the Llandaff Charters* (Royal Historical Society, London 1978). For other subjects, including the history of the Bible in the languages of antiquity, the best starting-point is *The Oxford Dictionary of the Christian Church*, or any other reliable encyclopaedia of Christianity with up-to-date bibliographies. There is a considerable literature about St Jerome, not all of it in English; for those prepared to read the master's elegant Latin, *The Letters of Saint Jerome*, ed. James Duff (Browne & Nolan, Dublin 1942) is a good selection. Again, for Latin readers who might like to discover more stylistic and arithmetical features for themselves, the standard text of the Vulgate is the 'Stuttgart' edition; *Biblia Sacra iuxta Vulgatam Versionem* (Deutsche Bibelgesellschaft, Stuttgart 1983). Older and less thorough editions do not necessarily include MS variants, which help to determine the most likely original readings. The broad-sweep history of Christianity in the Western provinces of the Roman Empire is constantly being re-written. Currently, readers may find a helpful and well-constructed survey in Richard Fletcher's *The Conversions of Europe. From Paganism to Christianity 371-1386 AD* (HarperCollins. London 1997).

Chapter 5

Again, no single modern work treats exclusively of Scotland's earliest religious history, nor its various categories of inscribed and/or pictorial stones. Sally M. Foster, *Picts, Gaels and Scots* is a good introduction to the mixture of peoples in the far North (Batsford/Historic Scotland, 1996) and chap.11 of my book *Christianity in Roman Britain* covers what was known to 1981 of the Lowlands in sub-Roman times from a Christian angle. Wider views are offered by the early chapters of Professor Alfred Smyth's *Warlords and Holy Men. Scotland AD 80-1000* (Edward Arnold, 1984). For Whithorn, Peter Hill's timely *Whithorn & St Ninian. The Excavation of a Monastic Town 1984-91* (Sutton/Whithorn Trust, 1997) collates all earlier reports and supersedes them with an account of far-reaching investigations; Hill's admirable chaps.1 & 2 provide a full range of current ideas, and a very clear illustrated summary of all that has been found.

The regrettably cursory treatment of Ireland should be remedied from Dáibhí Ó Cróinín's *Early Medieval Ireland 400-1200* (Longman, 1995), notably his chaps.1 , 6 & 7; a complementary and invaluable source-book, with everything translated, is Liam de Paor, *Ireland and Early Medieval Europe* (Four Courts, Dublin 1997). Damian McManus, *A Guide to Ogam* (An Sagart, Maynooth 1991), is now the standard account; it may have been written primarily for linguists and specialists but its first three chapters discuss ogam as a specific example among writing-systems and invented scripts, and all the theories about its origin. There is also a supplement (pp.68-77) detailing 21 ogam stones found since the publication of *CIIC*.

Chapter 6

The origin of mental images as *plans* of anything, from a city to a grave-plot, clearly resides in the Classical concept of *maps*, differing in many respects from our own today. At least two features of images as plans — placing East, not North, at the top, and including full or abbreviated titles/descriptions within the image — must be attributed to this derivation. O.A.W. Dilke, *Greek and Roman Maps* (Thames & Hudson, 1985) is the starting-point, and we now have Evelyn Edson's *Mapping Time and Space. How Medieval Mapmakers viewed their World* (British Library, London 1997), which does not entirely replace P.D.A. Harvey, *The History of Topographical Maps. Symbols, Pictures and Surveys* (Thames & Hudson, 1980). Since one starting-point for any display image must involve a perception of all the letters as separable into meaningful words, we can note that the Insular story of word separation (common in Late Roman times, partly retained *c*.500 in 421 *Rostece* but then generally lost for some centuries) remains to be studied, but essentially in the light of Paul Saenger's fascinating *Space Between Words. The Origins of Silent Reading* (Stanford Univ. Press 1997).

A link between images in profile, which cannot ever be better than skeletal depictions, and the art of the Roman world with its medieval sequel is less obvious. The standard survey for much of the latter is N. Davey & R.J. Ling, *Wall Painting in Roman Britain* (*Britannia* Monograph 3, 1982), usefully introduced by Professor Ling's *Roman-British Wall Paintings* (Shire Archaeology, Princes Risborough 1985). Two recent papers in *Britannia*, 37 (1957) are also relevant; V.M. Hope, 'Words and pictures; the interpretation of Romano-British tombstones' (245-58), and Roger Ling, 'Mosaics in Roman Britain: discoveries and research since 1945' (259-86). For those who would like a concise appreciation of how art, ideas and society came together in Late Roman times, chap.7 ('Art in Late Roman Britain') of Martin Henig's *The Art of Roman Britain* (1985) is recommended.

Chapter 7

The background to seventh-century Wales, setting of the three major inscriptions discussed, is given by Wendy Davies, *Wales in the Early Middle Ages* (Leicester 1982). Caldey, where possible explorations at the Priory site are under discussion, is described by Roscoe Howells, *Caldey* (Gomer, Llandysul 1948; bibliography 243-50). The final section must be seen as a preliminary note, based on simple observations, about a contentious and difficult subject. For one idea of what (reconstructed) neo-Brittonic verse forms might have been, see now John T. Koch, *The Gododdin of Aneirin* (Univ. Wales Press, Cardiff 1997). I have refrained from citing, or adding to, any of Professor Koch's restored stanzas because to do so would be to beg too many questions. Indeed, the section may have some other explanation altogether, but the features do appear to exist.

Chapter 8

Comparanda for the Penzance Cross (which from size, shape of head, wealth of panel-dotted ornament and crude figures and complete absence of true Romanesque features would anyhow be dated more or less as its chronogram implies) occur in A.G. Langdon, *Old Cornish Crosses* (Pollard, Truro 1896; the standard corpus still). Presence of English landowners this far west is amply documented in the Cornwall section of *Domesday Book*; and likely ecclesiastical centres, older monasteries that had become colleges of secular canons, in Lynette Olson's survey, *Early Monasteries in Cornwall* (Boydell, Woodbridge 1989).

Since 1051 Penzance is the latest of the relevant inscriptions, note that for written texts the latest identified example (from east Cornwall) is the work of Peter of Cornwall, *c*.1140-1221 (Howlett, *Celtic Latin Tradition*, 378-87). Peter wrote as prior of Holy Trinity, Aldgate, London but is likely to have received his education in the Launceston area. The account, here, of 1051, is somewhat compressed from a paper that also discusses 479 *Cunaide*; 'Christian Latin Inscriptions from Cornwall in Biblical Style', *Journ. Roy. Institution Cornwall*, new ser.II, vol.II.4 (1997), 42-65.

Envoi

The hypothesis of a reaction, on any scale, in the form of deliberately promoted 'Britishness' to the pre-800 English settlements has not as far as I know been aired in this form. David Howlett's *Cambro-Latin Compositions* (Four Courts, Dublin 1998) implicitly supports it by detailing the centuries-long literary accomplishments of the Britons in Wales, and for the second reaction (in Norman times) see Professor R.R. Davies's presidential address 'The Peoples of Britain and Ireland, 1100-1400' printed in four consecutive *Transactions of the Royal Historical Society* (6th ser., IV (1994) to VII (1997)). The passage quoted is from his part iv ('Language and Historical Mythology').

For the brief remarks on continuity from Roman to modern times, elements of historical repetition, and the real (but politically not always acceptable) 'multicultural' inheritance of the United Kingdom, together with our massive exploitation of this as a tourist industry, the most readable source is Professor Peter Fowler's *The Past in Contemporary Society.Then, Now* (Routledge, 1992). Present-day reassertions of Britishness, against perceived Anglocentrism, have veered away from devolution debates but are harder to find. Many interesting sidelights on the post-1900 viewpoint from Cornwall appear as papers in *Cornish Studies*, 2nd ser., 1-5 (Univ. of Exeter Press, 1993-7).

Glossary: Insular and Other Inscriptions in Biblical Style

Some words and terms here are used in epigraphy and palaeography, but others have been invented to describe features for which there are no descriptive labels. Examples are numbered from *CIIC*.

A (as *alpha*)	First letter of Greek alphabet, shown as Roman capital A, paired with O or rounded -W (as *omega*), to denote God as the Beginning (creation) and End (resurrection, judgement).
acrostic	Words or names not evident in a display, given by reading vertically an initial, left side, or internal column of letter square or grid (rarely, a diagonal reading).
alliteration	Commencing of two or more words in proximity with same letter(s); 350 hic **IAC**et **I**dnert filius **IAC**obi.
allusive	Of numbers in a computus, or words in a text, those deliberately alluding to a Biblical number or to an identifiable (and relevant) passage of Scripture.
anagram	(*see also* split anagram) Re-arrangement of letters in a word(s) to give another word(s); INTRA = TRAIN, or from 970 OPINATISIMUS = OPTIMUS ASINI.
angle-bar A	(also angular A, (rarely) 'Greek' A) Capital A with its horizontal as pointed or shallow V-shape.
apicals	In a triangularisation of all or part of a text, three letters at angles or apices of a pyramid or inverted triangle.
assonance	(*see* consonance)
author	Otherwise composer, of an inscriptional text, credited with the model, and any modification of it as the display (hence also 'auctorial self-reference', inclusion of author's name within a text, usually concealed by one or more devices).
Biblical style	General term for a compositional mode in Latin (and other languages) using stylistic, metrical and mathematical features (the last, 'arithmetical adjuncts'), exemplified by the Vulgate but of earlier origin and subsequent long duration.
bookhand	In inscriptions, general term for letter forms other than capitals.
capitals	Latin *capitalis*, further classifiable (monumental, rustic, etc.), as letter forms surviving from the Roman period.
chiasmus	Stylistic feature (adj., chiastic) comprising a short or long statement followed by a re-statement in reverse or inverted order (hence 'inscriptional chiasmus', specialised form for short texts, extending to paired or grouped inverted letters).
chi-rho	Monogram of Greek capitals X (chi) and P (rho), from ΧΡΙΣΤΟΣ, Latin *Christus* '(Jesus) Christ'; first form (as 520), early fourth century onwards; second form combining + and P (as 393) overtakes or runs alongside first from late fourth century.
chronogram	A device, akin to a validated split anagram, that uses letters-as-numbers to convey an

absolute date; in 1051 Penzance, procu **M** b **V** nt **I** nfor **I** s, quicu **M** q **V** epaceven **I** th **I** ncoret, both give MVII = AD 1007.

cognomen In Roman usage the equivalent of a surname, family name, epithet or nickname; in post-Roman Insular inscriptions, many were continued as equivalent of (single) forename.

coincidental LaN Uncommon device sometimes used to stress or repeat a key number; numbered position of a letter in a sequence made to correspond to LaN value (e.g. in HI**C** VE**R**GILIUS letters nos.3,5,7, C, E, G, have LaN values of 3,5,7).

composer Alternatively, the author (of a text).

computus General term (adj., computistic) for the mathematical or arithmetical, as opposed to stylistic, features within a text.

conjoined As opposed to ligatured, two or more letters that when cut (incised, pocked, etc.) in a display share a continuous or run-on line, usually angular; i.e., run into each other.

consonance Correspondence of sound (in inscriptions, frequently also *visible* correspondence) between syllables and parts of words (e.g. 986 **IN** s**IN**done; 520 domin**UM** laudam**US** latin**US** annor**UM**).

contraction In display, deliberate abbreviation of a word by the omission of internal letters, but retaining initial and last (e.g., 986 TREMDUM = TREM**en**DUM).

conventions In memorised number sets or sequences used to find extreme ratio, those other than strict Fibonacci number sets; 5.7.12.19.31.50 is commonest, but 4.9.13.22.35.57.92, and one that uses three square numbers (7.9.16.25.41), are also encountered.

corner (letters) In a display, or any devised re-arrangement of it, four letters (top right, top left, bottom right, bottom left) whose sum is intended to produce a meaningful LaN total.

cursive A bookhand script, with many varieties through time, generally corresponding to our informal handwriting.

cutter The person (mason, chisel-user, artisan) assumed, by copying a first original or modified model text, to have realised a composer's intended display on a surface; it is not supposed that, e.g., a bishop undertook the work of a probably far less literate stonemason.

device Any individual mechanism, technique or trick within the whole range of inscriptional (arithmetical) computus.

devised (Of images) Generation of an intended image by exercising one or more devices produces a devised plan or profile, as opposed to any inherent in a display.

diagonals In triangularisation, the sloping sides of a pyramid or inverted triangle, all letters of which yield a LaN total.

digit A single graph functioning as a numeral, as our 1 to 9.

digraph Two graphs (letters) intended to convey a single sound, as our *th, ph*; probably in 375 DOTHORANTI the -TH- is a digraph.

display The complete superficial appearance, letters and any ornaments, of an inscriptional text on a surface; what viewers see at first glance; frequently differing in details like internal totals from the composer's first and unmodified model text.

disyllable A word or part thereof that, however written, is intended to be spoken as two distinct syllables.

Divine Names	Direct reference to the Deity in a text, generally as CHRISTUS, DEUS, DOMINUS, IESU(S), and also by *nomina sacra*, series of conventional abbreviations using both Latin and borrowed-Greek letters; DS, DNS(DNE, DNI), IHS, XTUS, etc.
duple ratio	Proportions of two quantities as 1:2, or 2:1.
elision	In counting syllables metrically or computistically, loss of one through conjunction of similar or identical sounds, often Latin short vowels; e.g., 520 quinque-et, two short e's elide.
epitaphic-I	(Jackson, *LHEB*) Spelling convention, related to IOC, in which (male) British names are given Latin second-declension gen. endings (as *domin-us, domin-i*) regardless of their etymology.
extreme ratio	Division of any total so that the unequal lesser and greater parts are in, or approximate, desired proportions of 1 to 1.618..., or 0.382... to 0.618...; otherwise, the 'Golden Mean'.
extreme section	The point within a total at which it is divided into unequal parts exhibiting extreme ratio; in, e.g., 89 as the sum of 34 and 55, extreme section falls at both 34:55 and 55:34.
Fibonacci numbers	
	Sets or sequences in which each, conveniently from the third upwards, is the sum of the two preceding; the higher the figures, the closer any two within their sum are to correct extreme ratio (first set is 1.2.3.5.8.13.21.34.55.89.144...).
filiation	In memorial texts, recording of parentage through wording FILIA, FILI, FILII, FILIUS (plus second name); ogam equivalents are *MAQI* and, rarely, 362 FILIA plus ogam *INIGENA* (=daughter).
Golden Mean	Commonest of many terms (ideal proportions, Divine proportions, etc.) to denote proportions/division of extreme ratio.
graph	In displays, an individual unit or symbol of writing that, even when internalised or ligatured, represents a single phoneme (spoken language) or numeral; the smallest discrete segment in any text.
grid	Disposition of letters of a text in any rectilinear form other than a square, using all the spaces (regular grid), or leaving parts of lines blank (staggered or irregular grid), in both cases the aim being to produce acrostics, telestichs or LaN totals.
half-uncial	Variety of bookhand, not unlike our 'lower-case' letters, probably introduced to Ireland and western Britain in the fifth century as manuscripts; then developed into a specific Insular half-uncial, letters from which gradually and at an irregular rate were mixed with, and then overtook, capitals on inscriptions.
horizontal	Disposition of an inscription in horizontal lines, on the Roman model, usually displayed on the shorter axis of a surface.
horizontal I	Writing of final -I (rarely, also an internal -I-) on its side in relation to other letters in a text; apparently beginning in SW Wales by *c*.500, then spreading to (e.g.) Cornwall and Devon.
image (mental)	A pictorial, partly representational, and recognisable element in an inscription, generated in a viewer's mind either by the display (spacing and disposition of letters, etc.) or by any re-arrangement brought about by a device;

	further classified as a plan or profile image according to the assumed viewpoint.
indicate	Selected letters within a textual sequence of letters intended to give a reading (of a name or word) may be either those isolated or picked out between intervals (of unused letters, blanks) designated by a computus number set, or those indicated by similar intervals; e.g., a set 4.9.13.22, applied to the 22-letter phrase *from a dream or ruin of a day* would indicate the name 'Mary'.

Inscriptional Old Celtic (IOC)

In Insular inscriptional texts, fifth to eighth century, deliberate spelling of Celtic personal names that reflects their supposed pre-400 (British, less often Irish) etymology and largely ignores their contemporary spoken forms.

Insular   Portmanteau adjective = Irish and British together.

internalised (letters)

Writing or cutting of one or more letters at greatly reduced size, placing them within a textually-adjoining letter; a Roman-period alternative to ligaturing, but not found in post-400 Insular inscriptions.

intervals   In precession-and-interval, and anagrams, those strings of unused letters that come between letters comprising a reading.

inverted   Of cut letters, upside-down (as 487 CVNOWORI, where the seeming W is an inverted M); of texts, or inscriptional chiastic terms, when read backward or reversed.

inverted (triangle) One of the two rearranged formats of any text when triangularised; an equilateral triangle, point downwards.

key numbers   In a textual computus, one or more numbers (generally between 3 and 20) initially signalled and then repeated in various ways by computistic devices to the extent that it appears to act as a key to most interpretations and any hidden readings; key numbers may also be allusive, or taken from a stated age at death.

labelling   Conjunction of a text with any image generated by it, so that letters or part-words are made to refer correctly to any components of the image; by extension (e.g., 986, 1051), reference through letters or part-words to some other text, like the Bibilical names of the Disciples.

LaN (letters-as-numbers)

System, pre-dating both the Vulgate and the Insular inscriptions, where letters of a fixed-order alphabet (in Latin) possess additionally numerical values; 20-letter LaN, ABCDEFGHIL MNOPQ RSTU(V)X, values 1 to 20, used in the Vulgate, Roman period texts, and Insular ones until about the ninth century, when the alternative 23 letter LaN (with KYZ) took over. Greek LaN, with the full archaic 27-letter alphabet, employed the conventional numerical values 1 to 9, 10 to 90, 100 to 900. In 20-letter LaN, occurrences (Vulgate, etc.) of K,Z were treated as C, S; values 3,17.

LD   In analysis, the letter total of a display (as opposed to a model's); ligatures and internalised clusters are counted as single letters, and so usually are letters-as-numerals (e.g., 421, X I I I is four 'letters').

letter square   Disposition of a text, where the total of letters *LM* (sometimes *LD*) is a square number, in the form of a square; usually to allow acrostic or telestich readings, or LaN total or corners.

ligatures	Cutting of 2 or 3 letters (rarely more; *cf.*393, with MVL and INE ligatured) so that they share a vertical or diagonal stroke; widespread in Roman inscriptions, rather less so in post-Roman times.
LM	In analysis, the letter total of a full model, where necessary restored from a display by expanding ligatures, abbreviations or omissions, and LNu to verbal form (e.g., XIII is 4 letters, *LD*, but as *tredecim* 8 letters, *LM*). Rarely, as in 350, *LD* and *LM* are the same; usually *LM* is the greater, by a figure that may itself be significant.
LNu (letters-as-numerals)	In Latin texts, use of M D C L X V I to denote 1000,500,100,50,10,5 and 1; by extension, counting the occurrences of (mostly) I and V within a line, or whole text, to produce a significant LNu, as opposed by LaN, total.
mean ratio	Division of a total into equal halves, division by symmetry; written as '120, by MR 60.60', whereas division by extreme ratio is expressed '89, by ER 34:55', or shown by the convention '34:55 → 89'.
mental image	*see* image
model	As opposed to display (or 'as-cut'), the hypothetical but readily restorable original compositions behind a text, which the composer may or may not have written down but which must form the model, if necessarily modified, for the display.
number	As here opposed to numeral, the abstract notion of any figure or total having an arithmetical value; also the place assigned to any unit in a sequence (e.g., in IACIT, letter number five is T).
numeral	A graph that, regardless of its phonetic use if any, represents a fixed number, as (Roman) M D C L X V I; our own numerals 1 to 9 happen to be a non-phonetic set.
O (as omega)	Last letter of Greek alphabet (see A, as *alpha*).
overlining	Mark denoting abbreviation, usually by contraction, with small bar cut above relevant place in word (391, 392, 516, all imitating Continental usage on stone; 986, denoting loss of -n, later, and imitating manuscript usage).
parallelism	Stylistic feature comprising a short or long statement, which is then repeated, usually as a paraphrase or in a slightly different way; may be combined with chiasmus.
perfect (numbers)	Those, of which only the first two, 6 and 28, are relevant to inscriptional computus, in which the number is the sum of its factors including 1 but excluding the number itself (thus 28 = 1 + 2 + 4 + 7 + 14).
placing	Computistically governed construction of a text so that (e.g.) the precise location of a span or a split anagram allows detectable validation.
plan	Images, generated by inscriptions, describable as plans (as opposed to profiles) are those that in reality would suggest a view from above, looking down vertically at anything; a ground plan of a structure or site, a bird's-eye view from above, etc.
points (puncti)	Visible dots, pits or holes on a display placed between words, like modern full-stops; 421 is a rare post-Roman instance.
precession-and-interval	A device to produce the reading, in a text, of a concealed word or name (usually reading backward); to succeed, the correct intervals must be ascertained from the

	computus where they are likely to be either key numbers or an extreme ratio sequence.
profile	Images describable as profiles (as opposed to plans) are those that in reality would suggest a side-on view, looking horizontally at anything; a standing Cross, a cairn of stones (393).
pyramid	One of two rearranged formats of any text when triangularised; an equilateral triangle, point upwards.
quadruple ratio	Proportions of two quantities as 1:4, or 4:1.
quartering	Division of a text, not necessarily by clauses or semantic units, into quarter-totals of the words.
reversed	A reversed (or inverted) reading of a text, starting with its last letter, may be signalled by inclusion of split anagrams of Latin *rursus, retrorsum,* or both.
rhymes	In inscriptional texts, a not very common consonance of final syllable(s); e.g. 970 sapien*tisimus,* opina*tisimus.*
scriptura (or *scriptio*) *continua*	
	Any text with lines of continuous letters, not indicating word-boundaries; general before the sixth century.
semantic	Pertaining to the sense of a text; semantic divisions, often part of a structure and computus, represent separable clauses.
sesquialter ratio	Proportions of two quantities as 1:1½ (2:3, 3:2).
sideways-R	Capital R, the upper D-loop not fully closed at its base and the diagonal being raised towards a horizontal plane.
span	A clearly-defined sequence of letters within a longer text, containing (e.g.) the length of a split anagram; placing of a span within a text may be governed by proportional rules, or validated.
split anagram	Anagram of non-contiguous letters, within a span that holds both unused and anagrammatic letters, the proportions between which are usually in extreme ratio.
staggered grid	*see* grid
suspension	Abbreviation by suspending, or omitting, one or more letters from the end of a word; e.g. 421 PA (display), for PA(CE).
syllable	An element of speech that acts as a unit of rhythm; in analysis, where S = total of syllables, all possible syllables are counted, expanding to a model, so that 391 PRSB (= *presbiter*) is 3 syllables, as is 520 IV (= *quatuor*). Computistic syllables are not always (stylistic) metrical syllables; *see* elision, synizesis.
symbolic (numbers)	Recurrent figures in a computus, yielded by counts and LaN totals, known to symbolise Biblical numerical statements and observations; e.g., 144, the Heavenly City, 12, the Disciples.
synizesis	In metrics, fusion of two syllables into one without forming a recognised diphthong; e.g. in scansion of 350 (…Idnert filius Iacobi…), the -iu- of fil*ius* becomes one syllable by synizesis.
telestich	Vertical acrostic reading of the last, right-side, column of a grid or square; in 393, 1051, used to name the author.
text	The totality of any inscription, display or model, regarded as the unitary prose or verse composition of its author.

transcribe	To record an inscriptional text in modern printed form, using standard conventions like / for line-divisions.
triangular (number)	
	The triangular number from N, written ΔN, is the sum of all numbers from 1 to N inclusive; it is found from either equation, $\Delta N = \frac{1}{2}(N^2) + \frac{1}{2}N$, or $\Delta N = \frac{1}{2}N(N + 1)$.
triangularisation	Disposition of letters, all or part of a text, whose total is a triangular, as either a pyramid or an inverted triangle; so that LaN addition of apicals, diagonals (most commonly), and bottom or top line (or combinations thereof), yields new totals that are symbolic, or multiples of key numbers.
triple ratio	Proportions of two quantities as 1:3, or 3:1.
trisyllable	A word or part thereof that, however written, is intended to be spoken as three distinct syllables.
uncial	Variety of bookhand of calligraphic quality and appearance, developed from the fourth century; uncial letters occasionally appear in Insular inscriptions.
validations	Computistic device, used to confirm the intended reality of readings not apparent in a display (normally by extreme ratio). In a 68-letter text containing a split anagram, the placing as: (13 unused letters)/(span with split anagram, 21)/(34 unused), would be validated by 13:21 → 34, 21:34 → 55 (from 1.2.3.5.8.13.21.34.55).
vertical	Disposition of an inscription in vertical lines, usually on the longer axis of a surface; the predominant convention was to read lines downwards, viewer's head turned to the right.

Indexes

(numbers in bold refer to illustrations)

Inscriptional texts by regions, CIIC nos & key names (other names, locations)

Concealed readings (CIIC nos; Lull = RIB 2448.6)

(ac = acrostic, telestich
an = anagram
pa = part-anagram, 'label'
pi = precession-and-interval
sa = split anagram
sr = split reading)

Mental images, details (CIIC & RIB nos)

Selected Latin words and phrases

Biblical references (editio Vulgata)

General Index

Names of persons and places, with selected
topics (key names from inscriptions omitted:
K = king, S = saint)